SMUGGLING
ON THE
SOUTH COAST

CHRISTOPHER McCOOEY

AMBERLEY

First published 2012

Amberley Publishing
The Hill, Stroud
Gloucestershire, GL5 4EP

www.amberleybooks.com

British Library Cataloguing in Publication Data.
A catalogue record for this book is available from the British Library.

ISBN 978-1-4456-0459-6

Typesetting and Origination by Amberley Publishing.
Printed in Great Britain.

Contents

Acknowledgements

Many people have assisted me in the research and writing of this book. I am indebted to them for their encouragement, help and advice.

I am particularly grateful to the late Dr Robert Beckinsale of University College, Oxford, who originally suggested I expand my undergraduate thesis into a book. When I came to choose the title for this thesis, Dr Beckinsale said that I could not just call it 'Smuggling' as the Examiners would not like that. My tutor came up with 'Socio-Geographical Aspects of Illicit Trading in Kent and Sussex During the Eighteenth Century' for the 15,000-word thesis. This original research was worked up into a full book and Dr Beckinsale's close interest in the work and his painstaking criticism and correction of the original manuscript were invaluable.

I am also most grateful to my writing colleague and friend Bowen Aylmer-Pearse, who read the original typescript and made a number of useful suggestions. And thanks too to my oldest friend from school days, Peter Maverley, for taking a number of the photographs, as stated in the captions.

Note on the Text
Detailed footnotes are omitted in order for the narrative to flow. The reader will find that references to the most significant sources are stated in the text.

Introduction

'The accursed thing, smuggling'
(John Wesley)

Most of us enjoy a gamble and it follows that most of us like smuggling, for essentially smuggling is a gamble, a risky undertaking for financial or material gain. Again most of us must have tried our hand at smuggling at one time or another – not declaring that taxable item bought abroad or returning through customs with a straight face and an extra bottle of spirits. Although to do this is against the law, it is not considered to be really wrong as we are not physically hurting anyone and the fraud is considered petty. However, petty smuggling only became a feature of illegal importation after the era of open smuggling came to an end during the middle years of the nineteenth century.

Yet even this petty smuggling excited in our Victorian forebears considerable condemnation, for it was an age renowned for pious self-righteousness and moral high-mindedness. A Board of Customs report of 1858 stated:

> Notwithstanding also the liberal construction now placed by our officers on the amount of new articles of apparel which may be allowed to pass free, there are not wanting some gentlemen, many ladies, and more ladies' maids, who are still silly and perverse enough to risk pounds that they save pence, and both incur and inflict endless trouble and annoyance for the tremulous and vulgar joy of cheating the revenue and evading the vigilance of the officers charged with its collection.

The scope of this book is the era of open smuggling which lasted from the end of the Middle Ages right through to the beginning of Victoria's long reign – the era when men were prepared to run the risks of fines, imprisonment and even death, because the potential profit on the enterprise made it a gamble worth taking; it was an era of corruption and violence when commodities were both illegally imported and exported on a massive scale.

Hundreds of people were directly involved in the trade, and many thousands more encouraged it by purchasing the goods from the smugglers. It was little wonder that it came to be known as the 'free trade', for that is precisely what it was as traders arranged for goods to be purchased at a fair price overseas and these then were shipped to Britain, landed and distributed with the maximum of efficiency and the minimum of fuss. But this free-trading operation was illegal, for the goods imported should have been subject to heavy custom duties which would have greatly inflated their retail price. It is not surprising that the free trader enjoyed the public's sympathy, if not their active support, for it was he who gave so many of them their breakfast tea, the tobacco for their pipe and their evening tipple of gin at a price they could afford.

The heyday of open smuggling was the eighteenth century, when Britain's territory and trade were expanding on a global front. To protect these interests, the country became involved in a series of costly wars. The majority of merchants and politicians, and most of the general public, believed that war was right despite the heavy financial burdens.

In fact, the trading policy was very much part of the foreign policy, and government attitudes to it were much influenced by a desire to hurt neighbours as well as a desire to benefit themselves. For this reason French goods were banned for more than a century, from 1676 to 1786, as part of a deliberate policy to damage the Bourbons. This necessarily gave a spur to smuggling, particularly in clarets.

When Britain declared war on Spain in 1739 a speaker in the House of Commons declared, 'A war may be honourable and advantageous and a peace infamous and destructive. As long as we have any foreign trade left we should be jealous of its honour and tenacious of its privileges.' The Prime Minister, Sir Robert Walpole, was one of the minority; he remarked, 'They now ring the bells, but they will soon wring their hands.' The war with Spain, like subsequent wars, was financed largely by taxes imposed on imported goods which the government considered to be luxury items. However, most of these so-called luxury items had quickly become commonplace even among the poorest working classes. As the cost of legally imported tea spiralled with every new tax increase, so the smuggler was increasingly guaranteed more and more of the market, for his tea (which had not been subject to duty) was still within the farm labourer's price range, particularly if he had assisted the free trader in landing it. Smuggling was such a serious rival to legal trade and work in some of the seaboard counties that farmers were unable to find workers. In the summer of 1733 the *Gentleman's Magazine* reported:

> In several parts of Kent, the farmers notwithstanding the low prices for all sorts of grain were obliged to raise the wages of their labourers and yet were distressed for want of hands to get in their harvest which is attributed to the great numbers that employ themselves smuggling along the coast.

Wages were low, with an ordinary farm labourer being paid one shilling a day during the winter and 1s 2d a day in the summer. It was little wonder that the free traders did not lack for want of assistance for they offered twice the week's wages for a night's work plus food and as much liquor as they could drink, as well as a dollop of tea. Assisting the master smuggler not only augmented their poor wages; running contraband also added excitement to a normally dreary and dull life which was an almost non-stop round of work, and more work.

Suggesting ways to raise money to finance the wars and reduce the National Debt were common topics in the journals and magazines of the day. One writer to the *Old England Journal* of February 1748 proposed a tax on 'all idle frequenters of the road, in coaches and chairs and on horseback on Sundays', while another proposed that the tax be taken off soap and candles and one levied on kept mistresses instead. A sliding scale would operate: every duke would be taxed £500 per annum, a marquis and earl £400, viscount and baron £300, a baronet £200, all esquires £100 and every private gentleman £50. The writer suggested that 'the venerable judges, the reverend body of the clergy, and all above dukes (to avoid giving offence) are to be exempted'. These proposals were not taken up; instead more and more tax was levied on tea, brandy, tobacco and gin.

Gin had quickly become the national drink and drunkenness was commonplace as the amount consumed was enormous. The order of the day was, 'Drunk for 1d, dead drunk for 2d, straw for nothing.' After two years as a London magistrate, Henry Fielding wrote in 1751:

> Gin … is the principal sustenance (if it may so be called) of more than a hundred thousand people in this metropolis. Many of these wretches there are, who swallow pints of this poison within the twenty four hours: the dreadful effects of which I have the misfortune every day to see, and to smell too.

Drunken driving was a problem then as nowadays. One case was reported in a Bristol newspaper of 1770:

> The London Mail did not arrive so soon by several hours as usual on Monday, owing to the mailman getting a little intoxicated on his way between Newbury and Marlborough, and falling from his horse into a hedge, where he was found asleep, by means of his dog.

Many deplored the general drunkenness and debauchery and poems were published lamenting Britain's apparent sorry state of affairs:

> When Britons with the lark arose and slept
> Not midnight hours over gaming tables kept,
> When barleys strengthening juice, and beef man's meat,
> Not champagne, or ragoos, were drank or eat,

E'er nerve-impairing tea or pois'nous gin
Had made a race not half what men had been,
Then, then a Briton through the world was fear'd,
And Britain's flag triumphant rode rever'd.

Another vice common to eighteenth-century Britain was that of corruption. It was commonplace and accepted, especially in the middle and upper classes. Politicians were particularly pliable and even the highest in the land never escaped slanderous gossip.

Most people did not regard corruption with the sort of moral opprobrium which the word seems to indicate today; in the late eighteenth century it was a necessary part of running government. The situation was succinctly described by the great Whig statesman Sir Robert Walpole when he referred to pretended patriots by saying 'all those men have their price'. Few men were prepared to tackle the dishonesty of the day and when they did they were invariably defeated. William Shepherd, who was an unsuccessful political candidate to represent the borough of Southwark, brought a case of bribery and corruption against a brewer of Barnaby Street in 1734. Despite considerable evidence suggesting the case was proven, the jury did not want to return a 'guilty' verdict as they thought it would create a precedent and lead to 'a great number of such kind of prosecutions all over the kingdom'. There were some conscientious people. Prime Minister Pitt received a letter in 1784 which contained £300 in banknotes; the writer wished the money to be applied to public service, for he in his younger days, when he followed the seas, injured the revenue as most seamen do.

A man who strove tirelessly to rescue his fellow man from contemporary corruption and debauchery was the Anglican cleric John Wesley, who founded Methodism. Before he died in 1791 he had travelled 225,000 miles and preached 50,000 sermons, often drawing hysterical crowds of up to 80,000. His message was clear: if the Bible was the word of God, every Briton was doomed unless he repented. Unlike many men of the cloth who turned a blind eye to the smuggling trade, he was not prepared to condone it.

The great evangelist described the trade as 'this accursed thing, smuggling'. His hatred of smuggling led him to refrain from drinking tea and to publish a strongly worded pamphlet in 1767, entitled *Word to a Smuggler. This tract is not to be sold, but given away.* 'Thou shut not steal,' he exhorted the smuggler; 'the duties appointed by law are the King's right, as much as your coat is your right … therefore you are as much a thief if you take his duties, as a man is that takes your coat … Every smuggler is a thief-general, who picks the pockets both of the King, and all his fellow subjects. He wrongs them all'.

But his words repeatedly fell on stony ground because it is in the nature of mankind to be fond of forbidden fruit, and all but the most ardent Methodist found it difficult to refuse a bargain. Charles Lamb expressed the more popular view when he wrote about the smugglers of Folkestone: 'There are, or I dream there are, many of the latter occupation here. Their faces become the place. I like a smuggler. He is the only honest thief. He robs nothing but the revenue, an abstraction I never greatly cared for.'

The public's imagination has always been captured by the smuggler. He is often thought of as a bold and jolly seafarer in the Robin Hood mould who robs the government, who fear him, to give to the poor, who love him. Poems and novels have always tended to romanticise his illegal activities. 'The Smuggler King' by Eliza Cook is one of many poems that give a far from accurate picture of the adventurous free trader.

> There's a brave little bark stealing out in the dark,
> From her nest in the bristling bay;
> The fresh breeze meets her dingy sheets,
> And swiftly she darts away;
> She never must run in the eyes of the sun,
> But along with the owl take wing,
> She must keep her flight for the moonlight night,
> For she carries the Smuggler King.
> A monarch is he as proud as can be
> Of a strong and mighty band.
> The bullet and blast may go whistling past,
> But he quails neither heart nor hand.
> He lives and dies with his fearful prize
> Like a hunted wolf he'll spring,
> With trigger and dirk, to the deadliest work,
> And fight like a Smuggler King.
> Back from the wave, to his home in the cave,
> In the sheen of the torches' glare;
> He reigns the lord of a freebooters board,
> And never was costlier fare.
> Right firm and true were the hearts of the crew,
> There's faith in the shouts that ring,
> As they stave the cask and drain the flask
> And drink to the Smuggler King.

Undoubtedly some of the people involved in the free trade displayed qualities of boldness, courage and leadership; undoubtedly many involved in shipping the goods were excellent seamen and masters of their hazardous profession. But these qualities were displayed in defying laws which, although admittedly not good laws, were still the laws of Britain. And the smuggling trade, as shall be seen, often attracted the criminal element of society, people who were prepared to secure and protect their business not with boldness but with cowardice, not with courage but by intimidation; and it is little wonder that the smugglers forfeited the public's sympathy on the occasions when their arrogant depravity went too far. An eighteenth-century writer records:

> It is no wonder, indeed, that when once a set of men commenced as smugglers, that they should go on to commit the vilest excesses; for when a man wrought himself into a firm persuasion that it is no crime to rob his country, the transition is easy to the belief, that it is no sin to plunder or destroy his neighbour; and therefore we need not be much surprised that so many of the smugglers have turned highwaymen, housebreakers, and incendiaries, of which we have had but too many instances of late.

Throughout the eighteenth century, the government received numerous recommendations and reports suggesting ways to prevent smuggling. Invariably the main recommendation was the obvious one of reducing the tax on the commodities concerned and so making it unprofitable to smuggle. Both Walpole and Pitt endeavoured to do this when Britain was not at war. Both politicians realised that peace abroad was required before reform of the tax system at home could be achieved. However both were unsuccessful, as will be seen. Walpole was defeated by political machination at home and Pitt was forced to increase taxes once again when France declared war on the Old Enemy, England, in 1793. The third major attempt to bring open smuggling to an end came after the end of the Napoleonic wars. This time it was successful, although the close of the era was bloody and violent.

This book begins with a survey of the history of Custom in this country and then traces that of smuggling, which has its roots in the illegal export of wool to the Continent. Another little-known commodity smuggled abroad was Cornish tin, as widely prized in the sixteenth century as it had been by the Phoenicians 2,000 years earlier. Some three-quarters of the total output was believed to have been illegally sent abroad. Most of the tin found its way to Lyon in France, or to Holland, where it was worked and re-exported. The tin was normally conveyed to London from Cornwall by small coasting ships and hence there was plenty of opportunity for diverting the cargo across the Channel. The chief destination for legally exported tin was Italy and the Ottoman dominions, but very little was honestly exported. During the twelve months ending Michaelmas 1593, the Crown received only £28 in export duties levied at the outports, so rampant was the lawbreaking.

The next three chapters are devoted to the three main commodities that were smuggled into this country, namely tea, tobacco and spirits. The sixth chapter looks at whisky, the spirit unique to the British Isles, and traces its illegal distillation and distribution. The succeeding chapters describe smuggling activities throughout the eighteenth and early part of the nineteenth century and attempts by the authorities to curtail them.

This book is intended as a history of a fascinating era, that of open smuggling. Although a factual account, I have endeavoured to make it more readable by allowing the 'imp of association' to be present. This imp impels me to include Kipling's wonderfully romantic 'A Smuggler's Song'. May the poem serve as an introduction to my topic and may the chapters that follow stimulate further the reader's interest in that infamous traffick.

If you wake at midnight and hear a horse's feet
Don't go drawing back the blind, or looking in the street,
Them as asks no questions isn't told a lie,
Watch the wall, my darling, while the Gentlemen go by.

Running round the woodlump if you chance to find
Little barrels, roped and tarred, all full of brandy-wine;
Don't you shout to come and look, nor take 'em for your play;
Put the brush-wood back again, they'll all be gone next day.

Knocks and whistles round the house, footsteps after dark,
You've no call for running out till the house dogs bark.
Trusty's here and Pinchers here, see how dumb they lie,
They don't fret to follow when the Gentlemen go by.

If you meet King George's men dressed in blue and red,
You be careful what you say, and mindful what is said,
If they call you 'pretty maid', and chuck you 'neath the chin,
Don't you tell where no one is, nor yet where no one's been.

If you do as you've been told, likely there's a chance
You'll be given a dainty doll, all the way from France,
With a cap of Valenciennes, and a velvet hood
A present from the Gentlemen, along o' being good.

Five and twenty ponies trotting through the dark,
Brandy for the Parson, 'baccy for the Clerk,
Laces for a lady, letters for a spy,
Watch the wall, my darling, when the Gentlemen go by.

1

The History of Custom and Excise

Rectae et antiguae consuetudinae

Customs duties gradually evolved from ancient dues which the Crown levied on both imported and exported goods. This due was known as 'prise' or 'prisage', and one of the first levied was by Richard I, who placed many heavy burdens on the people in order to finance his Crusade to the Holy Land and his war against Saladin. Richard's prise was an import duty on wine and he used the money raised to defray the cost of his personal and household expenses. Customary levies, however, probably go back to pre-Norman times and even to when the Romans occupied Britain; for, according to Tacitus, the Britons had to provide 'tolls in kind' – corn, fodder and so on – for the Roman army of occupation. There is very little written evidence before the twelfth century, but it is fair to assume that levies were made. In the Barons' Magna Carta, sealed by King John at Runnymede on 15 June 1215 in obedience to their insistent demands, reference is made to the *rectae et antiquae consuetudinae* – in other words, the ancient and rightful customs.

Edward Carson, librarian and archivist at King's Beam House in London, traced the history of the English Customs service in his book *The Ancient and Rightful Customs*. It shows how King John made the first real attempt to set up a centralised system of custom collection. At the Winchester Assize in 1203 he imposed a duty of one-fifteenth on the imports and exports (the *quindecima*) and provided for officials to be appointed to deal with it. In each port of England six or seven or more of the wiser and more learned men of substance of the port and one knight and one clerk were to be chosen along with a further official, who should not himself receive any money but should keep rolls against the bailiffs who received the *quindecima*. This tax was imposed from July 1203 to November 1205 at thirty-five ports; the yield from London was £1,336 12s 10d and the next greatest amount was from Boston (£780 15s 3d), followed by Southampton (£712 3s 8d) and Lincoln (£656 12s 2d).

Edward I, nicknamed Longshanks, was a very active king who went on a Crusade in 1270, completed the conquest of Wales and overcame the Scottish opposition by executing William Wallace and receiving the submission of Robert Bruce. At home, when not subjugating or making war, he promulgated many wise laws and it was during his reign, 1282 to 1307, that the triangular system of control was initiated, a system which worked so well that it has continued with some modification until the present day in the United Kingdom. The same system was retained in the United States of America after their Declaration of Independence, and has been adopted by Commonwealth and other countries. The basis of this system is the separation of the processes of the examination of goods, the collection of the duties and the checking of the accounts. So-called Customers were set up in the ports in 1297; their job was to receive the monies transmitted to them by the Collectors and to make payments as directed by the Exchequer. Two years later the office of Searcher was established; his duty included the examination of goods and the preparation and returning of accounts.

Again during Edward's reign, in 1275 a new custom duty was imposed on goods destined for export: half a mark for each sack of wool (364 lb), half a mark for every 300 woolfells (sheepskin with the wool attached) and one mark for every last of leather (240 hides). Later on in 1297, Edward imposed a further tax of 40 shillings per sack of wool exported and 5 marks for every last of leather. Intended as a temporary measure to raise money to finance a war, it was levied without the sanction of Parliament and was known as the *Maletote*. These steep increases in rates roused much opposition and the tax was eventually abandoned and the King renounced the right to levy such a tax without the consent of Parliament.

Apart from export duty on wool and leather, there were two duties on imported goods: the first, on wine – imposed at so much a ton (a ton or tun was a barrel containing 252 gallons) – was called 'tonnage'; and the second, on all other goods – imposed at so much a pound of their supposed value – was called 'poundage'. The first complete legal grant of tonnage and poundage imposed by full Parliament was in 1373 and the subsidy of poundage (as it was called) was one shilling in the pound. This subsidy rarely varied from the established rate of 5 per cent; but tonnage, the duty on wine, fluctuated considerably. The normal method of revenue collection during this period was farming, whereby the farmers would make a fixed payment to the King for the rent of the farm of the Customs duties; the collectors and controllers were required to keep an account of the goods. It was usual for the farmers to appoint their own officials in the ports, and two local officials were elected to represent the King. The collector had one half of a seal known as the 'cocket' and the King's official, later known as the controller, held the other half. This seal was used to seal the licence required to export wool or hides.

The farmers, it appears, were not slack in using their position to further their private means. As Adam Smith said, 'In countries where the public revenues are in farm, the farmers are generally the most opulent people and their wealth alone would excite public indignation.' With the creation of this system of examination, collection and checking, malpractices by Customs officials occurred. As early as 1424 it was found necessary to impose penalties on Customers, Collectors or Controllers who 'should be attainted or convicted of falsely concealing the King's Customs or Subsidies, entered or paid'.

In spite of this early regulation governing their conduct, it would seem that the Customs officials were becoming deliberately slack in their observance of the rules, for it was stated in 1442 that:

> Of late divers Customers, Controllers and also Searchers have divers persons to be their clerks, deputies and ministers, some have ships of their own and some of them meddle with the freighting of ships and also buy and sell divers merchandises and thereof occupy to their own use divers wharfs and keys, being by the water's side where common discharge of divers merchandises is had in ports of this Realm, by which the great deceit and damages daily do grow to the King of his Customs and Subsidies … Also many hold hostelries and taverns and also keep wharfs and they and their servants be factors and attornies for merchants, denizens and aliens by which great damage and loss doth grow to the King … by favour that such clerks, deputies and ministers holding such hostelries, taverns and wharfs do to the merchants and to other their guests.

On conviction of any of these devious practices, the penalty was £40.

Regulations were coming into force designed to protect home production and to prevent the sharp practices carried out by the merchant traders and officials. In response to a petition from artisans, an Act was passed early in the reign of Edward IV prohibiting the importation of a wide range of articles, including wool, metal, dice, tennis balls, playing cards, daggers, knives, shears and scissors. A year after this another statute limited the vessels in which wool and woolfells could be shipped to galleys and carracks, and later anti-smuggling regulations governed the minimum size of vessels allowed to import merchandise. In 1472 an Act ordained that cloths imported should be sealed and counter-sealed by the Collector and Comptroller in the port of delivery before being exposed for sale, on penalty of forfeiture.

As trade increased so did the regulations controlling it, and these regulations gave further scope to the merchant adventurer to evade them and so secure a bigger profit. In 1496 Henry VII signed a treaty with the Netherlands which included an article providing that

> the officers of either country appointed for searching for contraband goods shall perform it civilly, without spoiling them or breaking the chests, barrels, packs and sacks, under pain of a month's imprisonment. And when the searchers shall have opened them, they shall assist in the shutting and mending of them, etc., nor shall they compel the owners to sell or dispose of the same against their own inclinations.

It was also Henry VII who in 1507 saw the introduction of the first official Rate Book (the forerunner of the present-day 'tariff') in which the official value of the goods was shown.

On his accession, James I had appointed a committee under the Great Seal to enquire into the reasonable values and prices of imported and exported goods from which, of course, he received a percentage of the Custom duty. By bringing the valuations up to date, James was able to ensure a higher revenue. A Levant merchant called Bates, who dealt in currants, claimed that the higher valuation given to this commodity was tantamount to an increase in taxation and could not therefore be imposed without the consent of Parliament. Custom duty was one of the major sources of royal revenue, and was therefore attacked by the Commons because their financial leverage over the Crown was their only weapon. If the monarchy could have made itself financially independent, the Commons would not have been able to exercise any control over royal policy. The question of Custom duty was therefore a highly political one. The case was heard in the Court of Exchequer in 1608, and after lengthy discussion the decision was given against Bates. The Court decided that he who had power over the cause must have power over the effect: the seaports were the King's gates which he could open and shut to whom he pleased.

A new Book of Rates was issued by patent in 1611 and of particular interest was the fact that the patent authorised the payment of drawback – that is, a refund of duty on the exportation of goods that had been previously imported. This is a system which still exists today and it has played a great part in easing the development of the processing trade in this country. It also opened the way for more abuses and possibilities of defrauding the Revenue, of which more later.

The Civil War, which involved both sides in great expense, saw the introduction of a tax which was intensely disliked right from the start. Excise had arrived. It was imposed by the Long Parliament in 1643, and also in the same year by Charles I in Oxford. It was imposed not only on goods produced in England (spirits, beer, cider and perry) but also on imports in addition to the Custom duties. The tax was meant as a temporary measure for the duration of the war, but the war proved so costly that the Excise duties were retained in spite of many complaints and objections. The Customs service was finally taken out of farm in 1671 and six commissioners were appointed to the Board of Customs, each with an annual salary of £2,000. Twelve years later the same action was taken with regard to the Excise. Dr Johnson described excise as a 'hateful tax levied upon commodities, and adjudged not by the common judge of property, but by wretches hired by those to whom the excise is paid'.

During this early period of 'farming', a system of collecting Custom and, latterly, Excise taxes had evolved which was reasonably successful in that those merchants who had secured the farming rights from the King carried out their task diligently, particularly as they were lining not only the Exchequer's coffers but also their own. Abuses did of course occur, and reminders from King and

Parliament appear simply to have made the merchant collectors more careful and discreet. The farmers themselves were disliked by the other traders and merchants because of their obvious riches from collecting the duty. With the abolition of farming and the creation of a Board of Customs, antipathy was diverted from the old to the new Collectors.

But a very significant development in relation to the history of Custom and Excise begins to appear after the dramatic events of 1688. James II, a Catholic, had reigned for three short years but during that time he had lost any popularity that he might have had by attempting to secure better conditions for his co-religionists in a predominately Protestant country. The chief statesmen of the land had hoped that James, who was fifty-one when he came to the throne in 1685, would not live long and that on his death, his daughter, a Protestant, would succeed to the throne. But James's second wife, Mary of Modena, gave birth to a son, who would certainly be raised as a Catholic, and this meant that his daughter Mary would now have to give way to her infant brother. Because of this, coupled with the unsuccessful Monmouth rebellion, the subsequent Bloody Assizes of Judge Jeffreys, the Declaration of Indulgence and the trial of the seven bishops, it was resolved not to wait for James's natural death, but to send at once to Holland and invite Mary and her husband William of Orange to come to England with an army and rescue the country 'from popery and slavery'.

William of Orange, although a stranger to England, was closely allied to the reigning royal family as his mother, Mary Stuart, was the King's sister and he himself the King's son-in-law. He was a wise, quiet man who spoke little, but a prudent prince and an able and courageous general. All his life he had been the protector of the Protestants in Europe, and had been defending the United Provinces of Holland against Louis XIV. William set out for England and, carried down the Channel by a 'Protestant' wind, landed at Torbay. As he moved methodically towards the capital, many rallied to him. At first James could not be made to believe that his throne was in danger; but one by one his courtiers, his friends and even his army deserted him. Finally, when he heard that his daughter Anne had gone over to his enemies, he fled with his wife and infant son to the court of his cousin Louis XIV. Thus was brought about, without bloodshed, the Glorious Revolution of 1688.

James II had fled his realm but he had not released his right to the throne of England. Both he and Louis XIV, and the predominately Roman Catholic Irish, considered that the Stuart line was the legitimate and rightful royal family to sit on the throne of England. From 1689 to 1697 the English were united with other Protestant countries of Europe in making war on Louis XIV. This long war with France began the National Debt in 1692 and the next century saw Britain embark on an unprecedented number of costly wars, beginning with the War of the Spanish Succession and coming to a gruesome finale of carnage at Waterloo in 1815. Between 1689 and 1815, a period of 126 years, Britain was at war for no less than 75 of them. These wars were fought not only on the Continent but also in places as far apart as Bunker's Hill in North America and Plassey on the Indian subcontinent. They were all partly maritime, with the Royal Navy playing decisive roles in the Channel, the Atlantic, the Mediterranean and the Indian Ocean. To pay for them, Britain during this period was subjected to an unprecedented amount of taxation; and it is simply staggering to marvel how she did not by weight of arms, by blood, sweat and gunpowder, grind herself into irretrievable bankruptcy. But survive she did and the struggle not only ensured Britain's supremacy throughout the world but also, by reason of the heavy taxation, ensured that it was profitable to smuggle goods on an unprecedented scale. The eighteenth century and early part of the nineteenth was the heyday of smuggling.

These historical acts of expansion and protection of national territories overseas were coupled with an economic consideration that had an equal effect in contributing to the scale of smuggling. The British had a fierce, narrow mercantilism which ensured a jealous and often short-sighted protection of their merchants and ship owners. Such a policy of protection goes right back to the reign of Richard III, when an Act was passed ordering the King's subjects to employ only 'ships of the King's allegiance'. Obviously this was intended to encourage the growth of the English mercantile marine. The spirit of mercantilism was evident in the Navigation Laws which had existed in one form or another since the days of Elizabeth I. These laws restricted trade with the Plantations, as well as inter-plantation trade, to British ships, although foreign ships were allowed to carry produce from the country to which they belonged direct to the Plantations, and to take goods from the Plantations to any foreign port. Certain ports, however, were designated 'free ports' and foreign trade into the Plantations was limited to them. Certain goods from Europe, such as wine, timber, corn, brandy, tobacco, oil, dried fruit, salt, flax and hemp, could only be brought to the United Kingdom in British ships, or, directly, in ships belonging to the country in which they had been produced. The Navigation Laws were finally repealed in 1849 and freed the Customs service from a great deal of non-revenue work concerned with their application.

These laws were restrictive and cumbersome and simply served to encourage the traders' inventiveness to circumvent them. Adam Smith, himself a Customs official, in his *Wealth of Nations* states categorically:

> The Customs Acts might have been described as acts of suppression of colonial timber, furs, sugar and fisheries, for the extinction of the English manufacturer of hats, silks and paper; for the extension of adulteration in the necessaries of life; for the promotion of the honourable profession of smuggler; and for the general advancement of frauds, abuses and riots among all ranks of his Majesty's subjects.

With the commencement of the National Debt in 1692, the government was forced to consider new ways in which to raise money for public spending. William III required more money for his war with France and the government therefore offered to borrow money from private persons, for which it was willing to pay a small fixed yearly interest. The usual plan then was to enact a new source of revenue (for example, a 5 per cent subsidy on a luxury item) for a term of years or in perpetuity, and for the government of the day to raise upon the security of such duty whatever capital sum of money might be authorised in the Act. The other ways of raising money, the land tax, window tax (which replaced the hearth tax in 1697), and stamp duties, all caused great public outcry, particularly the hearth tax which opened every house for inspection by the hated tax official. The raising of 5 per cent subsidies on goods which were supposed to be luxuries (tea, coffee, spirits, silks, tobacco) afforded a reasonably quick return without much controversy. The government, rightly in their estimation, argued that these goods were not necessities of life, that nobody would starve to death without them, and that anyway the nation was at war and fighting for survival.

The result of this revenue system meant that as more and more money was required, each commodity taxed was subject to an increasing number of subsidies. The process of paying duty gradually became a matter of such complexity as to place the public entirely at the mercy of the large official hierarchy. This sprang up as the necessary result of a system which none but experts could possibly understand, and under which every mistake in a computation might be construed as an attempt to defraud the Revenue; conviction of such an offence resulted in heavy penalties.

During Anne's reign, finance for the war of the Spanish Succession was in part obtained from duties and subsidies that were placed on pepper, raisins, spice, hides, skins, parchment, vellum, cards, dice, soap, hops, paper mill boards, linens and sail-cloths. There was even a duty on whale fins, which in 1702 raised £14,604 out of a total English Customs of £1,285,605. By the time that the first Hanoverian reluctantly accepted the offer of the British crown in 1704, the English fiscal system was already approaching what one eminent historian described as 'an ungodly jumble'.

The first two Georges were more interested in their possessions in Hanover than the affairs of Britain and were content to leave the governing of the country to their statesmen and chief ministers – one of whom was Sir Robert Walpole, a shrewd and clever, but by no means high-minded, man. He was wise enough to see that what Britain most needed now was rest and peace, and during all the many years he was in power there was for the most part peace both at home and abroad. This enabled him to persuade Parliament to turn its attention to reform at home and to peaceful policies for the encouragement of commerce and manufacture. However, he did not believe in anyone's incorruptibility and bribed and flattered and bought without scruple and without shame.

Walpole hated the merchant class, for they continually smeared his name with corruption and ranted about his greed. In 1733 his personal animosity towards the merchants manifested itself in a Bill that he introduced in Parliament; it was intended to reform the present system of paying Custom on wines and tobacco but in reality was a huge indictment of the dishonesty of the entire merchant community. In effect he proposed a strictly enforced and efficiently run excise system, which involved the present custom duty on imported wine and tobacco being reduced and replaced by an excise on home consumption, which would prevent smuggling, reduce frauds and yield a greater revenue than the present custom duty. It would also be for Walpole, if carried by Parliament, an immensely satisfying personal revenge.

In his speech to the Commons, Sir Robert Walpole, as Chief Minister and Chancellor of the Exchequer, proposed a small duty still to be paid on imported tobacco and to substitute for previous customs aggregating six and a third pence per pound an inland duty for four pence per pound to be paid when the tobacco was withdrawn from bonded warehouses for sale to the public. This scheme, he boldly declared, would not only give relief to the oppressed planters in America and benefit the honest trader injured by the frauds of others, but would also help the national revenue and make London a free port and by consequence the market of the world.

Walpole, expecting considerable opposition to these proposals, had made sure of his facts and delivered one of his finest speeches. He gave information to the House from Cope's investigation into smuggling, which had found that only 2,208 hogsheads of tobacco had been condemned by the Customs officials between 1723 and 1732, though it appeared from depositions on oath that in the space of two years 4,738 hogsheads had been run in Hampshire, Dorset and Devon alone. Bitter opposition was expressed in the House over a national issue involving many, not only party but also personal, conflicts. The debate between Whigs and Tories was furious. One speaker declared, 'This seems to be a step towards introducing a general excise, which is inconsistent with the liberties of a free people.' Sir John Barnard was more poetic in his denunciation of the scheme: 'They have indeed gilded the pill a little, but the composition within it is still the same; and if the people of England be obliged to swallow it, they will find it as bitter a pill as ever was swallowed by them since they were a people.' He went on to ask the House, 'What necessity is there for applying this new, this desperate remedy? A remedy which is certainly worse than the disease.'

Sir John Barnard, a London MP and no doubt with merchant trading interests, led the opposition and strove to prevent the acceptance of the proposals. After his speech he called in the Commissioners of the Customs and asked them what value the tobacco frauds amounted to each year. One of the Commissioners put a value of between £30,000 and £40,000 annually on frauds which came to the Commissioner's knowledge. The Commissioners agreed with Barnard that if the officers of the Custom service performed their duty diligently and faithfully the majority of the frauds would be prevented and that this could be brought about if they (the Commissioners) were given the same powers as had been given to the Commissioners of Excise.

Such powers 'would contribute to making them more exact and faithful in the discharge of their duty'. Barnard concluded by saying that the dangerous scheme proposed was not warranted when the existing laws, if carried out effectively, would prevent the frauds and that the 120 to 150 new Excise officers required (if the Bill were made law), not to mention the necessary warehouse men, would add to the swarm of tax gatherers already established and imperil the liberty of the nation's subjects still further. The division was taken. Two hundred and five members were against the proposals and two hundred and sixty-six were for them. The House rose at two o'clock in the morning on Thursday 15 March after one of the bitterest verbal battles it had ever witnessed. The proposals had been passed and a Committee had been appointed to bring in a Bill. But the Bill was destined never to become an Act.

Following Parliament's acceptance of the proposals there immediately ensued a great public outcry: posters, woodcuts, essays, poems and bawdy ballads satirised Walpole and condemned Excise. The press waged a campaign of unparalleled fury and unprecedented success. The issue kindled such extremes of passion and hatred that one Member of Parliament was confident that Walpole's political career was ended. 'You know we have long labour'd, in vain, to destroy this monster of power, this domineering Minister: but now he has destroyed himself. Excise will sink him; you see we have set all the Nation against him.' And so it seemed. Opponents of the Bill published satires and cartoons. One showed a many-headed dragon eating up the fat of the land, converting it into gold and spewing it into the lap of Walpole. Accompanying this visual attack was a verbal onslaught, 'Britain Excis'd':

> See this Dragon EXCISE
> Has Ten Thousand Eyes,
> And Five Thousand Mouths to devour us,
> A sting and sharp claws
> With wide-gaping Jaws
> And a Belly as big as a Store-house
>
> (Chorus)
> Horse, Foot and Dragoons,
> Battalions, Platoons
> Excise, Wooden Shoes and no Jury:
> Then Taxes increasing,
> While Traffick is ceasing
> Would put all the Land in a Fury.
>
> This Monster, Plague rot him!
> The Pope first begot him
> From Rome to King Lewis he went:
> From a Papist so true
> What Good can ensue
> No wonder he'll make you keep Lent.

From France he flew over
And landed at Dover
To swill down your Ale and your Beer
Now he swears he can't dine
Without Sugar and Wine
Thus he'll plunder you Year after Year.

Grant these, and the Glutton
will roar out for Mutton,
Your Beef, Bread and Bacon to boot;
Your Goose, Pig and Pullet,
He'll thrust down his Gullet
While the Labourer munches a Root.

And so it went on, combining detestation of Excise with anti-Catholic feeling. However, the country was not swept by a sudden hysteria in 1733. Excise merely provided the excuse upon which the opponents of Walpole fixed their hate. Walpole fought on against ever-mounting odds with great obstinacy, for he, too, was driven by hatred … for his political foes.

The outcry was so great and accompanied by such serious rioting that Walpole acknowledged defeat and withdrew the Bill a day before it was to have had its first reading in the House. The attempted Excise reforms were a wise scheme undone by political machination; a powerful minister was coerced by clamour and public feeling, whipped up by pamphlets and the newspapers. The withdrawal of the Bill contributed to the increased fraudulent practices in succeeding years and to the increasing amount of clandestinely imported goods. Walpole had lost a certain amount of face with the defeat of his Bill; but, with a resilience shown by many a later politician, he had not lost his office despite his unpopularity. His enforced resignation came nine years afterwards in 1742 when it was thought that, in a war which he had only reluctantly agreed to support, he was not doing enough to ensure success. It was left to Pitt the Younger nearly fifty years later to make the next serious attempt at reforming the Custom and Excise laws.

In 1751, a Mr Cooper, described as 'a very competent authority', made the following observations on the Custom and Excise complexities:

What a maze our merchants must be in if we consider the many regulations, and regulations of regulations for collecting the Customs and for paying the drawbacks on goods re-exported, we must conclude it impossible for any merchant in this country to be master of his business if he be what we call a general merchant; consequently he must trust to those honest gentlemen called Custom House officers for the duties he is to pay upon importation, and the drawbacks he is entitled to upon exportation. Can we wonder at the decay of our commerce under such circumstances. Should we not rather wonder that we have any left.

These complexities are best illustrated by a specific example. In 1784 a merchant imported 2,000 ells (a measure of 45 inches in length) of Russian linen. The total payment of duty had to be painstakingly built up in the following manner:

	£	s	d
By the Old Subsidy (5 per cent on the rate)	6	0	0
By the Additional Duty	3	0	0
By the New Subsidy	6	0	0
By the One Third Subsidy	2	0	0
By the Import 1690	4	10	0
By the Subsidy 1747	6	0	0
By the Subsidy 1759	6	0	0
By the Act 1767	30	0	0
By the Import 1779	3	3	6
By the Import 1782	3	3	6
Total Net Duty	£69	17s	0d

And this example is a comparatively simple one of a duty payment. Many were far more complex, and involved much labour to arrive at a result, because many articles and commodities were liable to a larger number of 'branches' of duty than those enumerated in the foregoing entry for linen. The total number of these branches in 1785 was sixty-eight and in addition there were five Plantation Duties and twenty-seven Expired Duties. The accounts of the latter had to be kept open for many years because of arrears due to the Crown.

Despite Walpole's failure at introducing much-needed reform in the 1730s, it is surprising that the government's next attempt at reforming the administration of the Custom and Excise Service was not made for another half-century. There had been a period of twelve years between the end of the Seven Years' War and the Declaration of Independence by the United States when Britain was at peace and had had an opportunity of carrying out reforms at home, but no serious attempt was made at Custom Law reform. The Seven Years' War had cost Britain an enormous sum and heavy taxes were necessary to discharge some of her debts. In 1783, the year of the signing of the Peace of Versailles, William Pitt, son of Lord Chatham, was made Prime Minister at the remarkably young age of twenty-four. He remained in office for eighteen years, until 1801, a longer period of office than had been held by any minister since Sir Robert Walpole. Pitt was a grave, haughty man, of immense power and will.

'His noble figure, his flashing eyes, his majestic voice, the fire and grandeur of his eloquence, gave him a sway over the House of Commons far greater than any other minister has possessed,' said one contemporary. After Pitt's first speech in the House, it was felt that he was a worthy son of the great Chatham. 'He is not a chip of the old block,' said Burke; 'he is the old block itself.' As soon as he was in the highest office, Pitt gave all his great gifts to the good of the country. He had extraordinary skill in the management of money, and was able to do much for the encouragement of trades which in recent years had been advancing with such giant strides that, in spite of the great wars, Britain was richer than she had ever been.

In Pitt's first year as Prime Minister he received a report by George Bishop entitled 'Observations, Remarks and Means to prevent Smuggling' which left the government with no illusions about the extraordinary scale of smuggling. The situation certainly was serious and had not improved since Lord Pembroke's remark of 1781: 'Will Washington take America, or the smugglers England first, the bet would be a fair and even one.' Washington had taken America and Bishop's report suggested that the smugglers were virtually running England:

> The practice of smuggling has of late years made such rapid and gigantic strides from the sea coasts into the very heart of the country, pervading every city, town, and village, as to have brought universal distress upon the fair traders, from the most opulent and respectable, even to the smallest shopkeeper, and requires the united efforts of every honest man to aim at suppression of it; foreign states have been enriched at the expense of this country and the destruction of many fair traders.

Bishop maintained that the many thousands of sailors engaged in smuggling who were clothed and fed and had their vessels repaired in foreign ports could be useful members of the community if the practice was discontinued. He calculated that 'sixty thousand of the youngest men and best able to labour' were employed in smuggling and one thousand women and children in retailing and hawking spirits and tea about the country. Also he considered that between one-fifth and one-sixth of all the horses kept were used for smuggling and the cost of feeding them at one shilling each day per horse amounted to the annual figure of £1,820,000. Bishop stated:

> Instead of a contraband let us have a legal trade with all our neighbours, and treat with them to lower the duties on the manufactures of these kingdoms, by lowering and permitting the manufactures and produce of their countries to be imported here, on paying small duties, which will increase the trade and commerce of this country, employ the poor and lessen the parish rates, to the very great interest of the landed property.

Bishop estimated that the Revenue lost £3 million in 1783 and he pointed out the disparity between the taxes paid in the inland districts with those on the coast, where the inhabitants have 'their tea, spirits, wine, currants, raisins, starch, soap, china, glass, and tobacco mostly smuggled'. The report closes:

> If the 160,000 that now carry on this trade were employed in fishing, agriculture, etc. the labour of sixty thousand men at one shilling and sixpence per day each, and

the women and children at sixpence per day each, amount to £2,464,000 annually, what an emolument to the trade and commerce of the kingdom; from those who are now supported in drunkenness by this iniquitous traffic, obviously productive of so numerous a train of evils, that prudence, common honesty, decency, order, and civil government united, cry loudly for redress. I am of the opinion, after thirty years remarks on this trade, the best and most certain method to prevent it, and to increase the revenue, is to lower the duties.

Following on from George Bishop's report to both Houses in 1783 came another report, two years later, prepared by the Committee of Public Accounts. This Committee drew attention to the 'intricacy and perplexity that involve the collection and accounts of this part of the Revenue', which had become an object of high and urgent importance for the attention of the legislature. They suggested that the obvious answer was to reduce the number of rules and branches to a simplified unity. The result of all these recommendations was Pitt's Bill of 1787 in which he repealed all the existing compound duties and consolidated them into single rates for each article. Thus, for the first time, Custom and Excise taxation was reduced into such a codified form as could be understood by ordinary men. All duties furthermore were to be paid into one single fund, the Consolidated Fund. Great as was the simplification produced by this consolidation, in comparison with modern tariffs the Rate Book of 1787 was still a formidable list of duties, the payment of which was still governed by numerous and complicated regulations.

Pitt, like Walpole, tried to keep the country at peace, and for the first years of his ministry he was successful. But the Revolution of 1789 in France eventually led to war being declared by that country on Britain four years later and all Europe was plunged once more into a series of terrible wars. Pitt had virtually put an end to tea smuggling by reducing the duty on that commodity so that it was no longer profitable during peacetime, but because of this war heavy additions to Custom taxation were made in quick succession, including an increased duty on tea. In 1793, the year of the declaration of war, the Custom Revenue produced £3,557,000 for the Exchequer; by 1796 the amount had risen to £7,056,000, nearly double.

The tariff of Great Britain was again codified and consolidated in 1803 by Acts which brought into one fund, the Consolidated Fund, the several additional duties imposed since Pitt's reforms of 1787. But the outbreak of war after the short-lived Peace of Amiens necessitated fresh alterations. The conflict now was with Napoleon Bonaparte, who, without formally declaring war, seized and imprisoned 10,000 British people who were peacefully travelling in France. In 1803, and for the next eleven years, these unfortunate people were kept, to their sorrow and discomfort, in close confinement. Fighting soon began again on both sides as vigorously as ever. Bonaparte, who had proclaimed himself Emperor in 1804, resolved to conquer the whole of Europe and to make himself the chief person in it. 'I must,' he said, 'make but one nation of all the countries in Europe, and Paris shall be the capital of it, and of all the world.' He had already carried out a large portion of his plans, and was threatening to land in England. So sure was he of success that in readiness for the event he had a medal struck which was inscribed with the words 'Landing in England 1804'.

This insolent threat roused the British. From the Isle of Thanet to Cape Wrath men rallied to their country's defence and an army of 10,000 volunteers was prepared to meet the invader. To finance this new struggle, additional 'temporary' or 'war' duties were added. They comprised a general increase of 12.5 per cent on most duties, with sugar, tea, wine and timber dealt with separately.

When peace came over a decade later, Britain and Europe needed time to recover from this long and expensive war. The population had increased rapidly during the war, but food was still the main item in the working man's budget. During years of poor harvests, there would be great distress and often rioting in the countryside. There was also much unemployment after the war, not only because of troops returning from the campaigns in Europe, but also because of new machines replacing workers, particularly in the cotton industry. Many people drifted into smuggling as a means to earn money. An enormous National Debt, amounting to millions that had been spent on armaments and on paying Britain's allies, ensured that import duties remained comparatively high and that smuggling was profitable. Those in charge of running contraband cargoes could afford to pay many ex-servicemen.

Endeavours were made in 1823 and 1826 to codify and simplify the Custom Laws. Mr James Deacon Hume reduced the numerous laws to eleven Bills, further dealing with every branch of Custom business and including a consolidated tariff for the United Kingdom. These Bills became law and took effect from the beginning of 1826. Thus, steps had been taken to lighten the number of duties and reduce the long list of articles prohibited from being imported or which could only be imported under severe restriction. The ultimate triumph of legitimate free trade came as late at 1860 when the Chancellor of the Exchequer announced to the Commons following the Commercial Treaty with France, 'England engaged, with a limited power of exemption, with respect to only two or three articles, to abolish immediately and totally all duties upon manufactured goods from the face of the British tariff.'

Throughout this period of open running of contraband goods, the government made rather vague and pathetic attempts to prohibit or at least reduce the practice. But apart from Walpole, who was defeated by political machination, and Pitt, who was undone by the declaration of war by France, the chief ministers lacked convictions strong enough to break the neck of the free trade. The laws they did enact, designed to save the Revenue millions, were of little use because the government would not release the mere thousands of pounds necessary to ensure that men of sufficient ability and keenness were employed to enforce them. The government ordained certain measures, but never tried seriously to see that they were carried out. Many of the laws were so ambiguous that a conviction was unlikely. Vessels were not to 'hover' (a sort of maritime loitering with intent) near the coast. 'Suspicious' ships were to be boarded by officers; persons going 'disguised and armed' were liable to arrest and imprisonment. Other Acts were more exact but no less difficult to interpret, particularly by members of the Preventive Waterguard, who had the right to seize illegal types of vessels on sight, on a wild and windy night in the Channel. No person, for example, was to have in his possession boats that could be rowed with more than four oars and no vessel was to have a bowsprit exceeding two-thirds of the vessel in length. It was not until the end of the Napoleonic Wars that the authorities finally recognised the magnitude of the problem and scale of open smuggling, threw down the gauntlet and entered the fray with a vengeance. But that violent end to an era is the subject of a later chapter.

2

Wool

'England's Golden Fleece'

For centuries England's chief raw material was wool, the indispensable basis of her greatest industry and the most highly prized of her products by other countries. Every class in the community, whether landlord, farmer, manufacturer or artisan, had a direct interest in wool and it was justly accorded the titles 'Goddess of Merchants' and 'England's Golden Fleece'. In an earlier chapter it was explained how the export of wool and woolfells quickly attracted a tax which became the main source of royal revenue; Edward I imposed in 1275 a custom duty of half a mark for each sack of wool exported. On the Continent the main centre of cloth making was in the valley of the Schelde in Flanders, where English wool was highly prized for its texture and length of staple and was used in the manufacture of the best-quality cloth. Spanish wool, though fine, was short and required an admixture of English or Irish wool to make fine thin cloth. Most other kinds of wool, German or French, were so coarse that the cloth was not merchandisable unless mixed with British wool. The long staple of 'combing' wool in particular was claimed to be 'absolutely necessary in some of the French manufacturers'. Occasionally an embargo was placed by English rulers on its export, but the prohibition was usually short-lived; and even when nominally in force, it was easily evaded by the purchase of licences, granted for revenue purposes, allowing wool to be sent abroad.

With this governmental interference and the levying of custom duty on goods sent abroad, the door was opened to the beginning of an era of smuggling. The violent heyday of the illegal import of luxury goods in the eighteenth century has its roots in the illegal export of wool, which began with the first restrictions in the thirteenth century.

At this time wool sent to the Continent had to be shipped to a Staple port. In the early days the Staple was at Bruges and later oscillated between St Omer, Antwerp and Bruges. Towards the end of the fourteenth century, Calais, then an English possession, had become the headquarters of the Company of the Staple and the export of wool elsewhere was forbidden. However, there were certain difficulties, the prime one being to ensure that the wool was in fact exported to the Staple port and not to other ports. To ensure this happened, orders were sent in 1320 to the Collectors in various ports, reminding them to be 'very strict in the swearing of the exporters', which was a rather ambiguous yet obviously official reminder that certain merchant exporters were not doing as the government had decreed.

The conditions and restrictions relating to wool export continued to accumulate during the fourteenth century. In the third decade of that century, a Charter laid down that 'ships laden with wool, woolfells or hides', on which Great Customs were due, should clear out only from that port where the King's Seal was kept and where the Cocket Seal was held. Edward III, in an effort to raise money for his long and bitter wars with Scotland and France, was able to persuade Parliament to agree to the presage of 50,000 sacks of wool as a temporary measure, although the prise of wool was abolished soon after in 1344. The King also levied the Cloth Custom in 1347 against the wishes of Parliament, and in answer to a petition against this imposition maintained that it was just as proper to tax cloth as well as wool, on account of the proportion of wool it contained. Edward III, one of the ablest of English monarchs, in fact did much for the commercial interests of the nation. In 1353 the statute of the Staple was introduced, as a result of which certain places in England and Wales were designated as Staple towns or ports and had the monopoly of the dealings in wool, woolfells, hides and, strangely enough, lead for export.

In 1374, towards the end of the reign of Edward III, one of the greatest English poets was at the centre of the business on the side of the law. For twelve years Geoffrey Chaucer was Controller of the Customs and Subsidy of Wools, Hides and Woolfells and of the Petty Customs of Wine etc. in the Port of London, on the condition that he made the entries with his own hand. But perhaps more significant was Edward's introduction of large numbers of Flemings into this country and these immigrants fostered the expansion of the English cloth industry, growth which had a very important effect on the export of wool.

The development and growth of the woollen industry enlarged the home market for English wool and caused a natural shrinkage of the export trade, which one writer described in 1601 as 'almost wholly decayed'. After the loss of Calais (1558), the Merchant Staplers still carried on operations, but they no longer enjoyed 'an assured place of residence' abroad. Furthermore, the increasingly complex system of licences and heavy duties handicapped legitimate exporters and simply served to encourage a clandestine trade, which did not yield any revenue to the Exchequer. The fact that the normal and revenue-producing channels of the trade were thus drying up brought about a reorientation of policy. In the seventeenth century the carrying of English and Irish wool overseas was forbidden, not as a temporary expedient but as a permanent feature of the new commercial and manufacturing system. It was James I, 'upon information of the setting up of clothing and drapery in the United Provinces, and the exportation of great quantities of wool into those parts', who issued proclamations in 1614, 1617 and 1621 for the 'restraining of the wool of this realm from exportation'. These proclamations were repeated by Charles I and Cromwell and were embodied in an Act of Parliament at the Restoration that prohibited the exportation of wool in 1660. The fact that this Act remained on the statute book until 1825, for reasons both political and economic, is a striking testimony to the importance of the woollen industry, regarded both as raw wool and as finished cloths.

This total prohibition gave increased impetus almost immediately to illegal exportation. It also heralded the beginning of the rivalry of interests between the wool producer and the clothier. The embargo on wool originated in the desire to secure an abundant supply of cheap material for the native manufacturer who claimed a natural right to monopolise the use of native products. Hence the woollen manufacturers protected their own interests and, in a highly organised and efficient way, exercised the utmost vigilance and exerted considerable pressure to ensure the government acted in their best interests. The wool farmers, on the other hand, raised a violent agitation against their confinement to the home market, and an interminable argument was carried on in an increasing stream of pamphlets, letters and broadsheets.

One of the first measures introduced after the prohibition of wool exporting at the Restoration was the curiously named 'Burial in Woollen Act' of 1666. By this extraordinary Bill the clothiers persuaded Parliament to demand that all burial shrouds 'were to be of wool only' and after each burial two witnesses had to go before a notary and solemnly sign or make their marks on a certificate, swearing that 'the corps was not put in, wrapt or wound up or buried in any shirt, shift, sheet or shroud made or mingled with flax, hempe, silke, haire, gold or silver or other than what is made of sheep's wool only'. It was incredible to what extremes the government would go to protect its home woollen industry. Its legislation followed the citizen even beyond death.

Ephraim Lipson, in his *Economic History of England* (Vol. III), sets out the arguments for and against the embargo on wool. This, it must be remembered, was the beginning of the period of mercantilism when Britain jealously protected her industry and manufacturing at home. James I's proclamation of 1614 marked the beginning of this change in commercial policy as regards wool, as it was intended to check the growth of the Dutch woollen industry 'so that we may not be killed with arrows from our own quiver'; and later, French competition came to be greatly dreaded owing to the cheapness of French labour. Two propositions were accepted as axiomatic: namely that trade depressions were caused, or aggravated, by the export of wool, 'whereby the stranger's wheel is set going'; and that foreign competition could be extinguished by refusing to supply other countries with raw materials. Accordingly the discussion centred on the question of whether English wool was indispensable for the continental textile industries. The general consensus of opinion was that English and Irish wool was the finest.

The prohibition of wool was therefore defended on economic and political grounds alike. If we manufactured all our wool, ran the economic argument, 'we should have the markets of the known world to ourselves and at our own price'; if France were denied supplies of English and Irish wool, then our national enemy would be unable to carry on her manufacture 'since bricks cannot be made without straw, and we should be saved from falling a sacrifice to universal monarchy and arbitrary power'. As one writer put it in 1741:

> Our Fathers bravely pulled down the exorbitant power of France at the expense of their blood and their treasure, but never thought of the way to give her a more deadly wound than she could receive by the loss of ten battles and twice as many towns.

The export of wool, protested the English manufacturers, would be an unparalleled disaster: it would 'change the current of our wealth, destroy our industry and enterprise, deprive the poor of their employment, add to the poor rates and diminish the rental of the land'. Fantastic estimates were made as to the depreciation in the value of our woollen manufactures due to smuggling. One 'very moderate computation' was that 'the nation loses no less than 42 millions sterling yearly'. One panic-stricken 'Cheshire Weaver' in 1727, having recounted the fatal consequences attending the smuggling of wool, begged hysterically 'that it be stopped 'ere the next generation England will be no more'.

The advocates of free trade, on the other hand, with equal fervour, endeavoured to show the folly of a system in which the 'coveted vineyard' was 'watched with as much care and jealousy as the Golden Apples of the Hesperides'. The policy of protection was denounced as an evil legacy of the Great Rebellion. It was the work of Cromwell's Commonwealth party, which had 'been assisted in the Civil Wars by great numbers of the wool-workmen, who liked much better to rob and plunder for half-a-crown a day than toil at a melancholy work for sixpence a day', and which prohibited the export of wool in order 'to encourage and reward them, and to weaken the gentry'. These last words were written in 1677, obviously by a Royalist landowner and wool producer. His assertion that the Commonwealth introduced the embargo on wool export is incorrect; the first Stuart was responsible for the first proclamation against its export.

The leading exponent of the argument that free trade in wool would not harm the English manufacturers was John Smith, whose *Memoirs of Wool* (1747), though written to provoke controversy and discussion, provides a valuable storehouse of historical material. Sheep farmers and landowners thought the book 'ought to be printed in letters of gold' and considered that Smith deserved 'the universal thanks and applause of his country'. Predictably, the clothiers and manufacturers attacked it vehemently. Smith sought to combat the notion that foreign nations could not carry on their textile manufactures without English or Irish wool. In fact, he affirmed that England and Ireland no longer possessed the much-wanted superiority in wool over all other countries and therefore England gained no benefit from prohibiting its export. However, it was difficult to induce Englishmen to abandon the tradition, which had acquired almost the sanctity of a dogma, that English wool was the best in the world. This superiority in all things, which the majority of eighteenth-century Englishmen considered they possessed, was expressed by a great writer of the time, with complete conviction and without a trace of irony. Dr Johnson, according to Boswell, 'was of the opinion that the English nation cultivated both their soil and their reason better than any other people'.

The tradition went back to early times. Dionysius Periegetes, a geographer of antiquity, stated that the fleece of the sheep was 'so soft and fine' that it was spun until it was 'comparable to a spider's web'. In 1551, the Venetian envoy had remarked that among England's chief endowments was her 'very fine and most excellent wool', while Lambard, a traveller to Kent in 1576, boasted that 'the exceeding fineness of the fleece passeth all other in Europe at this day'. This opinion seems to be borne out by a Venetian merchant, who one year later wrote, 'Spanish wools cannot be compared to it.' However, in the seventeenth century English wool began to lose its pre-eminence. The reasons for the deterioration in the quality of English wool were disputed. The sheep farmers contended that it was due to the wool laws, which made it less profitable to concentrate on the fleece, but it was more commonly attributed to enclosures and the breeding of larger sheep in place of the 'ancient small breed of English sheep'. 'So long as English men are fond of fat mutton,' it was said, 'they must not expect to grow fine wool.' The best English cloth now contained a large admixture of Spanish merino wool; and our dependence on Spain deprived us of our former monopoly, and placed us on the same footing as other manufacturing countries. However, there was one kind of wool, as the advocates of free trade sometimes admitted, which was still fine and much sought after on the Continent and that was 'the soft, the snow white and the long-grown flake' of the combing wool.

The second main reason for free trade was the contention that the embargo on wool depressed its price in this country, and the low price encouraged illicit trading since the 'un-natural artificial cheapness' of the material at home made it worthwhile to smuggle it abroad. In 1675, it was represented that the price of some wool had fallen from £12 to about £4 a pack (240 lb). The fact that wool in England was kept below 'its natural value' served as 'an advantage, in the nature of a premium, to the exporter of woollen goods; yet at the same time it affords equally a premium for the runnage of wool'. 'This in a word,' maintained John Smith, 'is the mainspring of the owling trade.' Owling was the name given to the illegal exportation of wool, presumably because it was usually carried out under cover of darkness. The ultimate word on this second argument remains a trading truism: 'They that can give the best price for a commodity shall never fail to have it.'

There remained the final plea that it was the duty of the nation to preserve the landed classes, the 'masters and proprietors of the foundation of all the wealth in this nation', who maintained great families, bore the burden of taxes, and filled all the magistracies and public offices. This was a very important point, and it must be emphasised that a holding of land was a fundamental requirement for political involvement. The ruination of the landed interest was deemed the more indefensible because it was 'the most considerable national interest', and wool was its 'principal' support. It was therefore on the grounds of injustice that the wool growers denounced 'the oppression which the grazier suffers under this iniquitous system of monopoly'. A Lincolnshire grazier in 1727 put their case bluntly by asking:

> If he that combs, dyes, weaves, works or exports wool thrives, why should he that grows it be impoverished? Why must the grazier be the only sufferer, where all other dealers in wool are gainers by it?' The manufacturers replied that the welfare of the landed and industrial interests 'mutually depend on each other.

They further argued, though somewhat tenuously, that the value of land depended on trade inasmuch as a prosperous trade increased the demand for agricultural produce such as corn, beef, mutton, etc. Hence, in their opinion, the farmers were compensated in other directions if the wool sold at a lower price at home than it would fetch abroad. Smith retorted that the embargo on the export trade in wool might benefit the export trade in cloth, but it certainly created a monopoly against the grower, and 'whether thus robbing Peter to enrich Paul is of any real public benefit, that is the point to be considered'.

Arthur Young, in his *Annals of Agriculture*, was conspicuous for the vigour with which he repudiated the alleged identity of interests between agriculture and industry: 'Let us hear no more from wool men of the prosperity of land and manufactures being the same.' He bitterly deplored the fact that that the gentlemen of the landed interest had quietly laid themselves down to be fleeced by the wool men, like their sheep; and he scathingly declared 'that the sweets of a monopoly of their raw materials' had made the woollen manufacturers indolent and devoid of the 'ardour of enterprise' or 'the spirit of adventure'.

Another protection for the English cloth industry was that the export of fuller's earth was prohibited. Most of the fuller's earth was quarried from a sandstone ridge near Maidstone, Kent, and it was in great demand in other English cloth-making areas, especially East Anglia. Nearly all the Kentish earth left from Millhall and New Hythe direct for the East Coast; almost none was distributed through London because of the low specific value of the earth. Nonetheless, throughout the seventeenth century large amounts were dispatched illegally. Sometime in the 1630s, the Customer responsible for the Port of Rochester was prosecuted in the Star Chamber for allowing 4,000 chaldrons of the earth to leave the port since 1627.

That a Parliament dominated by landowners should have made the sacrifice which the wool laws entailed indicates that it was not incapable at times of subordinating class interests to what it considered to be the national interest. For, in spite of their arguments, the efforts of the wool growers to secure a limited legal exportation of wool proved unsuccessful. In 1788 the penalties on the export of sheep or wool were made more stringent despite strenuous efforts by Arthur Young in opposing the Wool Bill. Throughout the wool-manufacturing districts there was great rejoicing when the Bill became an Act and a contemporary account records that the 'bells were set a ringing'. The severity of the penalties imposed at one period or another called forth Adam Smith's bitter reflection that the laws, 'which the clamour of our merchants and manufacturers has extorted from the legislature for the support of their own absurd and oppressing monopolies', may be said 'like the laws of Draco to be written in blood'.

The great political and economic debate in Westminster meant little to the sheep farmers and landowners of Romney Marsh. While people like John Smith were arguing passionately for the right to trade freely, the menfolk of the South Coast were doing just that, and in fact had been free trading for centuries. The law of Westminster was not the law of Romney Marsh. The free trader of the South Coast considered himself above the Proclamations, Acts and Prohibitions; he considered it his right to go across the sea, free to buy and sell without the inconvenience of observing statutes made by politicians in London. And, particularly during the early period of this illegal wool exporting, the free trader found a whole society, from the gentry and squires (who were the graziers, or sheep farmers, and landowners) down to the farm labourers (who unloaded and loaded his boats at night time), who, if not openly condoning the trade, were not sufficiently motivated to speak out against it. A guinea in the palm usually secured silence anyway. A contemporary author in 1677 described the wool-producing landowners as 'A militia, that, in defiance of all authority, convey their wool to the French shallops lying off the coast with such strength, that the officers dare not offend them.'

During the first half of the seventeenth century sheep farming in Kent expanded rapidly, especially on Romney Marsh, where the digging of drainage ditches and dykes produced excellent pastures. The national wool market was in London and wool was first sent to Canterbury and then dispatched via the ports of Milton and, more particularly, Faversham. Wool from the sheep on the Thames-side marshes and North Kent was sent to market via Faversham. The inhabitants of this port do not seem to have enjoyed a very high reputation, for Defoe wrote in his travel journal that the people of Faversham are said to have grown 'monstrous rich' by 'that wicked trade', implying that the legal distribution of woolpacks was not the only business they were involved in.

There was one person, however, who was determined to reduce the amount of wool being illegally exported from Kent. For many years in the second half of the seventeenth century, the indefatigable enemy of the owlers was William Carter, a Custom House official, who by the written word and by determined action endeavoured to bring the law of Westminster to the windswept, open pastureland of Romney Marsh. In a pamphlet of 1669 he described the owlers' methods:

First, in Romney Marsh in Kent, where the greatest part of rough wool is exported from England, put aboard French shallops by night, ten or twenty men well armed to guard it, some other parts there are, as in Sussex, Hampshire and Essex, the same methods may be used but not so conveniently. The same for combed wool from Canterbury; they will carry it ten or fifteen miles at night towards the sea with the like guard as before.

Two years later Carter was more emphatic:

The misery of England is the great quantity of wool stolen out of England. In the town of Calais alone, there have been, within two years, brought in 40,000 packs of wool from the coasts of Kent and Sussex, for the men of Romney Marsh, seeing the ease and profit with which they can sell their own wool, have now become wool merchants as well, buying wool as far as twenty miles inland, bringing it down to the shores of the marsh and shipping it of.

Britain's policy of export prohibition or raw material conservation had almost forced these men to break the law to preserve their own livelihood.

Sometimes, as a measure of precaution while the wool was afloat, it was pressed into barrels with screws, and then the barrels were 'washed over with brine-water' in order that they might pass for beef or herrings. Carter reported, 'These barrels are not put on board in ports where they are liable to be examined but conveyed into creeks from whence they are shipped off.' Another device to export wool illegally was to manufacture goods very loosely so that the wool was easily unravelled once it was sent abroad.

According to one statement (1703), wool in its raw state (fleece wool) was worth in Ireland 4d per pound and combed wool 10d. However, in France the first was sold for half a crown a pound, the second for 5s 6d or 6s. These facts prompted a member of the House of Lords to remark, 'The temptation is really almost too great to be withstood, especially by such who only measure their consciences by gain.' However, profits fluctuated quite considerably, particularly when a state of war added yet more risks to the enterprise. Overseas markets suffered from trade fluctuations just as home ones did. One ship's captain told the House of Lords (1704) that a 'glut of wool' brought down the price of combed wool in St Malo from 5s 4d to 3s 9d per pound. John Smith, in his *Memoirs of Wool* (1747), gave a more conservative estimate of a profit of 3d a pound on English wool, which amounted to 50 per cent or 60 per cent in regard to the capital employed.

Shipping wool to the Continent involved a considerable financial outlay for the clandestine wool-trader and it is hardly surprising that he would resort to violence to protect his own goods. The diligent Customs officer became inured to violence. On one occasion William Carter arrested a smuggler in Folkestone, 'But the women of the town came out of their houses and gathered up stones upon the beach, which they flung about my ears so violently that having no help I was forced to quit my prisoner, hardly escaping myself.' During 1688 the soon-to-be-deposed James II issued a proclamation which denounced those who 'by open force and violence with armed companies of men conveyed wool beyond the seas'. In the same year the intrepid Carter had another unpleasant experience at the hands of the Marsh folk. This incident served as further notice to the authorities that the free traders would brook no interference from men who had the courage to confront them directly but lacked the means of defeating public apathy and corruption. It was an ominous prelude to the ugly violence of the next century.

During December, Carter got word that a number of men openly and in broad daylight were taking wool by packhorse to a beach somewhere between Romney Marsh and Folkestone, where it was going to be shipped on board French boats and taken to the Continent. The openness and audacity of this operation were too much for the indignant Carter to bear and, having secured the necessary warrants and a party of men to assist him, he rode to Romney, seized the ten smugglers involved red-handed, delivered them to the Mayor of Romney and requested they be imprisoned to await trial. The owlers' incredulity at an interloper daring to interfere with their trade was immediately shared by Carter when the Mayor promptly set the men free on bail. It is hypothetical to conjecture the motive behind this astonishing act. The Mayor was placed in a difficult position but the law was quite clear, and it would appear that he was more concerned with what would happen to him if the prisoners were not released, for the owlers' methods of persuasion were based on violence and corruption rather than reason and integrity. One writer asserted that probably the Mayor was financially involved in the operation, although this must remain as supposition.

After such an unexpected development Carter prudently realised that Romney was no safe place for himself and his men and so they rode to Lydd, four miles away across the Marsh, where they intended to spend the night. Lord Teignmouth takes up the story:

> But if they had fondly expected peace and shelter there they were woefully mistaken, for a Marshland cry of vengeance was raised and a howling mob of owlers, ululating more savagely than those melancholy birds from which they took their name, violently attacked them in that little town, under cover of night.

The 'howling mob of owlers' were clearly bent on impressing upon Carter that his interference was not only imprudent but extremely unpopular. The Mayor of Lydd's son, displaying a questionable mixture of virtue and good sense, visited Carter and his men and advised them to quit Lydd as soon as possible and head for the greater safety of Rye, across the Sussex border ten miles away. The advice was heeded and on 13 December the unlucky men representing the authority of the Crown stepped out at first light. They were hotly pursued by the furious owlers. The deep and muddy tidal estuary of the Rother lay between Carter's party and the sanctuary of Rye and as the Guildeford Ferry was not in evidence his men commandeered some rowing boats. Leaving their horses behind, they tumbled in and hurriedly rowed across just before the owlers arrived. A contemporary writer records that the town of Rye had been 'put into much fear' and acknowledged, with marvellous understatement, that 'had they not got into the boats, Mr Carter would have received some hurt, for many of the exporters were desperate fellows, not caring what mischief they did'.

Officialdom appears to have left Romney Marsh to itself for the next few years. After Carter's abortive trip and lucky escape in 1688, it seems likely that he did not wish to risk his neck again for a government that appeared content merely to denounce the illegal trade rather than provide a force adequate to implement the laws against it. However, the slumbering lion of government stirred in 1696, but only long enough to flick its tail. Parliament, realising the contempt shown to its earlier laws, reduced the severity of the penalty for illegal wool exporting, in order, hopefully, not to deter the prosecution of offenders. Two years later, in 1695, ships were appointed to 'constantly cruise on the coasts of England and Ireland to seize vessels exporting wool'. This laudable aim was in fact supported by a ludicrously small number of ships and in 1700 the Admiralty reported that they had not taken a single contraband vessel, while they had lost two of their own and expected to lose others, and the cost involved amounted to £2,400 a month.

The situation in Kent and Sussex merited special attention because these two wool-producing counties enjoyed a close proximity to France. In the 1698 Wool Act, there was a section which decreed that no person living within fifteen miles of the sea in the counties of Kent and Sussex would be allowed to buy any wool without first entering into a legal bond, with sureties, that none of the wool he bought would be sold by him to any persons within the same fifteen miles of the sea. Also the growers of wool in those counties within ten miles of the coast were obliged within three days of shearing to account for the total number of fleeces shorn, and to state where they were stored. To enforce this law, there was appointed for all England a total of seventeen Surveyors (for nineteen counties) and 299 Riding officers – such a force would have been barely sufficient for Kent and Sussex alone. The service cost £20,000 a year to run and the Supervisor of the Riding officers for Kent and Sussex was Henry Baker.

In April 1698 Baker wrote to the Commissioners of Custom in London, informing them that within a few weeks there would be shorn in Romney Marsh and the adjoining levels about 160,000 sheep. Their fleeces would produce about 3,000 packs of wool, 'the greatest part whereof will be immediately sent off hot into France, it being so designed, and provisions in a great measure already made for that purpose'. It is evidence of his own and his Riding officers' ineffectiveness that these remarks were simply observations. The large well-organised gangs still exported their wool as before and some of the wool-buyers, with a token gesture of adherence to the law, first took the wool over fifteen miles inland and there carried out a farcical sale before carting it off to where they pleased. In the first year following the new Act only ninety-one packs of wool were seized in Kent and Sussex and of these only twenty were successfully condemned as forfeit to the Crown. In the same period the Romney Marsh graziers alone probably exported 3,000 packs illegally.

The owling continued and in the years that followed the authorities had little more success. In 1702 the situation warranted Mr William Symonds of Milton, near Gravesend, in his *New Year's Gift to Parliament or England's Golden Fleece Preserved*, to submit a list of twenty-five proposals designed to prevent the illegal exportation of wool. His first proposal was to create six staples or register offices at Tonbridge, Ashford, Faversham, Maidstone, Gravesend and Dartford, and these places would strictly control all aspects of wool trading. Again in 1717 an Act was passed that directed those found guilty of wool smuggling to be transported if they could not pay their fine. Convictions were made as the following case shows, but they do not seem to have deterred the main body of owlers.

One night in September 1714 a sloop came over from France and discharged a cargo of brandy at Cooden Halt, near Bexhill, without any official interference. The sloop then sailed westwards under the white cliffs to Cuckmere Haven to pick up a load of wool for shipment to France. The horses duly arrived on the beach carrying their packs and the wool was taken aboard. The captain, Pierre Zoussay, was just about to give orders to weigh anchor when out of the dark a Revenue vessel appeared commanded by Captain Toddman, who seized the sloop, the wool and the crew in the King's name and took them into Hastings. Zoussay, his four French crew and an Englishman, John Spice, were committed to Horsham Gaol and at their subsequent trial they were each fined £60, a sum they could not possibly hope to raise. They were returned to gaol, where they found themselves in the company of Thomas Wisdom, who had been committed for a riot and assault upon His Majesty's Customs officers and for recapturing some smuggled wool.

The story has an interesting sequel. Being committed to gaol in the eighteenth century for non-payment of a fine (and with little prospect of getting money to pay that fine) meant that the debtor faced a long period of confinement with poor food in cramped and filthy conditions, so all in all it would have been a very miserable time for the Frenchmen. John Collier, Surveyor General of the Riding officers of Kent and Sussex, wrote a report to the Commissioners on their condition, stating that

> all six lye in a miserable, starving condition, having not shirts to their back or hardly any other clothes. The keeper of the gaol affirms that they have received no remittance since they have been in gaol and they must have all perished if the charity of the townspeople of Horsham had not prevented it.

In their petition to the Lords of the Treasury, twelve months after conviction, the prisoners, 'having no clothes to cover our nakedness and now starving at the point of death humbly beg for God's sake that your Lordships will take pity'. It may be presumed that their Lordships did take pity and that the Frenchmen, after enduring a year in an English prison, were not tempted to run the risk of such confinement again.

But we should return to Henry Baker, who during his years in charge of the Riding officers of Kent and Sussex seemed singularly incapable of comprehending the actual degree of smuggling. It was during his period of authority at the turn of the century that the nature of the smuggling trade began to change, as the Cuckmere Haven incident showed. Wool was still exported but the free traders were beginning to realise there was equal, if not more, profit in the importing of luxury French goods such as brandy, silks and laces. Baker knew about this new trade but he failed to see, maybe did not want to see, the shift in emphasis from export smuggling to import smuggling. At a time when an augmentation of the Preventive force was needed, Baker was writing to his superiors and recommending, incredibly as it may seem, that, in his view, reductions in the service were in order:

May it please your Honours, in obedience to your Honours, commanding me to consider how the charge of the Riding officers appointed for the guard of the coasts of Kent and Sussex may in some measure, be reduced without prejudice to her Majesty's service, in preventing the exporting of wool, etc., from these coasts. Upon consideration thereof, and from observations I have made of the state of that and the smuggling trade, I have observed and do believe that the neck of the owling trade, as well as the spirits of the owlers, is, in a great measure, broke, particularly in Romney Marsh [where] wool used to be shipped off from thence and from other parts of that country by great numbers of packs weekly, there are not now many visible signs of any quantity being transported. But for fine goods as they call them (viz. silks, lace, etc.), I am well assured that trade goes on through both counties as have been formerly brought in. I mean in those days when (as a gentleman of estate in one of the counties has, within this twelve months, told me) he had been at once, besides at other times, at the loading of a wagon with silks, lace, till six oxen could hardly move it out of the place; I do not think that trade is now so carried on as 'twas then. Therefore, I humbly propose: That whereas there are now, for the security of those coasts, fifty officers appointed from the Isle of Sheppey in Kent, to Emsworth in Hampshire, which is coastwise more two hundred miles £60 per annum, with an allowance to each of them of £30 per annum, for a servant and horse, to assist them upon their duty in the night, the whole amounting to about £4,500 per annum, my opinion is ... that the said allowance of £30 to each of them ... may be taken off, which will completely reduce one third part of the whole, and leave it then at about £3,000 per annum: and for some kind of supply in their nightly duty, instead of their servants, and that the course of that may not be broken, especially in Romney Marsh, where the mischief has most prevailed, I further propose that the dragoons now quartered in Kent ... be detached into several parts of the Marsh, to assist the officers ... as from time to time I shall direct ... To all this, if your Honours can obtain the guard of cruisers for those coasts from the North Foreland to the Isle of Wight, and shall be pleased to remove your weak and superannuated officers, as soon as you can provide otherwise for them, and … that the officers be kept to a strict and diligent discipline in the performance of their duties. These methods being taken, I am humbly of opinion both coasts may be ventured with a single guard, so as aforesaid, during the war, or for one years trial etc.

December 1703　　Hen. Baker

It must be remembered that their Honours had decided on economies and it appears that Baker felt obliged to supply suggestions as to how these were to be effected. Even so, his letter shows his inability to take stock of the true situation. Admittedly the owling business may have diminished but, as Defoe observed twenty years later, this was probably due to economic rather than legislative reasons, for the French were getting their wool from Ireland rather than the South Coast 'with much less hazard, and at very little more expense'. But if the owling neck had been broken then the body was still very much alive, and the body now belonged not to an owling exporter but to a gin-swilling tobacco-smoking importer.

Despite the apparent reduction in owling, or (more correctly) the increase in import smuggling, the clothiers continued to petition Parliament for greater vigilance against the clandestine exportation of wool. They stated with sanctimonious disgust that it was 'feared that some gentlemen, of no mean rank, whose estates bordered on the sea coast, were too much influenced by a near but false prospect of gain' to wish for the application of a remedy proposed: namely the registration of all wool at shearing time, and a complete system of certificates until it was manufactured 'so that no smuggler or owler would venture to purchase it, by reason he would have no opportunity of sending it abroad in the dark'. To support their case the clothiers presented facts and figures which showed how necessary it was to keep the raw wool in England, where it could be worked up into woollen goods.

	£	s	d
One Man to sort and dry it		8	0
To clean, dye, etc.	1	10	0
4 Men + 2 boys to scribble it	2	8	0
30 women and girls to card and spin it	6	0	0
4 boys to spool and wind quills		10	0
4 Women to burl it		12	0
4 Men + a boy to scour, full, row shear, rack and press it	3	4	0
8 men to weave it	4	16	0
	19	8	0

One pack of long combing wool (a pack weighed 240 lb) from Kent – made into fine stuffs, serges, Sagathies, camblets and long ells for the Spanish and Portuguese trades – was estimated to give full employment for one week to 158 persons, who would have earned £33 12s 0d. Another pamphleteer in 1740 complained that the wool-trading ports of Bristol, Minehead, Barnstable, Braintree, Norwich, Yarmouth, etc., had all declined in recent years because Dutch and Spanish merchants no longer came to them to buy their woollen manufactured goods. The same writer estimated that the loss to the nation was a staggering £42 million pounds a year.

A proposal for a national scheme was rejected by the Commissioners for Trade and Plantations in 1732 on the ground that it would be very expensive and involve a 'multiplicity of accounts'. Nevertheless, a few years later the idea was revived; and in response to a petition from the Lord Mayor and Aldermen of London expressing 'unspeakable grief' at 'so great and crying an evil', the House of Commons passed a resolution (1741) declaring that 'a public register of the wool grown in Great Britain and Ireland is the most effectual method for preventing the exportation thereof to foreign parts'. No machinery, however, was instituted for implementing the resolution and smuggling went on unchecked. The severity of the penalty did not deter those who boasted that 'if a gallows was set up every quarter of a mile, yet they would carry the wool off'.

Wool smuggling continued well into the eighteenth century. In 1745 a farmer at Sheerness, Mr Rose, was robbed of £1,500 worth of wool. A week after this happened a vessel was seized off the Kent coast carrying £3,000 of wool and eight people were taken into custody. In July of the same year a certain Simpson of Whitehaven in Cumberland was found guilty of running 2,700 lb of wool to France and fined £405. In July 1749 James Toby was capitally convicted for carrying wool to France. The hempen jig was assured for him when the court heard that during the last war he had not only supplied the French merchants with wool but also their privateers with swivel guns. In October the same year an 'eminent factor in woollen manufacturing' was apprehended for sending artefacts relating to the industry to Spain.

In April 1750 the government brought in an Act of Parliament which increased the penalties for enticing workers from the home woollen manufacturing industry to go and work abroad. The fine was increased from £100 to £500 for the first offence, and for the second offence this was increased to £1,000 and two years' imprisonment. On 4 July the same year a certain Richard Metcalf was found guilty of persuading four woollen workers to go to Spain and was given three months' imprisonment and fined £100. In 1758, during the Seven Years' War, the privateer *Ferret*, captained by Joseph English, brought into Bristol the *Two Brothers*, which was out of Dingle in western Ireland and bound for the enemy port of Brest. On board were seventy-five bags of combed wool, five bags of fleece wool, 300 firkins of butter, two bags of hair, 20 tons of coal and one cask of flannen.

The Riding officer for New Romney, W. Elliot, informed the Commissioners of the Custom in December 1781, at a time when most of the dragoons quartered in the Marsh had been removed because of the American War of Independence, 'I have heard that there has been a great deal of that business (owling) done lately on our coast. Wool is brought from the hills mostly on horses and lodged somewhere within five or six miles of the sea to be handy to put on board in the night time by a gang of smugglers', and, as a covering afterthought, he adds 'which are persons unknown to the officers'.

Adam Smith acknowledged in *The Wealth of Nations* that 'Government restrictions which dated back to the Middle Ages, meant wool is exported, it is well known, in great quantities'. The final word on this era of export smuggling must remain with that sage who wrote, 'Long experience hath demonstrated that the mere prohibiting of the exportation of wool is but a cobweb.'

3

The Early History of the Preventive Services

'We are very much infested with smugglers'

After 1671, as stated earlier, the collection of Custom was taken out of farm and a Board of Customs introduced in its place. The Commissioners, therefore, had to replace many of the officials of the 'farmers' with their own staff. By the beginning of the eighteenth century the staffing of the service had been more or less consolidated. There were three main categories: Headquarters (Custom House on the Embankment), London Port and the Outports. The Headquarters staff consisted of seven Commissioners appointed by patent; a Principal Secretary who attended to the Commissioners, reading such representations, petitions and letters as should be laid before them, receiving their instructions and drawing up answers for the Commissioners to sign. To assist him, the secretary had two clerks, one for the western ports from London along the South Coast to Milford in Pembrokeshire and one for the northern ports from London northwards along the east coast and down the west coast as far as Beaumaris in Anglesey. A solicitor plus his assistant was also appointed by patent and it was his business to prosecute all goods forfeited and illegally imported and all persons offending against the Acts of Trade and the Customs Laws. The Commissioners would also consult him on all legal matters before giving direction.

This hierarchy was backed up by a number of officials with imposing titles who ensured that the decrees issued by the Commissioners were carried out. The Receiver-General received all the revenue money collected throughout England and paid it weekly to the Exchequer; the Register-General received the copies of the ship's registers; the Inspector-General of imports and exports valued commodities and drew up an estimate of the balance of trade with every country and entered the details in a ledger; the Surveyor of the Outports received the quarterly books of imports and exports and the duties paid thereon; the Inspector of Prosecutions kept an account of all prosecutions by Customs officers and ensured that the King's moiety of all fines and forfeitures was duly paid into the Exchequer; and the Register of Seizures received information of every seizure made by Customs officers, and checked on them to ensure that collusive seizures or compromises were not made.

The establishment of the Port of London included two Collectors Outwards who had deputies and clerks in the Long Room at Custom House. Their business was to accept entries, work out the duties and receive them on all goods entered outwards. There were likewise two Collectors Inwards with deputies and clerks who carried out the same work with regard to goods imported. The Comptroller of the Port was required to check upon the collection of Customs duties and approve all merchants' securities in connection with duties which were bondable. There was a Comptroller of the Issues and Payments of the Receiver-General and a Surveyor who kept an account of the duties received and served as a check upon the Collector.

The London Searchers Office was made up of the Chief Searcher, six Under-Searchers and five Searchers, who worked together and were responsible for the shipping of goods at Custom House Quay. In addition there were nine Land Surveyors who supervised the thirty-one Land Waiters and nineteen King's Waiters stationed on the quays between the Tower and London Bridge. Eight Tide Surveyors supervised the boarding of tidesmen on ships and visited them from time to time. The two hundred tidesmen – or tidewaiters, as they were often called – were boarded on ships according to the type and value of the cargo, from two to eight at a time.

They had to ensure that no goods were 'run', that ships were properly discharged and that goods on which customs drawback was claimed were not re-landed. They were regularly sent to Gravesend to board ships from foreign parts but East Indiamen were boarded at Deal. The tidesmen were divided into two classes: 'preferable' and 'extraordinary', the first being in constant employment.

There were also seventeen Land Carriage men who were appointed to certain stations, where they could watch the inns to which the wagons and packhorses came from the various parts of the kingdom, and see that no dutiable or prohibited goods were brought except with proper certificates and permits. Lastly, seventeen coastwaiters had to supervise the landing and shipping of goods carried in coasting vessels and ensure that goods consigned coastwise did not go abroad and thus avoid the export duty.

In the outport headports there was normally a patent Collector (Customer), Controller and Searcher. The patent officials frequently nominated officials to act in their stead, particularly in the smaller ports or creeks, where some of the offices were often combined. Each port would have one or more landwaiter, tidewaiter and coastwaiter, whose functions were similar to those of the London officials. As in London, tidewaiters were supervised by Tide Surveyors.

As mentioned, the Wool Act of 1698 had brought about the establishment of a force of 299 Riding officers supervised by seventeen Riding Surveyors. This force was created specifically to keep a check on the movement of wool and to prevent its illegal export, but it also had to combat smuggling generally. The preventive measures were assisted by a small number of Revenue sloops specially commissioned to intercept suspected wool-smuggling vessels. These Revenue boats first appeared in 1680, during the reign of Charles II, and did not exceed ten in number at the beginning of the eighteenth century.

There were only two vessels to patrol the Kent and Sussex coast, where the bulk of the owling was carried on; one was stationed at Dover, and the other, *Amelia*, at Rye. However, under William III, Parliament enacted:

> That for the better preventing the exportation of wool and correspondence with France … the Lord High Admiral of England … shall from time to time direct and appoint one ship of the Fifth Rate, and two ships of the Sixth Rate, and four armed sloops constantly to patrol off the North Foreland to the Isle of Wight, with orders for taking and seizing all ships, vessels or boats which shall export wool or carry or bring any prohibited goods or any suspected persons.

Thus the assistance of men-of-war was enlisted specifically in suppressing the smuggling trade; however, they only assisted during the rare interludes of peace. The efficiency of the Preventive waterguard was further weakened by the fact that when England was at war, which was for the major part of the period between William and Mary's accession and the end of the Napoleonic Wars, frequently the Revenue sloops were called away as well.

Thus the Preventive force designed to combat the illegal importation and exportation of goods at the beginning of the eighteenth century consisted of three groups. In the ports and creeks there were the land and tidewaiters, Land Carriage men and coastwaiters who checked for smuggled goods both ashore and afloat. Patrolling the stretches of open coastline between the ports were the Riding officers whose task was to prevent the clandestine running of goods. At sea were the Revenue sloops intended to intercept the smuggling boats, if they should escape the attention of the other two groups. In theory and in London, this threefold system of prevention was adequate; in practice, and on the South Coast, it merely provided a mild irritant to the free traders who openly flouted the law and took little regard of the officers who were meant to enforce it.

Henry Baker was appointed Custom Supervisor for Kent and Sussex in 1698 and his career has been traced in some detail in an earlier chapter. It was he who believed that the neck of the owling trade was broken and in December 1703 there were not 'many visible signs' of any quantities of wool being exported. In the same report to the Board, Baker further believed that the running of fine goods (silks, laces, etc.) was not carried out on the same scale as before. He seems to have been incapable of comprehending the scale of smuggling at the time. Obviously the number of smuggling runs fluctuated for economic and physical reasons and his report of December 1703 might have followed two months of severe storms which would have curtailed smuggling activities, but he had been in charge of a force designed to prevent smuggling for five years now and during that time had failed to see that not only was wool still being exported but that the illegal trade in import goods was also growing fast. He reasoned in his report that cuts were justified and his economies would save the Commissioners £1,500 a year. These economies were illusory as the smuggling continued unabated, and free traders flourished.

Collier's first major duty on becoming Surveyor General, undertaken in 1734, was a general survey, which he repeated annually, 'to inspect into the conduct and behaviour of the several officers employed in that service and having likewise to examine into the entries and disposals of wool in that county within ten miles of the sea and of the registers kept for that purpose'. Under his jurisdiction in that first year of office were thirty-six Riding officers, four Supervisors of Riding officers, five wool registrars (one each at Margate, Whitstable, Faversham, Milton and Rochester) and one Revenue sloop stationed at Dover under the captaincy of a man called Pickering but, at the time of Collier's first report, temporarily out of commission because it was being repaired. Most of the Riding officers were allocated stretches of coast to watch from Dartford right round to Rye, but a few had inland jobs, such as George Herbert, stationed at Southborough near Tunbridge Wells, whose task was sublimely described as being 'to combat the quantities of run goods from the Sussex coasts', a massive undertaking for a man in his seventies.

Collier visited each of his men and wrote in his letter to the Board a progress report on each. Those he considered inefficient were dismissed. Richard Thunder of Birchington did not create a favourable impression with Collier, who described him as 'a poor, insolent man and one whom I believe doth little duty'. Thunder was allocated the six miles between Birchington and Reculver, while stretches of coast that were more favoured for runs were patrolled by Riding officers with a smaller beat, thus John Bridges and John Tucker were responsible for the seven to eight miles of coast between Dover and Deal. Even four miles of coast was a long stretch to watch all night and every night and it is little wonder that runs were effected with the minimum of interference from the Riding officers.

In his first report Collier noted that there had been 258,494 fleeces of sheep registered by his officials in the ports. This is a high figure, but with the accepted corruption and bribery of the day it is not unreasonable to assume there was appreciable inaccuracy. Furthermore, there was no guarantee that even if the wool were registered it would not end up as warp or weft on Flemish looms. The bookwork involved in keeping track of each fleece must have been so cumbersome that there was ample scope for fraudulent practices. Collier concluded his report with a stern warning:

I humbly observe to your Honours that the smugglers in Romney Marsh are associated into very large formidable gangs and that without the assistance of dragoons [I] believe that the Riding officers will not be able to guard the coast to prevent the clandestine running of goods.

The Commissioners seem to have been impressed by Collier's determined start to his duties, for after the request for dragoons there is a note in brackets: 'they are ordered'. Collier was pleased to write that his proposals were implemented to some extent since he noted at the end of his annual report:

> Since my survey and the report made thereon, there are nineteen dragoons come into Romney Marsh on the application of the Commissioners of the Excise and are quartered at Hythe, Romney and Lydd. The Cornet, who is the Commanding Officer, had intimated to the Customs officers that he had orders to assist them in the execution of their duty.

However, dragoon assistance was not the panacea for smuggling; in fact, Collier's worries were only just beginning.

The smuggling gangs were now assembling in large numbers and arming themselves not only with 'bats', stout sticks of holly or ash, but with firearms as well. The dragoon assistance was grudgingly given, for they disliked being seconded to this particular duty and had little stomach for waiting and watching on cold nights for elusive smugglers who knew the lanes and dykes of the Marsh intimately. Subsequently it was extremely difficult for the Revenue officers to do their duty since the local population was so hostile to them. This hostility even extended to the juries before whom offenders were brought. Collier gives a striking example of this when two soldiers were indicted for the murder of a smuggler.

Thomas Elgood and Robert Biscoe were two privates belonging to Brigadier General Cope's Regiment of Foot and were stationed at Hastings under Sergeant Angell to assist the Customs officers in the execution of their duty. On Friday 24 October 1735, suspecting that a large quantity of goods would be run, three Customs officers assisted by Sergeant Angell and his men went to a place called Hollington, three miles from Hastings, where they divided into two groups and hid in the hedges and trees bordering the highway. 'The moon was shining very bright' and about midnight they saw a person approaching whom they assumed to be a 'fore runner' sent ahead of the smuggling gang to see if the coast was clear. This assumption appears to have been correct, for in less than a quarter of an hour the men hidden in the hedgerow heard a great number of horses coming along the road from the direction of the sea. The small party nearest the shore, comprising Elgood, Biscoe, and two Customs officers, Hide and Bourne, let the gang go past. The gaggle of about thirty horses laden with goods and a great number of men moved inland.

Further up the road the other Customs officer, Thomas Carswell (murdered in 1744 during another affray with smugglers), and the rest of the soldiers were in hiding. Carswell boldly stepped out from the hedge and challenged the first rider to tell him the goods he was carrying. The man answered with a great oath, 'None for him' and so the Customs officer tried to grab hold of the horse's bridle.

The leading smuggler reined his horse round and shouted to his compatriots to retreat. The gang immediately rode off at full gallop back down the road. Carswell and his men gave pursuit and at the same time called out for Hide and Bourne to stop them. When the latter attempted to intervene the smugglers 'struck at the officers with the great ends of their whips and the clubs they had in their hands'. Unable to stop any of them or secure any of the goods, Hide called out to the soldiers to fire. This they did, but the smugglers got away, and as the officers and soldiers were pursuing them they saw something lying in the road at some distance from where the action took place. It was a body and the officers carried it to a nearby alehouse. At the subsequent inquest the dead man was identified as Peen, a carpenter who lived at Hawkhurst in Kent, but it was not known how he came to be at Hollington, nor on what business. The coroner said there was no proof that the deceased was in the gang and found that the soldiers (without naming any individually) were guilty of manslaughter and the case was committed to the assizes.

Surprisingly enough, there was a witness to this incident, a curious character who more than once agreed to take his life in his hands by testifying against the smugglers. Thomas Pettett, or Pettit, was a twilight person who skulked around the haunts of smugglers hoping to pick up information which he could sell to Collier and which would lead to an arrest and so a share of the reward or of the value of the seizure. He lived at Battle and on the day of the incident was at the Black Horse in his home town, 'an alehouse much frequented by smugglers', where he saw a great many persons he knew to be smugglers. He overheard that there was going to be a run and went to Hollington to watch them. In an affidavit he testified that he saw the gang pass and then heard shots and watched the smugglers gallop back in great disorder and confusion. Pettit heard two of them propose to go to Whatlington and conceal their goods in 'Turner's Hole', a barn belonging to John Turner, who kept an alehouse at Whatlington. This information he sent to the Hastings officers, who went to Whatlington and seized a quantity of tea.

Pettit wrote to Collier on several occasions and told him he was determined to give evidence regarding the Hollington affair, despite the fact that he feared retaliation. If his spelling is suspect his concerns are very real 'for if I should be smelt out, I moust louck to my selfe, it may cost me my life for them Holkhourst [Hawkhurst] gange are bloudthoursty fellows'. His letters were accompanied by requests for money and even clothes, for he could not or would not work in his native town. The endings were obsequious: 'I am your most dutiful servant to command the most abused Thomas Pettit.' Because of the threats from the Hawkhurst Gang he left Battle and betook himself first to Cranbrook and then to Biddenden. Unfortunately, Collier does not record the result of the Hollington case, but Pettit reappears next year when he again writes to the Surveyor General to tell him that he was on his way to Hastings from Rye when he just happened to come upon a gang of smugglers running a cargo at Fairlight. Some of them knew him as an informer and threatened to drown him but later decided to spare his life if he would swear not to betray them. He promised not to do so but later wrote to Collier, 'I shall breack my promas in what I promased them for it is a fost [forced] promas.' They placed him on a horse, bound him to one of their number and took him to Hawkhurst, where he was released and told that if any of the gang saw him in the county of Sussex they had made an oath to kill him. Collier does not record what became of Pettit, who might well have been murdered if he had persisted in his masochistic delight in informing on the smugglers.

The smugglers were becoming so audacious that if they lost some of their goods to the Revenue officers the position was not irretrievable. On 21 August 1736, the Jordan brothers of Folkestone, two of Collier's Riding officers, seized a consignment of tea, part of which was later recaptured by the smugglers. The Commissioners received a full report from the officers concerned and they directed that a reward of £20 be offered for 'any of the persons concerned in rescuing the said tea, with a promise of a pardon to the person who shall discover his accomplice'. These rewards often went unclaimed, for there were few people like Pettit willing to testify or betray their accomplices. The magistrates of Kent do not appear to have been very co-operative in dealing with the problem. The Petty Sessional records for Wingham during the eighteenth century reveal that at almost every sitting so-called 'informations' were laid by the Collector of Excise against persons found to have foreign brandy, rum or tea in their possession. The penalty was forfeiture and a fine of treble their value. However, the full fine was frequently mitigated, as, for example, two fines of £9 19s 6d and £5 5s 0d that were reduced to 10s in each case.

In his report of 1741, Collier complained to the Commissioners that he had been informed by his Riding officers on Romney Marsh that the Lydd magistrates were 'regardless of putting the Act … into execution against persons found lurking on the coast'. He wrote directly to several magistrates, pointing out to them the ill consequences to the nation of the Act not being enforced by the law. In the same report he also mentioned the refusal of the Justices of the Peace of the Port of Dover to convict a man in whose house smuggled tea was found.

There was a certain animosity between the officers of the dragoons and the Custom officials. Both blamed the other for being corrupt and accepting bribes of drink or a share of the run goods. In 1740 General Hawley criticised the way in which the dragoons were being used. He accused the Customs officers of actively helping to promote smuggling in various ways, and suggested that they ought to be used as 'advanced spies' to give the Army officers information about gangs of smugglers working the area. The Board told Collier to enquire into the matter and make a report. He consulted General Hawley and a number of dragoon officers and his conclusion was that there were 'no particular facts or particular charges against any of the Custom officers'. He appears to have been deliberately protecting his men if not covering up for them, which is not surprising as it was very difficult to get recruits and, once enlisted, wherever possible they were admonished rather than dismissed when they were disciplined. They invariably promised 'a future better behaviour'. Collier was of the opinion that more troops should be stationed on the coast because those stationed inland, as for example at Scotney House near Lamberhurst, 'have not answered the intentions'. However, he was anxious to calm the troubled waters, for he ended his report by stating that he had given 'strict charge to all your Honours' officers to behave with respect and civility to the officers of the Dragoons and to go out on duty with them on all occasions when required and to exert themselves on the due execution of their duty'.

Without doubt, the Riding officers had a difficult and dangerous job patrolling the coast at night. They were hated by the local people, who refused to co-operate with them in any way. The two officers stationed at Lydd, Henry Brackonbury and Brian Hodgson, had only managed to seize between September 1740 and June 1741 eleven half-ankers of brandy, three half-ankers of rum, and three and a half pounds of tea out of all the thousands of pounds' worth of goods that must have been run during this nine months. The four Riding officers and the Supervisor for Romney Marsh, Thomas Clave, all stationed at Hythe, were more successful. During the same period, they seized 111 half-ankers of brandy, 430 pounds of tea, five pieces of cotton and Holland (a linen fabric), and twelve handkerchiefs. Francis Riggs, a Riding officer stationed in the Hundred of Hoo in North Kent, had an unpleasant experience while on patrol one December's night in 1740. He came across a gang of smugglers who forced him to ride into a deep ditch full of water 'which with the hard frost and snow of that time occasioned him almost to perish'.

The situation was rapidly getting out of hand as Daniel Barker, a Riding officer of Tunbridge Wells, reported to Collier:

> We are very much infested with smugglers that go in such large bodies armed with blunderbusses and other offensive weapons, several of which have called at my house, swearing they would kill me or any other officer they should meet with. About a fortnight past we had an Excise officer shot at Plackstead, within five miles of Tunbridge, by 16 or 17 men armed as aforesaid and last Wednesday the Excise officer of Seven Oakes was taken prisoner by upwards of 20 smugglers, who beat him and carried him to the Bull head at Sprats Bottom near Farnborow, where they unloaded their goods, kept him all night till they loaded again, and went clear off, and last night Mr Griffin Supervisor of Excise, was going his survey with the Excise officer of Tunbridge, was beat and cut in so violent a manor that his life is dispard of by a large parcell of smugglers within a mile of Tunbridge. They likewise beat and miss-uses several private people in the road, making them kneel down in the mud and beg their pardons. Sir, I humbly beg your utmost endeavours we may be supply'd with some soldiers.

His composition, grammar and spelling are a little suspect, but the message is clear enough. Two years later he wrote again to Collier, 'While attempting to seize several horses loaded with run goods [I] was very much beat and wounded by the smugglers and that I cannot go out on duty for fear of being murdered.'

The Riding officer who had the unfortunate task of patrolling the coast from Dungeness to Great Stones on Romney Marsh was John Darby. He lived only a couple of miles inland at Lydd with his wife and family, who must have been made to feel uncomfortable to say the least, for it appears that most of the inhabitants of the town were involved one way or another in smuggling. In March 1742, Darby wrote to Collier:

> The smugglers have been very much our way of late and so impudent as to ride through Lydd town loaded with tea at 12 o'clock in the day time. There was eight and fifty horses and about thirty men with firearms. I know several of the men.

On another occasion Darby and a fellow officer, Dray, were carrying eighteen half-ankers of seized brandy to the King's warehouses when a party of smugglers running a cargo of tea came upon them. They were forced to give up the brandy, and were put in a boat which deposited them in Boulogne 'from whence they are since returned'. In December 1743 'the smugglers are got to that height of impudence at Lydd, that they drove Mr Darby, his wife and family from their habitation threatening to murder them if they can catch him'. Darby fled to Hythe, where four fellow Riding officers and a Supervisor were stationed. Collier wanted to question Darby about this matter at Rye but the Riding officer dared not make the journey and meet him as arranged for fear of being murdered.

Further evidence of the anarchy that existed on the Marsh at this time is provided by the Supervisor of Hythe, Mr Clare, who wrote a report to Collier in October 1743. He explained that he went to Lydd, surveyed the officers and examined their books. He was warned that there was a large gang of smugglers in the parish and therefore it was thought safer to stay at Romney. He arrived at Romney at about six o'clock and went to the Rose and Crown, where on going to bed down his horse he found the stable already full of horses. Suspecting them to belong to smugglers, all he could do was to retire to his room having first sent for the Romney officers. He examined and signed their books, and then questioned them about the horses in the stables and the notable lack of other guests at the inn. Apparently the officers were aware that a run was about to take place but were powerless to do anything about it. In Clare's words, 'We lamented our condition, that such quantities of goods must be suffered to be run before our faces, and we not able to prevent or take any of it.' At eight o'clock in the morning the smugglers arrived with sixty horses, all laden with dry goods, which Clare took to be tea. They were armed with brass musketoons, brass 'ffuzees' and pistols, and immediately took possession of the two inns, the Dolphin and the Rose and Crown, where they breakfasted and baited their horses for about two hours. They then left the town in a long procession.

In 1744 France declared war on England once again and in the same year Mr Patrick, Collier's clerk, visited Lydd and informed his senior that large gangs of armed smugglers frequented the town as much as ever. He said that the local smugglers had leave from the French government to go in and out of the French ports and harbours, and that since the beginning of the war there had been great quantities of contraband landed on Romney Marsh. The smugglers had been 'so impudent as to publickly drink the Pretender's and his Son's health, with success to their arms and confusion to his Majesty King George, and swore they will murder Darby where ever they meet him'. This action meant that not only were they committing unlawful acts by running uncustomed goods, but they were also guilty of the far more heinous crime of treason. However, the toast to the King 'over the water' was probably more bravado than true allegiance, for if the Stuart had been sitting on the throne the men of Lydd would still have been dealing in contraband.

A letter sent by the Supervisor at Canterbury to Collier in 1746 furnishes a curious insight into contemporary customs. It would appear that a man of the cloth miraculously regained the sight in his blind eye when some of his flock failed to contribute to the collection:

> The Rev. Patten of Whitstable has let the Commissioners know when some gangs went through Whitstable for Faversham. It is reported he formerly received tythe from some smugglers, but these gangs being such 'rugged colts' that nothing is to be got from them made him angry.

The large smuggling gangs that operated around the coast frequently joined together to outwit their common enemy, the Revenue force. The Poole affair demonstrated that gangs were prepared to travel long distances to assist in an operation with another smuggling gang which was to their mutual advantage. However, at least one instance of dissension among them has been recorded and is mentioned in a report sent by Mr Ketcherell, Customs officer at Canterbury, to his superior officer. There was a common agreement among smugglers that each party should remain on the beach until everything had been laden or loaded when making a run. Invariably, however, those that completed their loads 'shifted for themselves'. On this occasion the Customs officers, with some fifteen volunteers, appeared before the last of the smugglers had loaded, and their goods were seized. There were some Sussex and Hawkhurst men among them, who went home and returned with a gang of ninety-two men, all armed. They intended to make up for their earlier loss by capturing the contraband from the smugglers who had left the coast before the rest. The two gangs met at Wingham, where a pitched battle took place, leaving seven men wounded, two of them seriously. In the end the Sussex and Hawkhurst gangs were 'masters of the field' and carried off forty horses belonging to the Folkestone men and others.

In the same year, 1747, the Hawkhurst Gang were involved in another unsavoury episode. In December, John Bolton and two other officers had been taken prisoner by the smugglers at Shoreham and carried off to Hawkhurst, where they 'were whipped and abused in the most unmerciful manner'. They were then taken back to the coast and confined with chains before being forced to assist the smugglers in working goods at Lydd Lights. The Solicitor of Customs, Mr Simon, succeeded in prosecuting two of the gang involved, Tickner and Hodges alias Poison; both were sentenced to transportation. The alias serves to remind us that several of the smugglers had nicknames designed to enhance their reputations, namely Black Tooth, Slipjibbet and Bloodthirsty.

The fearful reputation enjoyed by the Hawkhurst Gang even affected Collier, who was usually single-minded and quite open in his efforts to reduce smuggling. He wrote to the Solicitor of Customs in October 1747:

> All I have heard in his favour [referring to William Gray] is that he showed some humanity and compassion to the officers apprehended at Shoreham in Kent, but is said to be one of the contrivers of that villainy. Tripp, alias Stanford, is another head of the Hawkhurst gang and had built a house costing about £700, and is one of the persons that stands indicted for the murder of Carswell [shot dead in an accident when two dragoons were also wounded in defending some tea they had seized from smugglers at Hurst Green] and had never been apprehended; indeed the smugglers either bought off the chief evidence, or else murdered him, so that there is not sufficient for conviction. This [the arrest of Stanford and Gray] will be striking a deadly blow and entirely destroy this nest of vermin; and now the affair is on the anvil, and carried on hitherto with success, I hope it will be continued. These persons, as I am informed, pretend to have intelligence if anything is taken out against them, and keep a person in perpetual pay for that purpose, so that there must be the greatest secrecy, and persons to take them must be sent from London. I hint this, but desire my name in regard to Wm Gray and Tripp alias Stanford, may not be made use of, nor known but only to yourself.

Stanford was taken into custody and in March 1749 the Solicitor of Customs wrote to Collier that allegations against certain Riding officers regarding corruption appeared to be true:

> Stanford (alias Tripp), finding his trial fixed, as far as I can understand begins to squeak, and it has been hinted to me that his first discovery will be of their keeping a good understanding, for a valuable consideration, with many of the Riding officers along the coast, higher up in the country and just in the neighbourhood of the town. This, if true, will make sad work, though at the same time such a collusion is truely infamous and the actors in it cannot but fall unpitied.

The Solicitor's letter must have caused many Riding officers an anxious few weeks wondering whether Stanford would in fact 'squeak'.

Collier's supposition that the wealthier master smugglers had a trained legal man working full-time was correct. A letter to Collier states:

> Ye person who is solicitor for the smugglers when in Newgate is one Kelly, an Irish Roman Catholic. He has the assurance from his country, and his principles from his religion, or from Hell itself: and to make a gentleman so accomplished completely a man of business, he has 40 or 50 fellows of his own country and religion at his command who are ever ready to swear whatever he cares to dictate.

Collier's men were in an unenviable position. Their job was a thankless task involving long hours of night work; wages were poor as the Commissioners expected their men to augment their finances by seizing goods and receiving a reward proportional to their value. If a seizure was made, the smugglers were so bold that they would often retake it before it could be brought to the Custom House and condemned. The Revenue men were hated by the farm labourers and villagers, and distrusted by the landowners and gentry. If a receiver or smuggler was brought before a local magistrate, the honest efforts of the Revenue men were invariably undermined by the Justice of the Peace dismissing the case or imposing a ludicrously small fine.

In 1756 Collier's health began to fail and, being in his seventies, he retired from the service. For twenty-three years, with a constant flow of letters, visits, reports and surveys, he had struggled valiantly to do his job. At times he must have been daunted by the enormity of his task, as if he had been ordered by the gods to empty the Channel with a bucket that had a hole in it. Nonetheless, he persisted against every setback, and his dedication and efficiency gradually began to improve matters. During the second half of the eighteenth century, with the trials of 1749 as a turning point, the smugglers could no longer consider the Preventive service a mild irritant. It was becoming a force to be reckoned with.

4

Tea

'A kind of black water, prepared from a decoction of a certain shrub …
The leaves are long and taper … and shrivelled like worms'

The practice of scalding dried leaves of small shrubs of the camellia family and drinking the resultant beverage originated in China, becoming quite fashionable during the T'ang Dynasty (AD 618–906). The Chinese called the drink *t'e* (tay) or *ch'a* (chah).

The drinking and cultivation of tea appears to have been confined to that country and Japan until the late seventeenth century, when the plant was introduced into Java. However, long before this the inhabitants of several areas in central and southern Asia may have acquired the drinking habit without growing their own supplies. For example, W. Milburn in his *Oriental Commerce* (1813) recounts how Olearius, a German traveller, found the habit of tea drinking prevalent among the Persians in 1633. He describes the strange custom with delightful, yet accurate, words:

> They drink a kind of black water, prepared from a decoction of a certain shrub called 'Char' or 'Ch'a', which the Black Usbeck Tartars import from China; the leaves are long and taper, measuring nearly an inch, of a black colour when dried and welked, and shrivelled like worms.

With the arrival of the Dutch traders in the East, tea first appeared as an article of commerce in Europe. From about 1610 onwards the East Indiamen began bringing back a few cases of tea as part of their cargo, mainly for its reputed medicinal properties.

Gradually, the drinking of tea became established in Continental Europe, but opinion was divided as to its medicinal qualities: some declared against it while others extolled its virtues. However, misgivings about its side effects were reduced in 1673 when Dr Cornelius Bontekoe, first physician to the Elector of Brandenburgh, declared publicly that he entertained the highest opinion of its salutary qualities and deemed it impossible to injure the stomach 'even if as much as two or three hundred cups were taken in a day'. The Dutch East India Company, no doubt anxious to promote tea as an article of commerce, were relieved that tea drinking had been freed from the many prejudices held against it as a result of this endorsement from an eminent physician; the doctor was accordingly sent what is described as a 'handsome pecuniary gratification'.

It is not known exactly when the habit of tea drinking began in England, but the first of the countless trillions of cups consumed was probably sipped about 1650. Nobility returning from trips to the Continent brought back with them packets of tea and probably introduced the habit.

The earliest advertisement in an English newspaper for tea was probably that in *Mercurius Politicus*, London, 1658. It ran, 'That Excellent and by all Physitians approved China drink, called by the Chineans Teha, by other nations Tay alias Tee, is sold at the Sultanese Head Cophee House in Sweetings Rents, by the Royal Exchange, London.' Soon the novelty of taking 'a dish to tea' became established. The first tea sets were of fragile translucent Chinese porcelain which consisted of a delicate handle-less cup and saucer. The earliest English silver teapot dates from 1670 and has a strange near-conical shape. Later, a Dutch craftsman settled in Staffordshire and when he made his first English teapot in 1693 a whole industry was born. Samuel Pepys makes several references to tea in his famous diary: '28 Sept 1660 I sent for a cup of tee (a China drink) of which I had never drank before', and in June 1667, 'Mr Pelling the potticary tells his wife that it is good for cold and defluxions'. It was an expensive luxury, costing £3 per pound in 1662.

As the habit became established, the British East India Company realised the trade potential of tea and secured the monopoly of its importation into the country, which they held until 1834. Extracts from the Company records show how the leaves, 'shrivelled like worms', began to be imported – the birth of a great British habit.

On 22 August 1664, the Company resolved 'to have presented His Majesty with, and that His Majesty may not find himself wholly neglected by the Company that ... a silver case of oil of cinammon ... and some good thea, be provided for that end'.

The Company's first order for importing tea was issued to their agent in Bantam 'to send home by these ships 100 lbs weight of the best tey that you can get'. The first importation made by them arrived from Bantam in 1669, when one of their East Indiamen carried among a cargo of silks, spices, cowries, peppers, and numerous other Eastern goods, two canisters of 'tey' containing exactly 143 lb.

Tea was first mentioned under an Act of Parliament in the reign of Charles II when 'for every gallon of chocolate, sherbet and tea made and sold [the tax was to be] eight pence'. However, Charles's Act was for coffee houses where the tea was drunk and it was not taxed on entry into the country until 1695, when a rate of a shilling per pound was decreed. By this time the imports were rising steadily as more and more people, from the middle classes as well, began to drink the beverage. The new custom was gathering momentum and becoming less of a novelty and more of an accepted habit. It was still considered a luxury, but a luxury increasingly hard to do without. With the first import tax, the enterprising free trader began to realise that perhaps he could buy tea cheaper on the Continent and still be able to sell it in England at a profit by evading the duty.

By the time the first of the Georges had succeeded to the throne, the luggers taking wool across the Channel had begun returning with bags of tea as well as ankers of brandy. The high value of tea in relation to its bulk, coupled with a rate of duty which often doubled the legal price, made this particular traffic exceptionally profitable. For a large part of the eighteenth century, tea was one of the staple goods of the free traders. They usually found it more profitable to import the coarser varieties of tea, both because the Excise duty weighed more heavily on cheap teas and because good-quality tea required greater care in packing and transport.

Once ashore, the tea was sold to distributors, who often had ingenious ways of concealing their contraband. From the record of the trial of Edward Roofs, master of the sloop *Mermaid*, it is reported that he made seven voyages to Ostend for tea, carrying about 400 pounds' weight a trip and returning to the Thames estuary, where he put the goods ashore either on the Chalk Marshes or some way up the Medway. Two ladies, Mrs Hunter and Mrs Maryfield, used to pay ten shillings a pound for the tea and carry it away, 50 lb at a time, to clients in London in bags tied under their petticoats. With equal cunning, the inhabitants of Deal in Kent carried on a profitable contraband trade with the East Indiamen riding offshore in the Downs. They would use small craft to collect the tea and then conceal it in specially made hats, waistcoats and thigh pieces with pockets which together held about 30 lb. Once ashore, these 'Duffers' (as they were called), their coats effectively quilted with inside pockets, took the tea to London, where it was sold.

Many retailers dealt with traders who only sold tea that had not paid duty. It was reported in the *Gentleman's Magazine* of 1733 that Gabriel Tomkins – then in Surrey Gaol, having returned from transportation before his time – had received that sentence for dealing for three years with grocers and shopkeepers in the City, Westminster and Southwark, to whom he sold between 15,000 lb and 20,000 lb of tea and coffee per year.

The popularity of tea can be judged by the change that took place in the public pleasure gardens of London at this time. These eighteenth-century gardens had originally been tea-less and not too respectable but changed their character by turning themselves into tea gardens, where members of the higher classes went to walk and amuse themselves and take tea, because it was the fashionable thing to do. Those people who could afford it, though not of the same class, went to Vauxhall or Marylebone or Culper's Garden (just south of Waterloo Bridge) to mingle with the rich, the literary and the famous. The popularity of Vauxhall Gardens, first opened in 1732, was at its zenith between 1750 and 1790 when Horace Walpole, Henry Fielding and Dr Johnson, 'a hardened and shameless tea drinker', used to go there with their literary friends for tea and *divertissements*. The gardens had a season from April or May through to early autumn and had a fixed admission charge of a shilling; refreshments were extra. But at Ranelagh – perhaps the most famous pleasure gardens of all, in Chelsea – in 1742, tea and coffee and bread and butter were included in the admission charge of 2s 6d, a lot of money at that time.

As well as going to the tea gardens, another peculiarly British habit was instituted about this time. Anna, the wife of the 7th Duke of Bedford, is thought to have been the originator of afternoon tea in the drawing room. In her day it was customary to eat a huge breakfast, while lunch was of little account and dinner was at eight o'clock or thereafter. It was not surprising, therefore, that around about five o'clock the Duchess used to get what she described as 'a sinking feeling'. She ordered tea and cakes to allay this feeling and the habit caught on.

By 1734, more and more people were drinking tea but less and less of it had been subject to duty. In that year a writer reported in the *Gentleman's Magazine* that tea was so cheap that 'a poor woman of my neighbourhood for whom I had some time before procured twelve pence per week charity, acknowledged to me, that she had tea every morning for breakfast and said, that except water, it was the cheapest drink she could get'. At this time many believed that tea was injurious to the health, and one writer to the *Gentleman's Magazine*, under the pseudonym South Briton, went further by declaring, 'If this unwholesome practice is not in some degree prohibited by the Government, I can expect nothing less, in one generation more, but that we must hire foreigners, as they do in Spain, to do our hard labour.'

The 'fair trader' was obliged to sell his tea at more than five shillings per pound as the duty on it amounted to 4s 9d, whereas the 'free trader' could buy his tea in Holland for two shillings per pound, with the Dutch having paid one shilling per pound for it in the East Indies. The fact was that many people with the right contacts, even among the poorer classes, were indulging in a supposed luxury.

A short extract from Russell Thorndike's exciting smuggling novel *Doctor Syn* sums up the situation well. The incorrigible Mr Mipps is talking with Mrs Waggetts, the garrulous landlady of the Ship Inn, at Dymchurch.

> '… And while she's gone I'll make you a nice cup of tea.'
>
> 'Throw your tea to the devil,' snarled the Sexton. 'One 'ud think you was a diamond duchess, the way you consumes good tea. When shall I knock it into your skull that tea's a luxury – a drink wot's only meant for swells? Perhaps you don't know what a power of money tea costs!'
>
> 'Come now,' giggled the landlady, 'not to us Mister Mipps. Not the way we gets it.'
>
> 'I don't know what you means,' snapped the wary sexton. 'But I do wish as how you'd practise a-keepin' your mouth shut, for if you opens it much more that wagging tongue of yours'll get us all the rope.'

The Session of Parliament in 1734 devoted a long debate to a petition from the 'Druggists' (grocers, Chinamen and others dealing in tea). They complained that they could not compete against the smuggler because of the excessive Excise duty, and pointed out that, unless the excise was withdrawn completely or at least reduced, within a few years the whole trade for the home consumption of tea would be in the hands of the smugglers and those dishonest retailers who bought from them. The Druggists further complained that the alterations made in the collecting of the duties by the joining of the Laws of Custom and Excise in 1724 had not caused the desired simplification and classification but had, in fact, had the reverse effect.

The Druggists' Petition produced figures which strongly supported their case. They claimed that the duty received by the Exchequer from the legal retail of tea was £60,000 in 1716, and had risen to £112,000 in 1723 and £162,000 in 1729. Since that date, despite increased consumption, the free traders had learnt new arts of deceit and new ways of defrauding the public so that in 1733 the duty had decreased to less than £120,000.

The debate was keen and the facts appear to speak for themselves. One member of the House took the opportunity, once he had gained the floor, to digress from the true course of the debate – no doubt on a hobby horse of his – by declaring:

> I shall indeed readily be for anything that may discourage not only the running but the importation of coffee, tea or chocolate; for I wish we would or could be made all to return to the good old way of our ancestors in breakfasting upon good English ale and bread and cheese. Both the men and women of those days were I believe as strong and as healthy as they are now, and yet what they made use of for breakfast did not carry one penny out of the country.

However, the question of referring the petition to a committee of the whole house was defeated by 233 votes to 155 and, as no question was put for ordering it to lie on the table, the petition was dropped. This seems a strange course of action for a petition which had brought to the government's attention a malpractice of considerable magnitude. In an age of widespread corruption and fraud, Parliament chose to look the other way, as is often the case when something too near the truth about popular public misdemeanour is uncovered, particularly when the uncovering could have repercussions throughout society and could disturb the accepted order of things. Parliament no doubt remembered the great public clamour that had been invoked by Walpole's attempted Excise reforms one year earlier and so the petition was set aside.

With the high duty remaining, tea smuggling continued to be profitable. Often the bulky ankers of brandy were taken on board mainly as ballast while the cargo of tea, sown up in waterproof oilskin bags, was the free traders' real money earner. The fair trader was still managing to eke out an existence and more petitions were put before Parliament demanding reform.

In December 1743 a pamphlet was published entitled *A proposal for preventing of running goods*. In it the writer pointed out that the duty which was now four shillings per pound brought on average £130,000 a year into the Exchequer, which represented duty on a mere 650,000 lb of tea. In fact, the real consumption, as everyone knew, was far greater than that. The writer estimated it at £1.5 million pounds. He went on to report that the Treasurer of the East India Company had received a letter from Holland intimating that an English sailor, who lived in the province of Zeeland, smuggled yearly to England no less than half a million pounds of tea alone. He was married to a woman who kept a china shop, a charmingly unassuming front to a profitable clandestine business.

Though this seemed incredible, the directors of the East India Company, upon inquiry, were convinced of this sailor's existence and that he had four sloops of his own constantly employed in smuggling. They further believed that the staggering annual export of half a million pounds of tea was not exaggerated and that the man had more guineas and other English money in his house than any banker in England. The remedy proposed by the pamphleteer was a tax on a sliding scale from five shillings to twenty shillings on all those families who drank tea. The proposition was rather impracticable because the average English man considered it fair game to avoid paying tax wherever possible and would have hidden the teapot and caddy when the Excise man called. Something similar had happened in 1697 when the tax on hearth money was repealed and replaced by a tax on windows, payable on more than six in a house. Often some windows were bricked up when the assessor was expected, and reopened after he had gone.

Eventually Parliament was forced to take notice of the increasing problem of illegal importation of tea. At the time when the Jacobites were fighting their doomed cause in the north, a Parliamentary committee was compiling a report to submit before the House on 'the infamous traffick'. The committee received evidence from Excise officers, tea traders and ex-smugglers, some of whom claimed to know the quantity of tea being slipped into England from Continental ports. A few months before the presentation of the report at midsummer 1745, the Excise duty on tea of four shillings per pound had been replaced by duties of one shilling per pound plus 25 per cent *ad valorem*. It was estimated that in the three years immediately preceding this reform, smuggling had reached a peak of 3 million pounds in weight a year, more than three times the legal sales, while in the months which followed illegal imports had fallen and now stood at about 1 million pounds per annum. The only direct evidence advanced in favour of the view that there had been such a substantial reduction of smuggling was the fact that legal sales had greatly increased.

Again the figures quoted must be treated with caution. However, W. A. Cole, in an excellent article in *Economic History Review* (2nd series, vol. 10, 1957, 395–410) which looks at the trends in eighteenth-century smuggling, considers that tea legally sold by the East India Company almost certainly represented only a small fraction of the total consumption and he speculates that at least 2 million pounds, or probably more, was sold by the free traders prior to the reforms of 1745. Judging also from the contemporary accounts, which were not seriously misinformed about the probable magnitude of smuggling, although some of them had good reasons for erring on the high side in their estimates of the extent of the traffic, the illegal imports must have been greatly in excess of imports through legitimate channels.

Cole's survey of the quantitative importance of smuggling helps us to assess the possible margin of error involved in the use of the official statistics. His admittedly speculative conclusions provide a valuable insight into the trends of tea consumption in the eighteenth century. In the 1720s the legal consumption of tea was rapidly increasing, although the price of tea was almost stationary. In the early 1730s there was a sharp drop in demand, which was followed after a few years of comparative stability by a temporary increase in demand at the end of the decade. A much larger increase in 1745 was followed by another period of comparative stability and a further upward movement during the Seven Years' War. In England tea consumption rose in the early years of the war, but fell again after 1760 and by 1763 was only 8 per cent higher than in 1756. In Amsterdam, on the other hand, the price of black Bohea tea, the variety most favoured by the smugglers, rose by more than 70 per cent in the course of the war. Hence, it is quite possible that the relatively high demand for legally imported tea in Britain at this time was at least partly due to the temporary scarcity and unusually high price of smuggled supplies. Then, after 1763, legal demand dropped sharply, and with the exception of the excise years 1768–72 (when the Excise duty of one shilling per pound was suspended on all black and single teas in an effort to reduce smuggling) remained at a low level until 1784 when there was another enormous increase.

Thus Cole shows that the two largest increases in demand of legal tea sales followed the tariff reforms of 1745 and 1784. In September 1784 Pitt the Younger, recognising that repressive measures alone would not put an end to the clandestine importation of tea, abolished the cumbersome tea duties of £55 15s 0d per cent and 1s 2⅘d per pound and replaced them by a window tax and a duty on tea of 12½ per cent (24 Geo III C38). This dramatic stroke certainly worried the Continental importers of tea; that included the East India companies established during the seventeenth and eighteenth centuries by the United Provinces (Dutch), France, Denmark, Scotland, Spain, Austria and Sweden. The Dutch, Danish, French and Swedish companies were believed to exist mainly to supply the illegal British demand for duty-free East India goods.

The British East India Company was awarded its charter by Elizabeth I on 31 December 1600. It was an association of 125 London merchants who had subscribed £721,000 to engage in direct trade with the East Indies in order to compete with the Dutch and, originally, to break their monopoly of the lucrative spice and pepper trade. At the British East India Company tea sales, which began on 16 Sept 1784, the Dutch, Flemings, Danes and Swedes, in conjunction with the

English smugglers, ran prices up excessively with a view to forfeiting the deposit and leaving the goods in the warehouse until the stocks in their own warehouses had been cleared. The authorities were forced to take action, having recognised this bidding agreement. The British East India Company dealt with this sharp practice by decreeing that the tea remaining at the end of the sale and not paid for *in toto* would be resold immediately.

During the mid-eighteenth century, tea continued to be drunk in increasing amounts despite the government's repressive and heavy duty. Official pamphlets endeavoured to prevent the habit spreading throughout the social classes. One such pamphlet, published in 1758 and entitled *The good and bad effects of tea considered*, was written by Wilkes and sold at 6d. The following is an extract:

> The physical qualities for tea are good for those who live on high food, drink plentifully of wine, and use little exercise; but bad for those who are obliged to labour for the necessaries of life and require more nutritious food than they can procure. Afternoon tea drinking is censured in the lower and middle classes as a waste of time and money and an occasion for gossiping, slander and sometimes intrigue, and a natural production to dram drinking, as it generally produces mawkishness and low spirits.

This official disapproval appears to have been heeded but little, if at all, for by the 1780s, when Pitt was examining the problem with a view to bringing in reforms, estimates of illegal importations of tea varied between 3 million and 7.5 million pounds.

The deputy accountant of the East India Company reckoned that from 1773 to 1782 the annual exports of tea from China to Europe had averaged over 13 million pounds, and since 'the best information procurable, estimates the annual consumption of tea by foreigners in Europe' at under 5.5 million pounds, he argued that at least 7.5 million pounds must have been smuggled into Great Britain and her dependencies each year. Another contemporary estimate for Britain was 7 million pounds, made by the Commissioners of Excise on the basis of returns from the officers at the outports of the number of ships engaged in smuggling, their size and the number of journeys made each year. Pitt himself directed a further estimate to be made and this produced the far more modest figure of 3 million pounds illegally imported.

Both the Commissioners of Excise and the East India Company had a case to establish and thus their figures probably tend to be overestimates. However, following Pitt's dramatic reduction in tea duty in 1784, the Continental imports in the 1790s amounted to 5 million pounds, a figure remarkably close to the estimate of European consumption which the East India Company's accountant had made ten years earlier. Again the company's dramatic threefold increase in sales after 1784 appears to confirm the accountant's assertion that barely a third of the home demand had been met by legal sales. The accountant also reckoned that apart from smuggled tea, several million pounds of dyed leaves of other species of plants were fraudulently sold as tea each year, making the total illicit sales over 12 million pounds compared with the Company sales of under 3 million. Further distortions of the figures must be allowed for, because of the practice of re-exporting large amounts of tea from England in order to claim drawback. Undoubtedly a considerable percentage of this tea was illegally re-landed in Britain.

Cole is more conservative in his estimates of illegal tea importing. He acknowledges that during the American Civil War smuggling may have reached greater heights than Pitt's advisers feared, but not quite the level claimed by the East India Company and the Excise Commissioners. Hence he estimates the illegal imports on the eve of the Commutation Act at between 4 million and 6 million pounds.

Pitt's reform of 1784 forced the enterprising free trader to look elsewhere for easy profits and smuggling continued in other commodities. However, the Act was a great blow to those who for generations had made their livelihood from its illegal importation. The wars with Revolutionary and Napoleonic France caused the duty to be increased on tea and it again became, for a time, a profitable commodity to smuggle, but it never regained the importance it commanded in the eighteenth century. The halcyon days of easy profit from 'the cups that cheer but not inebriate' were gone for ever.

5

Tobacco

'A custome lothsome to the Eye, hatefull to the Nose,
harmefull to the Braine, dangerous to the Lungs'

Columbus and his crew were the first Europeans to encounter the tobacco plant.
On his first westward voyage searching for Cathay in 1492, aboard the *Santa Maria*,
he was offered by the natives of the islands he discovered dried brown leaves as a
friendly gesture. In what is now Cuba, where the practice of chewing tobacco was
noted, two members of his crew saw natives smoking crudely made cigars. One of
these men, Rodrigo de Jerez, is reputed to be the first man to smoke 'the weed' in
Europe and was later imprisoned by the Inquisition for the 'devilish' habit.

Full details of the early history of smoking may be found in Alfred Dunhill's
The Gentle Art of Smoking. Accompanying Columbus on his second trip to the
New World one year later was a monk, Romano Pane, who reported that the
natives of the Antilles used smoke as a remedial and that they sniffed both smoke
and powdered tobacco through a Y-shaped hollow stick. This observation was
confirmed by the Spanish historian Fernandez de Quiedo, who after many years
in the West Indies published a history in 1526. He wrote:

> Among other evil practices, the Indians have one that is specially harmful, the inhaling
> of a certain kind of smoke which they call tobacco, in order to produce a state of
> stupor. The Caciques [priests] employed a tube, shaped like a Y, inserting the forked
> extremities in their nostrils and the tube itself in the lighted weed; in this way they
> would inhale the smoke until they became unconscious and lay sprawling on the earth
> like men in a drunken slumber. Those who could not procure the right sort of wood
> took their smoke through a hollow reed; it is this that the Indians call 'tobacco', and
> not the weed nor its effects, as some have supposed. They prize this herb very highly,
> and plant it in their orchards or on their farms for the purpose mentioned above.

Thus the name which referred originally to the pipe or tube was given by the
Spaniards to the plant.

Wherever the early explorers went in the Americas they encountered different forms of smoking. The two species from which modern tobacco is derived, *Nicotiana tobacum* and *Nicotiana rustica*, are believed to have originated in Brazil and Mexico respectively. But long before Columbus set foot on the sandy beach of San Salvador in the Bahamas (or Watling Island, as it is now called) the plant *Nicotiana rustica* was growing both east and west of the Mississippi. Indeed, Jacques Cartier, the French sea captain who discovered and explored the St Lawrence (1535–36), found stores of tobacco and pipes among the Indians of Canada.

Most of the Indian tribes of North America valued highly the rare tobacco plants and considered them gifts from their great god Manitou. When preparing the leaf for smoking they economised by blending with it sumac, the bark of dog wood, and herbs and oil which bound the dust together. The Indian priests and medicine men had different ceremonial pipes for special occasions. The chief of these, the 'calumet' or pipe of peace. was the traditional sign of friendship, hospitality and peace. The natives came to identify the plant with the supernatural, to feed the holy fires with it and offer it to their god Manitou, whose spirit was thought to be concealed in rising clouds of smoke. Many religious rites and customs of the Indians derived from the belief that smoke, through the mystery of fire, disappeared into the void which was held to be the home of the gods, to whom the breath of the pipe was sweet. Smoke, the North American natives believed, would calm waters and bring good fortune to fishermen; it would protect a warrior and cure a sick child. The pipe of peace was also placed into the mouth of a slain bear to placate its spirit.

Thus white men became acquainted with a plant which could either be snuffed up the nose, chewed, or set alight and the smoke inhaled. It had a mystery of the supernatural about it in the way that it induced trances and stupefaction. Also it had remedial qualities, being a supposed cure for catarrh and asthma. And, as the first European smokers no doubt found, it was a personal pleasure to relax with a pipe of tobacco. Thus the custom of smoking tobacco was carried back across the Atlantic by explorers, adventurers and sailors who manned the merchant boats from America to Spain and Portugal. By the mid-sixteenth century Lisbon was one of the most important Atlantic ports receiving new wealth and imports from the New World. The French ambassador there at this time was Jean Nicot, who noticed that the herbalists of Spain and Portugal were experimenting with the new plant in their gardens. He sent seeds to the Queen of France, Catherine de Medici, and helped to spread the news that tobacco would cure ulcers and similar complaints and that it was a vital ingredient in all gargles, powders, emetics, inhalations and dentifrices. Thus, he encouraged a new era of medical science for which service the botanical name of the plant, *Nicotiana*, and the later term 'nicotine' for the alkaloid in tobacco, commemorate him.

Tobacco's use as a strange and wonderful medicine was probably known in England during the latter years of Henry VIII's reign, but it was not until

Elizabeth was on the throne that the English first took to smoking the dried leaves. By the 1570s the habit was common among the English sailors at the ports. On Drake's return from Virginia in 1586 his men brought with them pipes, tobacco seeds and plants, and their example of what was at first called tobacco-drinking (taking the smoke into the mouth and apparently swallowing it) must have caused considerable excitement. In 1587, Sir Walter Raleigh received a letter, and some tobacco, from one of the colonists in his ill-fated Virginia colony of Roanoke and, by introducing smoking at Court, it soon became a mark of the fashionable courtier and man about town. The 'tobacconists' – or less complimentarily, the 'reeking gallants', as the early smokers were called – needed elaborate smoking paraphernalia. This consisted of a set of pipes ornamented with gold or silver, an ivory or metal box which contained up to a pound of tobacco, and silver tongs for lifting the glowing ember to light the pipe. Also needed were a pick, a knife to shred the tobacco and a small scoop for drying the leaf. All this equipment helped to secure for tobacco its important first foothold in the country. The 'divine weed' had arrived, giving birth to 'a pernicious habit'.

The habit was taking society by storm and consequently providing the butt for much satire for writers of the time. Ben Jonson's water-carrier in *Everyman in his Humour* makes the following observation about 'roguish tobacco':

> It's good for nothing but to choke a man, and fill him full of smoke and embers: there were four died out of one house, last week, with taking of it, and two more the bell went for, yesternight: one of them, they say, will ne'er scape it: he voided a bushel of soot yesterday, upwards and downward. By the stocks, and there were no wiser men than I, I'll have it present whipping, man, or woman, that should but deal with a tobacco pipe: why, it will stifle them all in the end, as many as use it: it's little better than ratsbane [white arsenic].

In 1604 the most renowned critic of tobacco, James I and VI of England and Scotland respectively, published his *Counterblaste to Tobacco*. The pamphlet proclaimed that the 'smoking gallants' were a social menace, that doctors regarded the habit as dirty and injurious to health, and that to foster the tobacco trade meant playing into the hands of our Spanish enemies. It concluded by stating that smoking is 'a custome lothsome to the Eye, hatefull to the Nose, harmefull to the Braine, dangerous to the Lungs, and in the blacke stinking fume thereof, nearest resembling the horrible Stigian smoke of the pit that is bottomelesse'.

This clever denunciation from the throne had the undesired effect of making tobacco better known and more popular. James's hatred for the weed continued, however, and he imposed an exorbitant duty of 6s 8d on each pound imported; it was with this imposition duty that tobacco smuggling undoubtedly began. A great deal was smuggled ashore by the crews of vessels tied up in the receiving port, and some was probably transferred to small boats before the inbound vessel docked.

Most of the early tobacco exported to Europe was of the popular Spanish type (*Nicotiana tobacum*), which was grown in the West Indies, Mexico and northern South America. Soon after the second attempt by English colonists to settle in Virginia in 1607, the Spanish variety was introduced there from Trinidad. It was touch and go whether Virginia would survive as a colony; but with the better Spanish plant successfully replacing the indifferent *Nicotiana rustica* and the perfection by John Rolfe (who married Pocahontas) of a method of curing tobacco, Virginia's exports of tobacco rose astonishingly in a very short time. A small cargo of tobacco was shipped to London in 1613. By 1619 the annual shipment had risen to 20,000 lb and a decade later it had soared to 1,500,000 lb. Succeeding years saw a continual increase and Virginia's financial future was assured.

The smuggling of tobacco has been traced in detail by Alfred Rive of Yale University in his 'Short History of Tobacco Smuggling' in the *Economic Review* (January 1929). James I's attempt to banish the smoking of tobacco had failed, but the King acknowledged this and was now especially concerned about the state of the illicit import of tobacco. So in 1620 he issued a proclamation providing for the 'viewing' of all tobacco – which, upon payment of custom and import, was to be sealed by the officers – and imposing penalties of forfeiture and trial before the Star Chamber for all those selling unsealed tobacco. Despite this gesture, smuggling continued and even increased, particularly when restrictions were placed upon the importation of Spanish tobacco. Large quantities were run ashore in the usual way and a great amount came in under the guise of plantation tobacco. Tobacco was carried from the Spanish West Indies to the Bermudas, and there reshipped for England, entering as the product of the English colonies. The Customs officers could not identify with certainty tobacco as Spanish or colonial. Rive cites an example of this by quoting a Governor of the Council of Virginia, somewhat irate, who wrote to inform the home government in 1626 that the 'petty English plantations on the savage islands in the West Indies … export large quantities of Spanish tobacco'.

James was fighting a losing battle against the illegal importation of tobacco. In September 1624 he issued another proclamation increasing the penalties for smuggling tobacco: 'some have imported secretly and by stealth great quantities of foreign tobacco for which they have payed no subsidy or other duty unto us'. To combat this, he decreed that no one was to purchase foreign (i.e. Spanish) tobacco and that all tobacco landed in England was to be put ashore at the Customs quay in the Port of London, and none landed elsewhere. The proclamation made shipmasters themselves responsible for checking smuggling. In the following March, the King announced a further elaboration which decreed that all subjects were to have profferers of smuggled tobacco arrested and that informers would receive half the value of the tobacco that they caused to be seized.

With Charles I's accession to the throne, the problem remained despite more official threats and warnings:

Certain persons have secretly imported much tobacco not grown in these places [meaning the colony of Virginia and the Somers Islands in the Bermudas]. No person is to use this foreign tobacco or to receive it under pain of law and of the Star Chamber.

Charles further prohibited the landing of tobacco seed and the planting of tobacco in England and Ireland. However, during the King's eleven years of rule without Parliament he attempted to impose taxes himself. Recognising that the tobacco habit would not be broken and requiring money for the royal coffers, he revoked his earlier proclamation against the importation of Spanish tobacco and decreed, 'Spanish tobacco is so much appreciated that it is smuggled and the Revenue from it lost. In future 50,000 lbs weight of Spanish tobacco may be imported by the Commissioners only as Royal merchandise.'

By Cromwell's time, despite earlier royal proclamations forbidding its growth such as that of James which considered tobacco 'an abuse and misemployment of the soil of this fruitful kingdom', tobacco was being cultivated in about twelve English counties. The orders were hard to enforce and the cultivators of the plant were anxious to preserve their right to grow what they liked. Pepys, again, writes how the inhabitants of Winchcombe in Gloucestershire 'did not only offer violence but had like to have slain the Sheriff, giving out they would lose their lives rather than obey the laws in that case provided'.

Despite the difficulties involved with the growing of tobacco in this country, the retailing of it was becoming a respectable trade comparable with that of mercers, tailors and chandlers. A licence to sell was obligatory for all those who traded legally in tobacco and with improved curing methods smoking consolidated its hold on the British public. A few women also enjoyed a pipe of tobacco, if only in the tavern and because the idea that it was good for the health persisted. During the Great Plague in 1665, tobacconists were supposed to be immune; consequently, those who looked after the stricken or who carted corpses out of the City smoked incessantly, and boys at Eton were made to smoke in the morning. The only proclamation regarding tobacco that appears to have succeeded during the seventeenth century was that prohibiting its cultivation, for by the turn of the century home-grown tobacco had largely disappeared. At Winchcombe, except in years when the Life Guard was sent to spoil the crop, great profits had been made from tobacco cultivation. But records from the time show that 'planting was restrained in the twelfth year of King Charles II, and the town decayed little by little, and is now poor and inconsiderable'. This abolition of a crop that grew so well and sold so profitably in England was a boon to smugglers.

At this time the government relied mainly upon the interest of private individuals for the enforcement of the law against smuggling. Whoever chose to prosecute a case and was successful received as reward a certain proportion, usually one-third of the confiscated tobacco, or its value. However, the procedure was expensive and it was not profitable to prosecute when the amount of smuggled tobacco was small. In the preface to *Index Vectigalium*, a work published in 1670 on customs duties and procedure, the author remarks on this and concludes, 'Some easier and cheaper way of proceeding against small and dubious cases is necessary … since the charge deters all men from prosecution. The aggregate sum of all these offences costs the revenue more than downright smuggling.'

Eight years earlier in 1662, Parliament had made some effort to prevent Kentish smugglers meeting merchant ships from the Plantations outside the Port of London and taking off part of their cargo of tobacco to be run ashore illegally and sent by packhorse to London. The decree stated, 'No vessel arriving from beyond the sea shall be above three days coming from Gravesend to the place of her discharge in the Thames, nor touch at any place between Gravesend and Chesterskey.' To combat the frauds involved, the Act further provided for penalties for evasion and false entries that may be made by the masters of the ships and the officers of the Customs.

In 1692 an *Essay on Bulk Tobacco* was published; it was subtitled *or some reasons why bulk tobacco from Virginia and Maryland ought to be prohibited from being exported thence or imported into England*. Considerable quantities of tobacco were exported from the plantations in loose bundles, a wasteful method which involved certain damage to a proportion of the tobacco, especially by saltwater. Yet it persisted largely because it facilitated smuggling and 'it is the only tobacco run by seamen'. The tobacco was smuggled directly into the numerous bays and creeks along the coast, thus evading the duty; or, if the ship came into port, 'every sailor and woman and little inconsiderable person can buy bulk tobacco on board the ship and squeeze over by little design part of the duties if not wholly run it, and then carry it, from shop to shop and sell it at easy and low rates'.

The essayist maintained that as a result of this smuggling of bulk tobacco legitimate merchants, who imported large quantities of tobacco and sold it both wholesale and retail, and always had large stocks on hand, had been ruined and 'destroyed'. Tobacco is sold in London 'a penny ha'penny per pound cheaper than such paying their first dues could afford it'.

Bulk tobacco is said to have supplied the demand of whole districts. In York and Newcastle it was peddled from door to door upon packhorses at prices below those prevailing in London. Again the demand in the north of Ireland and the west of Scotland was 'fully satisfied with bulk tobacco'. In the end the efforts of the merchants were successful and Parliament passed an Act prohibiting the importation of bulk tobacco:

> After 29 September 1700 no tobacco shall be imported from the Plantations or shipped there but in a cask, chest or case each containing 200 weight of neat tobacco at the least at 112 lbs weight per hundred, on pain of forfeiting such tobacco, and 6*d* for every pound weight thereof.

The Navigation Laws were responsible for much chicanery on the part of merchants who found numerous ways of making an easy, though illegitimate, profit. Under these laws tobacco, like other plantation commodities, had to be brought to England before it could be shipped elsewhere. On the re-export of the tobacco, duty was re-paid or drawn back and this 'drawback' system facilitated many deceits, such as shipping tobacco waste or other waste camouflaged as tobacco. It was then claimed as duty-paid tobacco which was being re-exported and the Searcher very often was unable to discern the deceit. Another method of obtaining duty-free tobacco was to make pretence of shipping it to a place which qualified for drawback and then to land it elsewhere on the English coast or transfer it to smaller coastal vessels for landing. If these ships were intercepted by Revenue or Naval vessels they merely claimed that they had been blown off course, a reasonable enough excuse in the days of sailing ships and one sometimes difficult to disprove.

In December 1734 Alderman Perry was brought to trial by the Crown, which sought from him the sum of £623 14s 3½d, which was drawback on 38 hogsheads of tobacco exported in 1725, ostensibly to Cadiz. The tobacco was in fact landed in Bantry Bay, Ireland. Other tobacco was 'exported' to Dunkirk or Ostend, where it was repacked in 100-lb bales and put on English vessels to be smuggled ashore. These vessels took out clearances from a Spanish or Portuguese port in case they were challenged off the English coast.

Edward Carson describes another attempted tobacco fraud in his *The Ancient and Rightful Customs*. The Collector at Liverpool in a letter to the Customs Commissioners in 1724 tells them he has discovered 'a most notorious fraud in this port in the exportation of roll tobacco to the Isle of Man'. He considered that the Revenue had lost £10,000 per annum by the shipping of tobacco stalks rolled up in a large twist and thinly covered over with tobacco, so that most of the rolls were filled up with sand, dirt and 'all manner of rubbish'.

Other frauds were highlighted by Sir Robert Walpole when he endeavoured to introduce his Excise reforms of 1733. He told the House not only about the re-landing of tobacco after it had been shipped off for export but also of the stealing and smuggling of tobacco out of ships after their arrival in the River Thames. Another fraud was the stripping of the leaves from the tobacco stalks and then, by means of a special machine, splitting the stalks which were then pressed and exported as tobacco leaf.

Many of Walpole's facts emanated from a committee headed by Sir John Cope, whose terms of reference were to investigate the frauds, particularly in the tobacco trade. Their report was submitted to the House on 7 June 1733. In it they highlighted the principal fraud, that of recording in the landwaiter's book (from which the duty is computed) a figure less than the actual weight of hogsheads imported. The planters in Virginia maintained that the utmost allowance for waste in the voyage was 8 lb in every hundredweight. The report cited an actual example: in June 1727 John Midford imported in the *William and Jane* from Virginia 301 hogsheads of tobacco, the weight of which as recorded by the landwaiters was 199,257 lb. However the true weight was 230,150 lb, or a difference of 30,893 lb, the duty on which was lost to the government.

The existing duty payable on tobacco was 6⅓d per pound, which had to be paid in ready money on importation with an allowance of 10 per cent discount on prompt payment or otherwise bonds given with sureties for the payment. Walpole wanted to reduce this to 4¾d per pound, not to be paid until the tobacco came to be sold for home consumption, so that if the merchant exported his tobacco he would be quite free from all payment of duty or from giving bond. As Chancellor of the Exchequer, he argued that these measures would put an end to those other frauds of merchants who failed to pay for their bonds on import, and also prevent those rich merchants paying cash on import, which entitled them to the 10 per cent discount, and then entering the tobacco immediately for export and securing drawback of the full duty, thus making 10 per cent profit on the total duty. His scheme would mean that tobacco for export would be reloaded without the fuss of cancelling the bonds or taking out debentures for the drawback. The much-needed reforms were not carried out for the reasons described earlier and Parliament's failure, or more correctly refusal, to acknowledge the corrupt situation allowed tobacco to remain one of the free traders' most profitable commodities for many more years.

Meanwhile, the government continued its efforts to check smuggling by preventing tobacco being shipped in small boats, or landed at outlying harbours from larger ones or passed from ship to ship at sea. In 1733 a number of ships were stationed between Gravesend and Rye to keep an eye on the Channel shipping, and hopefully to prevent any clandestine running of goods. Despite all these measures, petitions were still frequently received by Parliament from the legal tobacco trader. The merchants of Whitehaven complained, for example, that the tobacco running had greatly increased and 'it is now carried on with variety of methods and with such success [that] traders in Whitehaven and all fair traders everywhere are deprived of the inland trade of Great Britain, and the same is (almost wholly) now in the hands of the clandestine traders, who have stripped Whitehaven of the trade'.

The 1783 committee on illicit practices in the revenue reported that smuggled tobacco could be bought throughout the countryside at one half and in London at two-thirds of the lowest price at which legally imported goods could be sold. 'It is the opinion of the Commissioners of the Excise, from which we cannot dissent, that the Excise duties alone would, if smuggling could be prevented, increase the revenue three times.'

Stemming from this committee's report and from Walpole's original 1733 concept of an Excise survey, a system of permit and survey was applied to tobacco in 1789. The aim of the Excise was to discover smuggled tobacco rather than to prevent it being smuggled, and to this end the whole process of manufacture and transportation of tobacco was supervised. Excise officers had to be informed of the minutest details involved in the least operation of manufacture or the transportation of the smallest quantities of tobacco. As a practical measure of trade control, the regulations simply served to harass the honest trader. The smuggler still found outlets for his tobacco because small quantities were required in many places, such as public houses and shops, where no accurate check of sales could be kept. As a deterrent to smuggling, the excise proved a failure and was discontinued by the Act of 1840.

Tobacco smuggling continued well into the nineteenth century. However, methods employed by the smugglers became more and more ingenious and the use of false bulkheads and linings in ships, of hollow stones in the ballast and of tobacco made up to resemble rope reflects the increasing efficiency of the Customs officers. The gradual reorganisation of the Customs services with the attendant improvement in its personnel meant that the smuggling of tobacco in sizeable quantities was gradually rendered so difficult and risky as to be unprofitable. The bold runs on open beaches had become a memory of the previous century.

6

Spirits

Franciscus de la Boe (1614–1672), a seventeenth-century physician and professor of medicine at the University of Leyden in Holland, is generally credited with the invention of gin. Its creation was quite intentional and the professor's objective was strictly medicinal. Knowing the diuretic properties of the oil of the juniper berry (*Juniperus communis*), de la Boe, more familiarly known as Dr Sylvius, felt that by redistilling a pure alcohol with the juniper berry he could obtain its therapeutic oil in a form that would provide an inexpensive medicine. And he succeeded. Within a very few years all Holland was taking Dr Sylvius's medicine to cure an amazing variety of ills. He named the mixture 'Genievre' from the French for juniper. It also came to be known by other names, such as 'Hollands' after the country that claims its inventor, or 'Schiedam', a gin-distilling centre near Rotterdam. The English shortened and anglicised the word to gin.

Some authorities maintain that gin was being made in England before the end of the seventeenth century; barley or hops were used to make the alcoholic base, with juniper berries added for flavouring. However, its popularity and consumption appear to have been limited, although there was some demand for distilled spirits that were palatable and cheap. By Queen Anne's time, 1702–14, this demand was met by distillers who took the lees of wines and beers and distilled out the alcohol. But it was during her reign that the English began to acquire the taste for gin, no doubt partly because soldiers returning from the Continental wars of the Spanish Succession gave glowing reports of the new drink that they had nicknamed 'Dutch Courage'. Rapidly, gin became the national drink, and superseded ale beer, especially after Anne had raised the duties on French wines and brandies, and lowered the Excise tax on distilled spirits.

The early history of brandy, the other spirit much smuggled into Britain during this period, is more obscure. Technically, it is a potable spirit derived from the distillation of wine or a fermented mash of fruit, which usually has been suitably aged in wood. An interesting legend of how the spirit came into existence may be near the truth. During the sixteenth century there was a brisk trade between La Rochelle, outport of the Charente valley wine-growing area, and Holland. One thrifty Dutch ship owner hit on the idea of concentrating the wine and thus greatly increasing the amount that could be carried. By eliminating the water he could transport the spirit or 'soul' of the wine to Holland, where the water could be put back. Apparently on arrival with the concentrated consignment his Dutch friends tasted it and liked it as it was; the brandy trade had been born. The Dutch called it 'brandewijn' or 'burnt wine', presumably because fire or heat was used in the distilling process.

During the first three decades of the eighteenth century the consumption of distilled spirits in Britain increased so rapidly that the government began to be seriously worried about its adverse effects on the populace. The labouring classes had taken to gin, for it provided a relatively cheap way to escape from the reality of the drudgery, boredom and long hours of their working lives. Soon, all too frequently, gin and other spirits were drunk to excess, as Hogarth's famous 'Gin Lane' testifies. Gin, or 'geneva', got most of the blame; to its critics it was 'the grand preservative of sloth … which in a little time cures the tormenting sense of the most pressing necessities'. Drunkenness and debauchery became rife in some quarters and, as will be seen, many of the smugglers' most horrific crimes, such as the murders of Galley and Chater, were committed by men fired with copious draughts of gin or brandy. The government considered that many, if not the majority, of the country's ills could be squarely blamed on the excessive drinking of spirits, and measures were taken to eradicate this 'bane of the Nation'. Needless to say, like most prohibitions these measures were largely unsuccessful.

One of the first steps taken was the so-called Brandy Act of 1733. A committee had been appointed by Parliament to encourage the manufacture and export of home-made spirits and so promote the growth of corn (wheat and barley) in this country. This would save gold and English currency going out of the country to buy French brandies and other spirit-based liquors from the Continent. At this time the cost of one gallon of French brandy on the London market was between seven and eight shillings, of which six shillings and five pence was duty. The duty was so prohibitive that very few people paid it and much French brandy was smuggled into the country in ankers (8½ imperial gallons) and distributed to public houses and private individuals in the usual way. Another method of getting French brandy into England was for merchants to arrange for it to be sent first to Rotterdam or Ostend whence it was shipped as Flemish brandy, on which the duty was only four shillings per gallon. It was virtually impossible for a Customs officer to distinguish between the two types. The committee reported this fraud and recommended that there be a standard duty of five shillings on all foreign brandies imported and, furthermore, that a drawback or allowance of £6 8s 0d per ton ought to be paid on corn used for the distilling of spirits destined for export. These recommendations were ineffectual in reducing the clandestine importation of French brandy. The public had acquired a taste for it and in any event the new duty of five shillings per gallon ensured that the free trader still had a wide profit margin.

In the metropolis itself the problem was particularly acute; the Grand Jury of the Old Bailey Sessions of 1735–36 were so disturbed by the effects of spirits that they issued a public condemnation,

> That the daily increase of profanity and immorality is owing to the passions being inflamed by these spirits; the natural and common product of which is cursing, swearing and fighting in our streets: women throwing off all shame and modesty, in the open day, and in private, not common lust alone is satisfied but rapes and sodomy are perpetrated.

In April 1736 the government introduced a Bill which, it was hoped, would virtually put an end to the excessive drinking of gin. The Bill introduced into the House asserted that 'the excessive drinking of spirituous liquors by the common people tends not only to the destruction of their healths and the debauching of their morals but to the public ruin'. Its object was to restrict the consumption of spirits and consequently stimulate that of beer and ales, and the growing of corn used in their preparation. The Bill required all sellers of brandy, rum, arrack, usquebaugh, geneva and *aqua vitae* to take out a licence for £50, to be renewed annually, and to keep accounts of all wholesale purchases with no quantity less than two gallons (undiluted) to be purchased by the licensee.

The opponents of the Bill argued that it would lead to a much reduced contribution to the Revenue as smaller amounts of spirits would be sold. The government claimed that this was preferable if the moral standing of the populace would be improved; and besides, they believed that more beer would be brewed, which would mean increased acres under corn and more money and work for the landowners. The Bill was passed and the Act came into force on 29 September 1736. The day before, there were parades and marches through the London streets with 'Madame Genieve' being carried in a funeral procession to her place of lying in state; for such a solemn occasion several at the wake got surprisingly drunk and the Justices of the Peace saw fit to commit some of the more high-spirited mourners to prison.

The Gin Act did not achieve what the government hoped it would. True, in 1735 the 'official' figure for spirits distilled in this country was 5,394,823 gallons and for the first full year after the Act came into force in 1737 the total had dropped to 3,611,155 gallons. But the apparently significant reduction in the consumption of spirits was false. The Act had merely succeeded in driving the distillation of spirits underground and increasing the amount clandestinely imported.

The illegally distilled gin was far worse than that distilled legally and was known as the *labis infernalis*. It was also discovered that spirit could be distilled from other products of the British soil besides malt, 'though not equally pleasing to elegant palates with those of an exotic produce resembled them at least in their inebriating qualities'. By 1742, when the Act was finally acknowledged to be unworkable, the official (i.e. legal) distillation figure was 7,161,437 gallons or nearly 2 million gallons more in spite of the prohibition. Prior to the Act, London had an abundance of lunch houses where interesting gin-based drinks could be imbibed by merchants and businessmen. One side effect of the Act was the closure of many of these houses, whereupon some of their keepers went into the brewing business, some took taverns in the universities, others became apothecaries, and a few took out the necessary £50 licence. However, one punch seller in the Strand, a Mr Gordon, got round the new law by devising a new punch based on strong madeira wine, which he called 'saugre'.

When the Act first came in, convictions for selling spirits without a licence were frequent as the new law was interpreted with vigour. Fines were heavy for a successful prosecution and informers were paid £5 for their information. The *Gentleman's Magazine* for April 1737 reported that during that month eleven people in London were fined £100 each for retailing spirits without a licence. Few could pay such a fine and they simply languished in prison; so informers were rarely paid (by December 1738 over 400 still had not received their reward) and prosecutions quickly became less and less. In order to defeat the informers, dealers devised a password system, to be answered correctly, before the customer got his drink. One common system was for a customer to knock on a known retailer's door and whisper 'Puss', whereupon the retailer would answer 'Mew', and thrust out a drawer in which the customer inserted the money. Finally the drawer would be pulled in and returned again with a measure of gin in it.

A new Bill for altering the duties on spirits and permitting them to be sold with less restraint was introduced in 1743 and became law at the beginning of the next year. Under this Act there was a small duty per gallon laid on spirits at the still head and the licence to retail spirits was reduced from £50 to 20s and was only given to persons who already possessed an alehouse licence. The duty levied at the still head meant that the retailer would have to increase the price of his gin to his customer by about one-third. The supporters of the Act argued that the increase would put the liquor out of the price range of the working-class drinker; furthermore, the cheapness of the licences would encourage spirits to be sold in the proper establishments, i.e. alehouses. Penalties for retailing spirits without a licence were reduced to a fine of £10 but the barrels containing the stock were to be staved and the contents tipped down the gutter. In January 1752 one person from Radcliffe Highway in London lost 400 gallons in this way, when his stock of geneva, aniseed, plague waters, cinnamon and mint water, and cherry and raspberry brandy, were tipped away because he did not have a spirit licence.

This new fiscal approach did nothing to wean the working classes off 'Mother's Ruin', and the consumption of illegally distilled and illegally imported gin, and of that which was legally distilled in this country increased annually. In 1750 an authority estimated that there were 14,000 gin addicts in London; in the parish of St Giles-in-the-Fields, spirits could be bought in 500 out of the 2,000 houses in the parish. In 1751, and on succeeding occasions, the government increased the duty on spirits in the rather contradictory hope of reducing consumption and of raising extra money to finance the war with France (the Seven Years' War began in 1756). But the drinking of spirits, particularly gin, was firmly entrenched in the English way of life and the average worker, even when literate, paid little heed to the many pamphlets that condemned the habit. Among them was Dr Cheney's *Essay on health and long life* (1760) in which he warned:

> People who have any regard to their healths and lives, ought to tremble at the first cravings for such poisonous liquors; every dram begets the necessity of two more to cure the ill effects of the first; neither laudanum nor arsenic will kill more certainly.

During the 1760s the debate was revived on whether home-grown grain should be used in the malt distilleries. One side argued for the complete prohibition of malt distilleries and to leave spirit distillation to that derived from sugar in the colonies, while others advocated a controlled distilling from home-grown grain. Landowners were unfavourably disposed towards selling their grain to distilleries as generally a better price could be obtained for it if sold to the bakers or for export. One writer in the *Gentleman's Magazine* in 1760 estimated that annually 30,000 quarters of wheat were used for domestic bread consumption; 10,000 quarters were exported and 5,000 quarters went to the malt distillers. This writer believed that as long as the percentage of grain sold for malting was kept reasonably low it would not have an adverse effect on the grain market. He further pointed out that the grain for either export or for malting provided a good reserve which could be tapped when famine threatened.

The distillers, having a case to prove, were anxious to retain their share of home-grown grain and argued their case forcibly in the face of bitter criticism:

> The private adventurers, in this prohibited trade, have summed up every sophism to palliate the evils of which it stands accused, and to prevail both with the ministry and Parliament to espouse their cause against the voice of the public sufferers; who support their complaints against the pernicious use of spiritious liquors, by facts which make it necessary to continue that prohibition
>
> (*The Monitor*, 12–19 January 1760)

But there were many who were still greatly worried about the effects of alcoholism. 'How common was it to see the miserable ingenious artist intoxicated with gin, selling his own and children's clothes, and bed, to purchase that bewitching poison.'

Despite prohibitive duties and official warnings of the deleterious results, the populace rode triumphant over the law and continued to drink copiously gin and other spirits. Although home distillation was increasingly controlled and subjected to more stringent checks, there was no shortage of geneva, brandy or rum for those who knew, or frequented hostels and public houses supplied by, the right people.

From Beachy Head to Cuckmere Haven near Seaford in Sussex, a distance of about six miles, there are only three ways up the cliff. One, known as Crowlink Gap, from the beach to a lonely farmhouse near Friston church, was so celebrated for contraband that for years spirit shops in London advertised their stock of Hollands as being 'Genuine Crowlink'. Many of the Continental ports had established their own distilleries to serve the English smugglers. George Bishop, in his report of 1783 entitled 'Observations, Remarks and Means to Prevent Smuggling', estimates the scale of spirit smuggling. In 1773 approximately 2,500,000 gallons of geneva were smuggled to Britain out of Dunkirk and about that time geneva distilleries were established to supply the British smugglers in Goteborg, Nieuwport, Ostend, and Calais. By 1782 upwards of 4,000,000 gallons of geneva were smuggled annually and about half that quantity of brandy, besides rum and other spirits.

Gin and brandy were the main spirits illegally imported but rum and, to a lesser extent, French wines were also smuggled into Britain. Sir Robert Walpole was not averse to securing his favourite French claret by having illegal shipments brought up the Thames. Rum was freely available in the public houses of England by the middle of the eighteenth century; the unfortunate pair Daniel Chater and William Galley, murdered by smugglers in 1747, broke their ill-fated journey on a cold February day to take a couple of draughts of rum in the White Hart at Rowlands Castle. It was here that the landlady of the inn first overheard their conversation and by supplying them freely with the drink ascertained their mission.

Rum comes from a grass, the botanical name of which is *Saccharum officinarum* and the common name is sugar cane. The Spaniards introduced sugar cane to Cuba from the Canary Islands after Columbus arrived in 1492, whence it spread to the other West Indian islands. Rum is the spirit obtained by distillation of the fermented products of sugar cane, either pure cane spirit or more frequently molasses. Its manufacture developed in the British West Indies during the seventeenth century; in Barbados rum was certainly produced as early as 1647 and possibly earlier. First known as 'kill-devil' and later referred to as 'rumbullion' or 'rumbustion' by the Caribbean freebooters, it was known simply as rum by the eighteenth century, the term probably being a contraction of rumbustion or of the Latin word *Saccharum*.

In 1745 Admiral Vernon was concerned about the incidence of scurvy among sailors in the British Navy and one measure he instituted to curb it was to replace the small beer ration by a daily tot of the West Indian spirit. Long before the Admiralty gave rum their official blessing it was a popular drink and a valuable item of trade, particularly on the eastern side of the Atlantic. Many of the slave ships outward from North America were laden with the spirit to be bartered for negroes when the West Coast of Africa was reached. The French, British and

Spanish islands in the West Indies all sold rum or molasses to traders and it is easy to believe that some proportion of the spirit was smuggled before the ship reached its home port. It was, of course, the most popular drink in the West Indies and one eighteenth-century writer recorded the recipe for a punchbowl of gargantuan proportions.

A marble basin, built in the middle of the garden especially for the occasion, served as the bowl. Into it were poured 1,200 bottles of rum, 1,200 bottles of Malaga wine and 400 quarts of boiling water. Then 600 pounds of best cane sugar and 200 powdered nutmegs were added. The juice of 2,600 lemons was squeezed into the liquor. Onto the surface was launched a handsome mahogany boat piloted by a boy of twelve, who rowed about a few moments, then coasted to the side and began to serve the assembled company of 600, which gradually drank up the ocean upon which he floated.

Rum was overwhelmingly popular in the American colonies before 1775, much of it being illegally imported. It was estimated that 10 million gallons were consumed annually, which gave an average of three gallons per person for all spirituous liquors combined. One historian declares that the British Law of 1763, designed to make the American colonies give up Spanish West Indian rum in favour of the British product, caused the American Revolution – and a revolution might just as well be fought over rum as tea.

George Washington was elected on rum; he got into the Virginia House of Burgesses in 1758 not by campaigning but by distributing among the voters 75 gallons of rum; and it was the Virginia House of Burgesses that sent him to Congress. Another apparently authentic story recounts how Paul Revere set out on his famous ride in a morose silence and did not begin to shout that the British were coming until he had stopped at the home of a rum distiller, Issac Hall, for a draught of rum.

Gin, brandy and rum were all smuggled in considerable quantity during the eighteenth century. Today, the average tourist, if tempted to gamble against the likelihood of discovery by bringing in more than his duty-free allowance, usually favours a bottle of spirits. He works on the principles of relatively high value and relative ease of concealment. But in the halcyon days of contraband running, concealment was almost a sign of weakness and mismanagement.

7

Whisky

Smuggling usually implies the clandestine movement of goods in or out of countries with the express purpose of evading payment of border duty on these goods. However, there was in the late eighteenth and nineteenth centuries a movement of goods *within* Britain with the same intention of avoiding payment of excise. This, of course, was the illegal distillation and distribution of the one spirit unique to this country, *uisge beatha* in Gaelic, more familiarly known as Scotch whisky. In so far as the distillers were deliberately evading duty and illegally selling their product around the countryside, that means it comes under the heading of smuggling.

A drink whose virtues as a source of solace, comfort, cheer and courage have been so universally recognised and appreciated must surely be a gift from the gods, and tradition has it that Osiris, the son of Seb (the Earth) and Nut (the Sky), first revealed to poor humans the secret of distilling the water of life. If an Egyptian god does not take the credit for its invention, then the Chinese will, for the art of separating alcohol appears to have been known in the Far East from early times. A race who invented the manufacture of silk and porcelain, the mariner's compass, the art of block-printing and who developed gunpowder may well be allowed the credit of having invented the art of distilling alcohol. The art diffused westward and is reputed to have been first introduced into Europe by the Moors of Spain about 1150. The distillation of aromatic waters is said to have been known from very early times to the Arabians. The word 'alcohol' (*al-koh'l*) is Arabic, meaning originally 'fire powder' which was used for staining the eyelids and gradually came to mean 'essence' and 'pure spirit'. The meaning of 'whisky' is very similar. The term seems to have come from 'usguebaugh', a derivation from the Gaelic *usige beatha*, the water of life. Whisky, or whiskey in Ireland, was probably a post-Tudor contraction of 'whiskybae', a phonetic variant of usquebaugh.

Its early history involves the western and northern Gaelic parts of the British Isles. Following the invasion of Ireland by Henry II in 1170, the English found the Irish in the habit of making and drinking *aqua vitae* primarily as a medicine which was considered to be a panacea for all disorders. Physicians recommended it to patients indiscriminately, for preserving health, dissipating humours, strengthening the heart, curing colic, dropsy, palsy and other complaints, and even for longevity. It appears to have been used at one time to inspire heroism, just as opium was used among the Turks. An Irish knight, named Savage, about 1350, prior to engaging in battle, ordered to each soldier a large draught of *aqua vitae*. Four hundred years later we find Burns claiming a similar virtue for usquebaugh or Highland whisky:

> But bring a Scotsman frae his hill,
> Clap in his cheek a Highland gill,
> Say, such is Royal George's will,
> An' there's the foe
> He has nae thought but how to kill
> Twa at a blow.

There is no precise record of when whisky was first distilled in Scotland. The earliest direct account is found in the Exchequer Rolls of 1494, which list 'eight bolls of malt to Friar John for where with to make *aqua vitae*'. By 1609 the Island Chiefs were concerned about the consumption of strong wines and *aqua vitae* and in the 'statutes of Icolmkill' they point out that one of the chief causes of the great poverty of the Islanders, and of the cruelty and inhuman barbarity practised in their feuds, was their inordinate love of strong wines and *aqua vitae*, which they purchased partly from local dealers, partly from merchants of the mainland.

In the fifth statute, power was given to any person to seize, without payment, wine or *aqua vitae* imported for sale by a native merchant, and if any Islander should buy any of the prohibited articles from a mainland trader, he would incur the penalty of £40 for the first offence, £100 for the second, and for the third the loss of all his possessions and moveable goods. However, it was declared lawful for an individual to brew as much *aqua vitae* as his own family might require; and the barons and any wealthy gentlemen were permitted to purchase in the Lowlands the wine and other liquors required for their private consumption.

In 1622 a more stringent measure was passed; termed an 'Act that nane send wynes to the Ilis', it deprived the Hebrides of the wines of Bordeaux and in consequence whisky became a more popular drink than claret, although for the better classes claret remained the accepted drink until a duty was imposed on it for the first time in 1780. Noblemen stored hogsheads of claret in their halls and guests received a cup of wine when they entered and another on departure. Drinking to excess was expected; a landlord was considered inhospitable who permitted any of his guests to retire unaided on their own legs. Those who stayed for the night found in their bedrooms a copious supply of ale, wine and brandy to allay the thirst induced by their previous drinking bout. Those who insisted on going home were 'helped' on their way with a *deoch-an-dorius*, a drink for the door, from a vessel, as one contemporary account puts it, 'of very formidable proportions'.

Burns's song 'The Whistle' confirms that claret was the favourite drink among the better classes:

> The dinner being over the claret they ply,
> And every new cork is a new spring of joy.

The competitors having drunk six bottles of claret each, Glenriddle, 'a high ruling elder, left the foul business to folks less devine'. Maxwelton and Craigdarroch continued to contest and drank one or two bottles more, Craigdarroch winning the whistle. Burns is said to have drunk a bottle of rum and one of brandy during the contest.

Ian MacDonald, in his *Smuggling in the Highlands* (1915), asserts that wine, ale, rum and brandy (the latter two largely smuggled) were drunk more than whisky up to the late eighteenth century, and in consequence whisky manufacture and use must then have been limited. This conclusion can clearly be drawn from the small quantities charged with Excise duty. On Christmas Day 1660, Excise duty was first laid on whisky in Scotland, the duty being 2*d*, 3*d*, and 4*d* per gallon according to the ingredients from which the spirits were made. No record exists of the amount of duty paid until 1707, when it amounted only to £1,810 15*s* 0*d*, representing about 100,000 gallons at a time when the population was 990,000. No record of the quantity taxed exists until 1724, when the duty was 3*d* and 6*d*; in that year 145,602 gallons were taxed, the duty amounted to £3,504 12*s* 10*d*, and the population was a little over 1 million. However, these figures must be treated with caution and despite the small duty in the early eighteenth century it seems probable that more whisky was distilled than the official figures suggest, particularly as much of the whisky was produced in small stills within the homes where it was consumed. Moreover, it seems reasonable to assume that the average Scotsman would not go out of his way to part with money in payment of a tax imposed by Parliament hundreds of miles away in Westminster.

The duty on whisky remained at 3*d* and 6*d* per gallon from 1709 to 1742; it was then raised gradually until by 1784 it had reached 3*s* 11*d* and 15 per cent. In that year tax was paid on 239,350 gallons, the total duty came to £65,497 15*s* 4*d*, and the population of Scotland numbered 1,441,808. Owing to the difficulty and cost of Excise collection in the thinly populated areas, the duties, while low, had been farmed out for periods not exceeding three years. When the duty had increased appreciably the Commissioners took the management in their own hands and it was levied and collected by their own officers, much to the inconvenience and discontent of the people.

The high duties and stringent regulations prompted Burns to write his 'Earnest Cry and Prayer' (1785) and no doubt the poet's strong appeal helped the agitation;

before the end of the year, duty was reduced to 2s 7½d, at which it remained for two years. However, the enactments of the law were so imperfectly enforced that the duty was evaded to a considerable extent. In 1787, in order to facilitate and improve collection, Scotland was divided into Lowland and Highland districts and duty charged according to the size of the still instead of on the gallon. The duty was £1 4s 0d per annum on each gallon of the capacity of a still, the assumption being that a still at work would yield a certain annual produce according to its cubic capacity and the length of each complete distillation.

The Excise officers could see the impracticability of this law and wisely took no further trouble than to visit the distilleries occasionally, to observe if any other stills were in operation or if larger ones had been substituted for those which had been already gauged. The distillers soon outwitted the Excise authorities by making improvements in the construction of their stills, so that instead of taking a week to complete a distillation, it could be done in twenty-four hours and eventually in a few hours and even in a few minutes. To meet these sharp practices on the part of distillers, the duty was increased year after year until by 1814 it amounted to £7 16s ¼d per gallon of the still's capacity and 6s 7½d on every gallon made. This mode of Excise duty made it so much in the interest of the law-abiding distiller to increase the quantity of spirits by every means possible that the quality of the product was entirely disregarded. Not surprisingly, this encouraged a large increase of illicit distillation because of the better flavour and quality of the spirits produced by the illicit distiller, usually with small stills. In sheer desperation, the government in 1814 prohibited the use of stills of less than 500 gallons capacity. The restriction actually increased the amount of illicit distillation.

In 1789 Scotland's national poet obtained a part-time post as district Excise officer and when his farm at Mossgiel finally failed in 1791 he transferred to a full-time post, remaining in service until his premature death in 1796 prevented him from taking up the promotion that he had been marked out for. A popular poet, he was capable of writing lines that would not endear him to his superiors.

Thae curst horse-leeches o' th' Excise,
Wha mak' the whisky stills their prize

But he was also a conscientious and brave officer, performing at least one heroic deed. In 1792 a brig was smuggling in the Solway, and looked like presenting some difficulty to the little band of Excisemen and dragoons gathered on shore to prevent it. Burns was in the party and he waded into the water, sword in hand, and made for the boat. In spite of risks from quicksand and from the smugglers, he reached the brig, was the first of the party to board her, and helped to arrest the crew, and take the boat to Dumfries to be sold.

The illicit trading and traffic became so grave that in 1814 and 1815 meetings of the county authorities were held in the Highlands, and representations made to the government, pointing out the evil effects of the high duties on spirits, and of the unwise regulations and restrictions imposed. Among other things it was affirmed that the Excise restrictions were highly prejudicial to the agricultural interests of the Highlands because a still of 500 gallons' capacity would consume more than the disposable grain of its neighbourhood, and furthermore the area could not possibly afford to fuel such a still. In the face of so many difficulties the government gave way and the still duty was discontinued and replaced by the high duty of 9s 4½d per gallon. In 1816 stills of not less than 40 gallons were allowed to be used with a view to encouraging small distillers to act lawfully; in the next year the duty had to be reduced to 6s 2d. Yet illicit distillation continued to such an extent that in 1823 the authorities took what seemed to be the only effective means of suppressing it, and further reduced the duty to 2s 4d. In that year alone there were 14,000 prosecutions in Scotland for illicit distillation and malting; the military had to be employed in its suppression, and Revenue cutters had to be used on the West Coast. Later on, Riding officers were appointed.

This was a period in the Scottish history when lawlessness was particularly rife. Skirmishes between the authorities and the people were common, and both sides suffered serious losses and injuries. Cases occurred where not only individuals but whole communities never recovered temporal prosperity after successful raids by the military, cutters and gaugers. However, matters had now reached their worst and during the nineteenth century illegal distillation decreased. A high duty had operated as a bounty to the illicit distiller, and its reduction had reduced his profits. The permission to use smaller stills encouraged farmers and others with limited capital to engage in a legitimate trade on a small scale, which afforded a ready market for barley of local growth and provided whisky for local consumption. The relaxation of the Excise regulations led to an improvement in the quality of the whisky made by the licensed distiller, and the quality was further improved by the permission in 1824 to warehouse free of duty, which allowed the whisky to mature prior to dispatch for consumption. These and minor changes led to the decrease in smuggling in the Highlands shown in the following statistics. In 1823 there were 14,000 detections (duty 6s 2d to 2s 4d); in 1834 the total had dropped to 692 detections (duty 3s 4d); and in 1854 there were only 73 detections when the duty was 4s 8d.

Whiskey was causing problems on the American side of the Atlantic as well. The small farmers of Western Pennsylvania, mostly Irish and Scottish immigrants, had brought with them the knowledge of distillation and were in the habit of converting their surplus grain into whiskey which they could easily transport and sell. The federal government had passed a law on 3 March 1791 which placed an excise on distilled liquors. It was the brainchild of Alexander Hamilton, the Secretary of the Treasury in George Washington's cabinet, who saw the tax as a way to raise money to help pay the national debt and to assert the power of the federal government. The farmers of Western Pennsylvania resisted the tax and in 1794 resorted to violence by attacking and in some cases tarring and feathering the federal Revenue officers who attempted to collect it.

A law of 5 June 1794 designed to compel non-complying distillers to pay the tax touched off what appeared to be organised rebellion, which came to be known as the Whiskey Insurrection. In July about 500 armed men attacked and burned the home of General John Neville, the regional inspector of taxes. Some of Hamilton's followers saw in the insurrection a plot to destroy the federal government. Hamilton himself saw it as the first occasion to bring federal government strength against local defiance. Under authority granted by Congress, President George Washington on 7 August 1794 issued a proclamation ordering the rebels to return to their homes and calling for a militia from Virginia, Maryland, New Jersey and Pennsylvania. After negotiations between the federal commissioners and rebel leaders proved fruitless, Washington ordered some 13,000 troops into Pennsylvania's western counties. Opposition melted away and no battle ensued. Some of the rebels were captured and two were put on trial and convicted of treason but subsequently pardoned by the President.

Many Americans, particularly members of the opposition Republican Party, were appalled by the overwhelming force used by the government. They considered it unnecessary and feared that Hamilton sought to use the suppression of the insurrection as the first step to absolute power. To Federalists, however, the most important result was that federal authority had triumphed over its first rebellious adversary and had won the support of the state government in enforcing federal law within the United States.

It would be wrong to end an account of whisky smuggling by reference to the moonshiners of the New World. Any such history must end where it began, in the windswept Gaelic lands of Atlantic Britain. We must return to Scotland, where Ian MacDonald, himself an Inland Revenue official at the end of the nineteenth century, recounts some interesting stories about the illegal distillers and the unpopular gaugers.

A cask of spirits was once seized and conveyed by the officers to a neighbouring inn. For safety they took the cask with them into the room they occupied on the second floor. The smugglers came to the inn and asked the maid who was attending upon the officers to note where the cask was standing. The girl took her bearings so accurately that, by boring through the flooring and the bottom of the cask, the spirits were quickly transferred to a suitable vessel placed underneath, and the officers were left with the empty cask. On another occasion an officer came unexpectedly on a bothy where distilling was taking place; when he entered, the smuggler, who was the sole occupant, calmly asked him, 'Did anyone see you coming in?' 'No,' replied the officer. Seizing an axe, the smuggler said, 'Then no one will see you going out!'

Obviously the Highlanders had no love or respect for the British government and the law which made distillation illegal came to them in a foreign garb. If they were convicted and sent to prison, the sentence was not regarded as a disgrace, nor as much of a punishment. At Dingwall Gaol, smugglers were several times allowed home for Sundays, and one enterprising inmate petitioned to commence distillations within the prison to raise money to pay his fine. However, writers of the time were concerned not only with the physical injury caused by drinking an impure, immature whisky, the product too often of a hasty and clandestine distilling operation, but also with its moral aspect. Stewart of Garth wrote in 1821:

> Smuggling has grown to an alarming extent, and if not checked will undermine the best principles of the people. Let a man be habituated to falsehood and fraud in one line of life, and he will soon learn to extend it to all his actions. This traffic operates like a secret poison on all their moral feelings. They are the more rapidly betrayed into it, as, though acute and ingenious in regard to all that comes within the scope of their observation, they do not comprehend the nature and purpose of imports levied on the produce of the soil, nor have they any distinct idea of the practice of smuggling being attended with disgrace or turpitude. The open defiance of the laws, the progress of chicanery, perjury, hatred, and mutual recrimination, with a constant dread and suspicion of informers, men not being sure of nor confident in their next neighbours, which result from smuggling, and the habit which it engenders, are subjects highly important and regarded with the most serious consideration and the deepest regret by all who value the permanent welfare of their country, which depends so materially upon the preservation of the morals of the people.

MacDonald supported this swingeing denunciation and was happy to recount that 'the decrease in illicit distillation since 1823 … is a remarkable proof of the great improvement which has taken place in the morals of the Highland people'. He suggested that the change had been due to various causes but mainly to the spread of education, and the influence of enlightened public opinion. Landlords who had formerly turned a blind eye or winked at the practice embodied stringent clauses in estate leases against illicit distillation. In addition, the clergy refused Church privileges to those engaged in smuggling and in a few localities the smugglers' funds were exhausted by the frequent seizures made by energetic officers. Often, however, people were driven to smuggling by dire poverty.

Even when MacDonald was working for the Inland Revenue in the 1880s, illegal distillation went on and he quotes figures that must have provided a great temptation to the poor Highlander in the remoter localities. In 1880 barley could be bought for 23s a quarter from which could be obtained 14 or 16 gallons of whisky, which could be sold at 18s or 20s a gallon. Allowing for all contingencies, such as payment of carriage, liberal consumption during manufacture and generous treatment of friends and neighbours, some £8 or £10 could be netted from an outlay of 23s. Poverty, tradition and isolation were the main reasons why illegal distillation continued well into the twentieth century in many a wild and ill-frequented glen on the west coast of Scotland.

The Gaelic enthusiasm for illegally distilling whisky in secret bothies did not seem to diminish the Scottish interest in other contraband activities. Many Scots were not averse to the open smuggling of goods both in and out of their country; in fact, one author wrote that smuggling was their 'national besetting sin'. The Customs system in Scotland prior to 1707 had seen the country divided into a varying number (usually twenty-three or twenty-four) of administrative areas known as precincts. Of these, five were located along the border with England, ten centred on the coast ports, and three on inland towns selected to catch any goods that might have slipped surreptitiously through the outer net. Each precinct was administered by a Collector and a Surveyor who were assisted by a clerk and a number of tidewaiters varying from one in unimportant places like Perth to fourteen in Leith and Port Glasgow. As happened on the South Coast of England, smuggling took place with or without the connivance of the officials, with frauds and false entries common; where bribery was not successful the goods were brought ashore quite openly and distributed. The English authorities were particularly perplexed by the amount of wool being illegally sent across the border into Scotland from the northern counties. Violence was not uncommon between officials and the smugglers. In 1690 the Surveyor in Leith, who had gone in search of smuggled brandy, was 'thrust twyse in the buttock' by the sword of an infuriated skipper.

In 1707, with the Act of Union between Scotland and England, the English Customs system was introduced north of the border. The Scots were delighted, for now they were able to couple their traditional dislike of Customs officials with a patriotic ideal of cheating and outwitting the Sassenach. Smuggling suddenly escalated. Scottish merchants, perfervid Jacobites, relished the opportunity to defraud an alien government of tax and at the same time line their own pockets. While the new Customs system was having its teething troubles, the smuggling of foreign goods through Scotland into the rich English market proved only too easy. The canny Scottish merchants quickly realised this and so too did the French and Dutch.

The Isle of Man acted as a supply depot for much of the smuggled goods that did not come directly from Holland and France via the Scottish east coast. The Duke of Atholl took over the island from the Stanley family in 1736 and developed it into what was described fifteen years later as a great storehouse or magazine in which the French and other nations deposited prodigious quantities of wines, brandies, coffee, teas and other India goods. The Scottish smugglers called here, as also did slave ships out of Liverpool. Mackenzie in his *History of Galloway* writes:

> The illicit intercourse of smuggling with that island [Man] so much occupied the attention of the most intelligent and enterprising part of the inhabitants of Galloway, that the idea of acquiring wealth in a commercial line by fair and upright dealing, seemed to be wholly laid aside. Even the clergy at this period were adventurers in the free trade.

In 1765 the government bought out the sovereign rights from the Duke of Atholl for £70,000, but despite this the smuggling continued.

To complete this survey of smuggling *within* Britain, here is a quote from the greatest whisky poet. Where else on earth would an Exciseman extol strong drink and condemn his colleagues and remain beloved of all?

Scotch Drink

Gie him strong drink until he wink,
That's sinking in despair;
An' liquor guid to fire his bluid,
That's prest wi' grief an' care:
There let him bouse, and deep carouse,
Wi' bumpers flowing o'er,
Till he forgets his loves and debts,
An' minds his griefs no more.

The De'il's Awa' Wi' The Exciseman

The De'il cam' fiddlin thro' the town,
And danc'd awa' wi' th' Exciseman;
And ilka wife cry'd: 'Auld Mahoun,
I wish ye luck o' your prize, man'

We'll mak our maut, and we'll brew our drink
We'll dance, sing, and rejoice, man,
And monie braw thanks to the meikle black De'il,
That danc'd awa' wi' the Exciseman.

There's threesome reels, and foursome reels,
There's hornpipes and strathspeys, man:
But the ae best dance e'er cam' to our lan',
Was – the De'il's awa' wi' the Exciseman.

8

The Goudhurst Affair

'O, what are these, Death's Ministers?'

Having outlined the general nature of smuggling in the previous chapters, it is now time to look at some of the more arresting incidents in the smugglers *v.* government struggle. There is no doubt that it must begin with the notorious Hawkhurst Gang and the incredible Goudhurst affair of 1747.

The decade from 1740 to 1750 saw the smuggling gangs reach a peak of lawlessness, audacity, cruelty and terror. The authorities could do little against the armed and organised smugglers, who openly, with an arrogance instilled as much by geneva as by their contempt for the law, went about their business of running and distributing goods. Writers of the time, usually for obvious reasons in the form of anonymous letters, complained to the authorities about the state of affairs in the country.

The following is an extract written anonymously by a person in Sussex to Mr Pelham, brother of the Duke of Newcastle, Lord of Sussex. These two brothers succeeded Walpole and held office for twelve years until 1754. The letter is dated 14 June 1747:

> They [referring to William Gray and James Stanford (alias Tripp), notorious smugglers] are so immensely rich that they bribe ye private men. Both of Hawkhurst in Kent they have bought estates and, at this time harbour the outlawed persons in their houses and are the support of the whole affair … I've hope your Grace and your Honour will use ye utmost interest to save us from inevitable ruin; at present we are in as bad a condition as they were in Scotland when plundered by the Rebells; when they plunder houses they call it visiting of them and say ''tis only neighbours fare' (local proverb meaning the 'same bad luck') and hope they'll not take it amiss.

Another writer from Horsham, Sussex, on 23 August in the following year puts only his initials 'J. F.' to a letter in the *Gentleman's Magazine*. He begins:

Sir, I have frequently conversed with many gentlemen of fortune about these dangerous men and they assure me that the outlawed and other smugglers in this and the neighbouring counties are so numerous and desperate that the inhabitants are in continual fear of the mischiefs which these horrid wretches not only threaten but actually perpetrate all round the countryside. The outrageous proceedings which you see in the public papers are not a tithe of what they actually commit.

This same writer quotes from Milton (*Paradise Lost*, Book XI, lines 675 to 680) to describe the smugglers' callous inhumanity to man. God has declared that Adam and Eve may no longer stay in Paradise because of Eve's indiscretion. Archangel Michael is sent to convey this news and leads Adam up a high hill and sets before him a vision of what shall happen until the Flood. Adam sees violence, oppression and sword-law throughout the plain; he turns to Michael and laments:

> … O, what are these,
> Death's ministers, not men? who thus deal death
> Inhumanly to men, and multiply
> Ten-thousand fold the sin of him who slew
> His brother, for of whom such massacre
> Make they, but of their brethren; men of men?

Another writer, from Chichester, draws the authorities' attention to the likely outcome even if a smuggler was indicted:

If anyone of them happen to be taken and the proof ever so clear against him no magistrate in the country durst commit him to gaol, if he did he was sure to have his house or barns set on fire or some other mischiefs done him which has been the occasion of their being brought to London to be committed.

This appears not to be an exaggeration, for in 1748 William Fairall, a notorious member of the Hawkhurst Gang, was apprehended in Sussex as a smuggler and taken before a Justice of the Peace, James Butler, of Lewes. The JP, cognizant of the danger of putting so powerful a person as Fairall on trial at Lewes, where the jury would be too terrified to bring in an unbiased verdict, wisely ordered that he be sent to London and taken before Justice Hammond. However, the episode does not end with Fairall being dispatched to London. Mr Butler's action, as it turned out, had sinister repercussions.

Fairall's guards got him safely to London without incident but instead of pressing on and reaching Newgate Gaol that evening the party stopped at an inn just short of London Bridge, where they proposed to spend the night. This action and subsequent events suggest that the prisoner's escape was a result of complicity or bribery between himself and his guards. At the inn, Fairall gave his guards the slip and, since they had conveniently neglected to put him in leg-irons, he was able to run off down Blackman Street, at the end of which he leapt on to a horse tethered there and rode away at full gallop, scattering the startled onlookers. Even his fellow smugglers, it is said, were surprised to see him back three days after he had been carried off to London under a strong guard. So it does not seem that they had rescued him. It seems more likely that Fairall, by threat or bribe, or both, had persuaded his guards to stage the escape. Once back among the safety of the gang, a council of revenge was called and a course of action decided upon, designed to regain some of their lost prestige. A contemporary anonymous account, *Smuggling and Smugglers in Sussex*, published in Chichester in 1749, takes up the story:

> They [the gang] were no sooner met than he [Fairall] declared vengeance against Mr Butler, and proposed many ways to be revenged. First to destroy all the deer in his park, and all his trees, which was readily agreed to. But Fairall, Kingsmill and John Mills and many more of them, declared that would not satisfy them, and accordingly proposed to set fire to his seat, one of the first in the county of Sussex, and burn him in it; but this most wicked proposal was objected to by three of the gang, namely Thomas Winter, alias the Coachman, one Stephens and one Slaughter, who protested against setting the house on fire or killing the gentleman, and great disputes arose among them, and they parted at that time without putting their villainous proposals into execution; but Fairall, Kingsmill and some more of the gang were determined not to let their resentment drop, and accordingly they got each a brace of pistols, and determined to go and waylay him near his own park wall and shoot him. Accordingly they went into the neighbourhood, when they heard Mr Butler was gone to Horsham, and that he was expected home that night, upon which they laid ready to execute their wicked design. But Mr Butler, by some accident, happening not to come home that night, they were heard to say to each other 'Dam him, he will not come home tonight, let us be gone about our business.' And so they went away angry at their disappointment, swearing they would watch for a month together but they would have him.
>
> This affair coming to Mr Butler's knowledge, care was taken to apprehend them if they came again, and they, being acquainted therewith, did not care to go a second time without a number; but no one would join except John Mills and Jackson … as not caring to run into so much danger; and they not thinking themselves strong enough, being only four, the whole design was laid aside … They were all much chastened, and Fairall said 'Damn him, an opportunity may happen some time', that they might make an example of Mr Butler, and all others that shall dare presume to obstruct them.

Fairall appears to have been denied his revenge but, nonetheless, he certainly had his freedom, at least for another year. In April 1749 he stood trial at the Old Bailey, indicted with others for his part in breaking open the Custom House in Poole. This desperate ruffian, whose sadistic and perverted delight in evil was shared by a number of smugglers at this time, suffered the ultimate penalty. He was unable to cheat the hangman again by effecting an escape. But more of these events in due course.

Attention must now turn to Goudhurst, a small village which sits upon a hill in Kent. Here in April 1747 the local inhabitants decided to put an end to the ignoble subservience that the Hawkhurst Gang had instilled in the majority of the people of Kent and Sussex. The villagers and local farmers, who no doubt had benefited from the free traders in earlier, less violent years by buying from them tea, gin and tobacco at competitive prices, became weary of their insolence and arrogance. Horses of the farmers had been commandeered by mysterious strangers for the carrying of contraband goods, and payment, if made, was by leaving an anker of spirits; but this high-handed borrowing had latterly led to more desperate measures. Those that were foolish enough not to comply with the smugglers' requests had their houses or barns or hayricks burnt; the smugglers' fear and suspicion of informers meant that innocent people quite content to go about their everyday business and 'watch the wall' were terrorised and tortured even if merely thought to be working against them.

Thus the friendly feeling towards the free trader as a person who was tolerated if not actually welcomed, gave way to antagonism when good and reasonably honest folk became sick and tired of the increasing outrages. The event which precipitated a collective expression of this growing condemnation happened in Goudhurst in the spring of 1747 and it signalled the beginning of the end for the feared Hawkhurst Gang.

Mr Ballard, a gentleman from Tunbridge Wells, was riding through Goudhurst when he was set upon by a gang of ruffians, later identified as members of the Hawkhurst Gang. They robbed him of the money he had on him (£39), his watch, and a ring. Not content with this they whipped and kicked him. The attack took place in broad daylight, about midday in fact, and the robbers got clean away. Mr Ballard was carried home and died four hours later.

A few weeks before this incident took place there had arrived in Goudhurst, just back from the Army – from which he had procured an honourable discharge from Lientenant General Harrison's Regiment of Foot – a man called William Sturt, a native of the village. He was in his late twenties and according to his discharge papers he was held 'high in esteem by his officers for his great perfectness in the different manuals and evolutions, and every art of war which he had strictly applied himself to'. Sturt, for one, was so shocked by this callous murder and by the general fear that the smugglers had created among his friends and neighbours that he called a meeting of the village at which he informed them of his abhorrence of the present state of affairs, and of his proposal to set up a militia under his leadership for the purpose of defending themselves against the outrages of the smugglers. The local folk thanked him for his resolution and unanimously concurred in his proposals, and immediately had articles drawn up (17 April 1747) to which they respectively signed their names, agreeing 'to meet the enemy and fight them, as long as life remained'.

The Goudhurst affair is indicative of the complete mastery that the large smuggling gangs exerted throughout their territory. The puny force of Riding officers that had been created in 1698 were reduced to mere observers and continually went in fear of their lives; from time to time dragoons were drafted to the area by the government following appeals from the Commissioners of Customs to assist in suppressing the trade. For instance, on 28 July 1732 the Commissioners wrote to the Lords of the Treasury appealing for further military aid and giving information of 'divers vessels running large quantities of tea and brandy on the coasts of Suffolk, Essex, Kent and Sussex' and

of great gangs of smugglers well armed to assist them in landing their goods and in open defiance of the officers of the Customs and Excise, convey them into the country and that when the officers have attempted to seize their goods they have been confined until the goods have been carried off, or beat and abused in a barbarous manner and some of them murdered in the discharge of their duty.

In the year that this letter was written, there were stationed in Kent at four places forty dragoons – a very small number, particularly when they showed little relish for their task of hunting fellow Englishmen across strange and dark country. As Lt Henry Shore, R.N., says in his *Smuggling Days and Smuggling Ways*, setting dragoons to capture smugglers was 'like setting elephants to catch eels'.

Thus it was left to an ex-serviceman to form a band of volunteers to protect themselves when the official forces of law and order were incapable of doing the job. At first sight this may seem a fantastic state of affairs for a country nominally at peace. But it was a turbulent period and less than two years previously a government order of 5 December 1745 had called for the raising of a militia in Kent, to oppose Prince Edward Stuart, who was leading a band of rebels southward from Carlisle. In any event, the people of Goudhurst now resolved to stand firm, confident that their private militia would succeed where the government, the Army and the Customs and Excise Service had failed. And so it proved, but not without a fight.

There are several accounts of what happened that spring day in 1747 and no doubt many of them have improved the story in the telling. However, two accounts seem to be reasonably near the truth. The chief account is a petition sent to the Lords of the Treasury by the people of Goudhurst, who are claiming a reward after the incident. I have only seen a copy of this and was unable to trace it in the Public Record Office. The second is in a guide to Tunbridge Wells written by J. Sprange and published in 1780, only thirty-three years after the events described took place and when Sturt was still alive.

After the initiation of the Goudhurst Band of Militia on 17 April 1747, its members made Sturt their 'General' (a nickname which remained with him for the rest of his life) and the members swore to obey him. These events were meant to be kept secret but the network of smuggling informers ensured that it was not long before the Hawkhurst Gang found out. As soon as they got word they waylaid one of the militia and in typical Hawkhurst fashion, by confinement and torture, managed to ascertain the names of the other members of the band and their plan. It was at this stage that the Hawkhurst Gang made a serious mistake. Their incredulity that local folk should dare to question their authority appears to have prevented them from observing a basic concept of war, namely surprise. Instead of holding their informer prisoner and carrying out their evil plans under cover of secrecy, they released him, after making him swear not to take up arms against them, and, as Sprange put it, 'Desired him to acquaint his General, that they would (for his audacious attempt to repulse them) go immediately and get together one hundred or more smugglers, and besiege the town on a certain day which they fixed; then plunder every house, murder every soul therein, and lastly set the whole town on fire.' Their contemptuous naivety is shown by the fact that they not only fixed the day and time for the attack but they kept to it almost to the minute.

William Sturt, as his discharge papers stated, showed 'great perfectness in every art of war' and as soon as the smugglers' intentions were known, he immediately mustered all his men and 'addressed them with a suitable speech, and used every means to create animation in them, against the appointed dreadful day'. Once morale had been stiffened, battle preparations began. He ordered some of his men to cast musket balls (local legend has it that lead from the church roof was used) while others were sent out to collect all the firearms, good and bad together, that there were in the neighbourhood. Two hundredweight of powder was procured and with the balls he himself set to work and made up a sufficient quantity of cartridges. The smugglers had not only fixed the time and day for the attack but also, unbelievably, the direction; they were to come from Hawkhurst and so approach the top end of the village from the east. Again, according to Sprange, Sturt decided on the field of battle and barricades were thrown up and trenches dug in the little time left before the appointed hour.

On the morning of the day of the attack, the militia assembled in their entrenchments, with their general at their head. Sturt went among his men placing each one at his station and ensuring that each of the muskets was in working order and that there was a sufficient quantity of cartridges for each. In the petition the inhabitants state that they took up their stations in a house, possibly the Star and Eagle, and not in entrenchments in the open. However, this anomaly matters little; the important fact is that the Hawkhurst Gang did arrive, 'not one hundred or more smugglers' but about sixteen, galloping along, stripped to their shirts, with a handkerchief bound about their heads and armed with 'blunderbusses, carbines, pistols and hangers [short swords hung from the belt], and all the terrible weapons they could think of'. They had come to assert their authority. Full of rum, geneva or brandy and determined to make Sturt pay for his impudence, they rode into Goudhurst as arrogant as ever, swearing and firing off pistols. They left in complete disarray, several of them wounded, pursued by the militia men, and leaving two of their members dead in the village.

Above left: **1.** The exciseman or gauger. 'Wretches hired by those to whom excise is paid' (Doctor Johnson).

Above right: **2.** Adam Smith (1723–1790) in his sixty-fifth year, 1787. He was the Scottish economist who wrote *The Wealth of Nations* (1776).

Above left: **3.** 'The London Merchants Triumphant' – Sir Robert Walpole's effigy being burnt following the defeat of his Excise Bill, 12 April 1733.

Above right: **4.** Geoffrey Chaucer (*c.* 1340–1400) was appointed controller of customs in the Port of London in 1374.

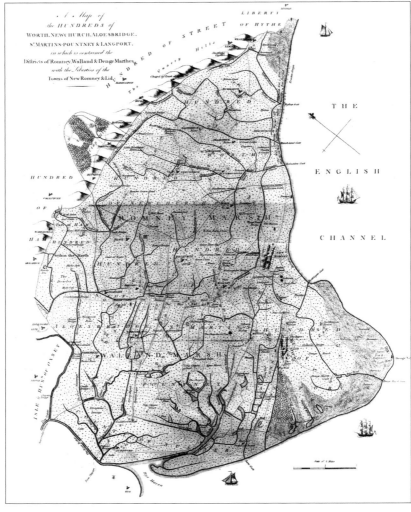

Opposite above: **5.** Scenes of the woollen industry first printed in the *Universal Magazine* in 1749. *Top left* sheep are sheared of their fleece, *bottom right* the wool is combed out, worked *top right* and finally beaten *bottom left* before being spun.

Opposite below: **6.** Map of Romney Marsh *c.* 1750.

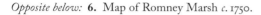

Top: **7.** John Collier, Surveyor General of the Riding Officers in Kent and Sussex.

Middle: **8.** Custom House, London Pool. The original building burnt down in the Great Fire of 1666 and was rebuilt by Sir Christopher Wren in 1671.

Bottom: **9.** The old East India Wharf at London Bridge, painted by Peter Monamy (1689–1749).

Above left: **10.** A Revenue cutter.

Above right: **11.** A Revenue cutter's rowboat retrieving jettisoned contraband; the crew were more interested in seizing goods than apprehending the smugglers. They would get a percentage of the auctioned goods.

Left: **12.** Lydd today. (Photo by Peter Maverley)

13. 'An English Smuggler'. Print published by Rodwell & Martin of London, 1822.

Right: **14.** A Coast Blockade officer wondering if the woman has bags of smuggled tea about her person. 'Why Polly! You an't on the smuggling tack, I hope!' Print by W. Heath, 1830.

Below: **15.** Vauxhall Gardens *c.* 1799 by Thomas Rowlandson. The two ladies in the centre are Georgina, Duchess of Devonshire, and her sister Lady Duncannon. The lady on the right of the picture in white is the actress and author Mary Darby Robinson with the Prince of Wales (later George IV). On the left, seated and eating, is Samuel Johnson with James Boswell on his left and Oliver Goldsmith on his right.

16. A satirical print on the heavy excise duty added to other burdensome taxes, 1773.

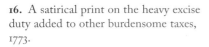

17. 'The Tea Phrensy', a cartoon of 1785 depicting the rush to buy tea when the tax was reduced.

18. A satirical print depicting a gentlemen's smoking club, 1792.

Above left: **19.** Hogarth's famous 'Gin Lane' print depicting the evils of drinking gin to excess, 1751. Over the doorway in the bottom left corner is written: 'Drunk for a penny, Dead drunk for two pence, Clean Straw for Nothing.'

Above right: **20.** Hogarth's 'Beer Street', which extols the virtues of drinking good English ale. Note that the pawnbroker has gone out of business (as contrasted with the previous print) and that the inn sign reads: 'Health to the Barley Mow'.

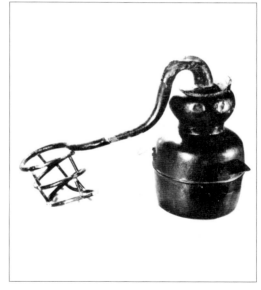

Above left: **21.** Old distilling utensils print, taken from *Smuggling in the Highlands* by Ian Macdonald.

Above right: **22.** A whisky still which, reputedly, belonged to General Gordon.

Top: **23.** Robert Burns (1759–1796).

Middle: **24.** An Excise logbook with Robert Burns's signature.

Bottom: **25.** An illegal whisky still in the Highlands, camouflaged to avoid detection. The artist was Maclan and the picture is of Sandy Macgruar's bothy in Strathglass and is taken from *Smuggling in the Highlands*.

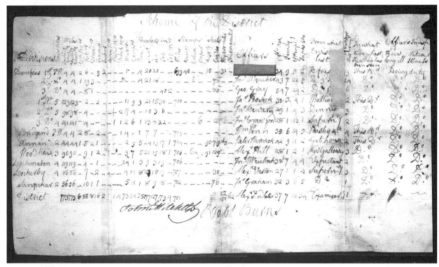

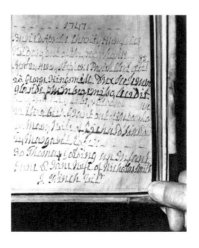

Top: **26.** A staged picture depicting a raid by excise officers on an illegal whisky still in a bothy. Taken from *Smuggling in the Highlands.*

Middle: **27.** Goudhurst today. (Photo by Peter Maverley)

Bottom: **28.** The Latin inscription in the Goudhurst register recording the death of George Kingsmill: *dux scelerum glands plumbi emisso cecidit* – 'leader of the scoundrels fell, killed by the discharge of a lead bullet'. (Photo by Peter Maverley)

29. Hawkhurst today. (Photo by Peter Maverley)

30. 'Smugglers', a print of 1799 engraved by J. P. Smith showing a somewhat romanticised scene of free traders leisurely going about the business of running ashore ankers of contraband spirits.

31. Print entitled 'Halt – Smugglers'. Taken from a painting by H. P. Parker in 1856, it is a romanticised depiction of Kipling's 'gentlemen' free traders.

32. Poole Custom House (right) today. (Photo by Peter Maverley)

33. A contemporary print showing the smugglers breaking open the Poole Custom House in 1747.

The IDLE 'PRENTICE Executed at Tyburn.

34. William Hogarth's 'The Idle 'Prentice Executed at Tyburn', 1747. Public hangings were a great spectacle for all classes, with the better off in the seated galleries.

Above left: **35.** After hanging, some bodies were put in iron cages and hung from a gibbet until the flesh rotted away or was eaten by crows and the bones fell through the irons to be taken by dogs and foxes.

Above right: **36.** The former Red Lion Inn at Rake, which is today a private house. (Photo by Peter Maverley)

William Galley, brought cross a Horse to a Sand Pit where a deep Hole is Dug to Bury him in.

The unfortunate William Galley put by the Smugglers into the Ground & as is generally believed before he was quite DEAD.

Chater, Chained in ye. Turff House at Old Mills is. Cobby, kicking him. & Tapner, cutting him cross ye Eyes & Nose, while he is saving the Lords Prayer. Several of ye other Smugglers standing by.

Above left: **39.** Contemporary print of Daniel Chater being hanged at the well in Lady Holt Park.

Above right: **40.** The former Dog and Partridge Inn at Slindon, which today is a private house. (Photo by Peter Maverley)

Right: **41.** Contemporary print of the murder of Richard Hawkins at the Dog and Partridge Inn, 1748.

Botom: **42.** Custom House notice detailing seized contraband to be auctioned, 1782.

John Mills alias *Smoaker.* & *Rich.ᵈ Rowland* alias *Robb. Whipping Rich.ᵈ Hawkins. to Death. at ỹ Dog & Partridge on Slendon Common; & Jeremiah Curtis. & Thoʳ. Winter* alias *Coachman: Standing by Aiding & abetting ỹ Murder of the said Rich.ᵈ Hawkins.*

Opposite bottom left: **37.** Contemporary print of William Galley being buried, probably while he was still alive.

Opposite bottom right: **38.** Contemporary print of Daniel Chater, the old shoemaker, being kicked and cut across the face by the smugglers.

NOTICE is hereby given, THAT at the CUSTOM HOUSE on Thursday, the 19th Day of September next, at Ten of the Clock in the Forenoon there will be put up to Sale, for Home Consumption, in sundry Lots:

110 Gallons of Geneva,
61 Gallons of Brandy,
2 Small Cutters and Furniture,
1691 Pounds of Wool, seized 15th of July, 1781.
240 Pounds ditto, seized 28th Feb. 1782.
3582 Pounds ditto, seized 10th March.
1258 Pounds ditto, seized 21st May.
359 Pounds ditto, seized 29th May.
715 Pounds ditto, seized 11th of June.

The Goods to be viewed the Day before, and Morning of the Sale.

N. B. 25 per Cent. will be required as a Deposite.

RYE, Aug. 31, 1782.

Top: **43.** A Revenue cutter chasing a smuggling vessel.

Middle: **44.** An eight-oared rowing galley running contraband ashore.

Bottom left: **45.** The gravestone of Robert Trotman, a smuggler, in the churchyard of Kinson, Dorset. The text reads: 'To the Memory of Robert Trotman, late of Rowd, in the County of Wilts who was barbarously Murdered on the shore near Poole the 24th March 1765'. The epitaph reads:

A little tea one leaf I did not steal,
For guiltless bloodshed I to God appeal;
Put tea in one scale Human blood in t'other,
And think what 'tis to slay a harmless brother

This epitaph is to free trade; although the tea was smuggled, it had been bought on the open market on the Continent and paid for accordingly.

Bottom right: **46.** Gravestone of William Green, a Revenue officer, killed on duty by smugglers in 1784.

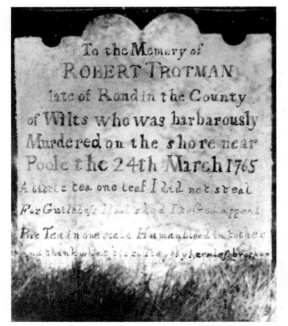

PARDON.

WHEREAS it has been humbly represented to the KING, that divers large bodies of Armed Smugglers have lately been feloniously assembled on different parts of the Coasts of Kent and Sussex, for the purpose of effecting the Landing of Uncustomed and Prohibited Goods;—And Whereas, upon such occasions, violent attacks have been made upon the Officers and Men in His Majesty's Coast Guard Service, and upon the Officers of Customs, in which several Persons have been Killed and severely Wounded;—And Whereas it is necessary to put an end to such Outrages and to bring the Offenders to Justice;—HIS MAJESTY, for the better discovering the Persons who have been guilty of these Felonies and Murders, is hereby pleased to promise His Most Gracious

PARDON

to any one or more of the Persons so assembled, (except those who actually committed violence upon the said Officers and Men) who shall discover his Accomplices, so that they may be apprehended and brought to Justice. **MELBOURNE.**

And the Commissioners of His Majesty's Customs are hereby pleased to offer the following

REWARDS

for the Detection and Apprehension of Persons who have been concerned in such Offences, that is to say,

£1000

to any Person or Persons who shall discover or cause to be discovered any Person or Persons by whose agreement or undertaking such companies were so illegally assembled, or the actual Perpetrator or Perpetrators of any such Murders.

£500

to any Person or Persons who shall discover or cause to be discovered any Person or Persons who was or were Armed with Fire Arms or other Offensive Weapons, and assembled to the number of Three or more for the purpose of running such Uncustomed and Prohibited Goods, and

£200

to any Person or Persons who shall discover or cause to be discovered any one or more of such Offenders who were concerned in the running of such Goods. The above Rewards to be paid by the Collector and Comptroller of Customs at the Port of Rye upon the conviction of any such Offenders.

Custom House, London,
2d March 1832.

THOS. WHITMORE, Sec.

[By Authority—J. Hartnell, Fleet Street, London.]

Above left: **47.** Notice of pardon and reward for informers, 1832.

Above right: **48.** A print, *c.* 1820, of smugglers about to be raided by Revenue officers and rushing to hide their contraband.

49. The Mermaid Inn at Rye has many smuggling connections. (Photo by Peter Maverley)

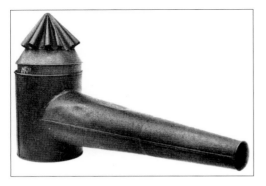

Above left: **50.** A smuggler's signalling lamp.

Above right: **51.** Notification of the murder in 1826 of Quarter Master Richard Morgan of the Coast Blockade in Dover while trying to prevent a gang landing smuggled goods. It is also an offer of a reward for the capture or naming of any of the smugglers involved.

Below: **52.** George Ransley's house, Bourne Tap, near Aldington, which is a private house today. (Photo by Peter Maverley)

CUSTOMS HOUSE, LONDON.

1ST AUGUST, 1826.

WHEREAS it has been represented to the Commissioners of his Majesty's Customs, that about one o'clock in the morning of the 30th ultimo, RICHARD MORGAN, a first-rate Quarter Master, and MICHAEL PICKETT, a Seaman, both belonging to the Service of the Coast Blockade for the Prevention of Smuggling, and stationed at the Casemates at Dover under the orders of Lieutenant THOMAS S. HALL, were out on duty on the beach, and observed a boat in the surf, upon which the said RICHARD MORGAN fired his pistol as an alarm, when several smugglers, armed with long Duck Guns, stepped forward from the body of smugglers collected near the bathing machine, within the Town of Dover, and fired at, and instantly killed the said RICHARD MORGAN; and with their fire-arms beat and wounded the Seaman RICHARD PICKETT; and that afterwards thirty-three tubs of Foreign Run Spirits were found and seized near the spot, and deposited in the Customs-House at Dover.

The said Commissioners are hereby pleased to offer a Reward of

FIVE HUNDRED POUNDS

to any Person or Persons who shall discover, or cause to be discovered any one or more of the said Offenders, so that he or they may be apprehended and dealt with according to Law, to be paid by the Collector of his Majery's Customs at the Port of Dover, upon conviction.

By Order of the Commissioners,

T. WHITMORE, Secretary.

Sturt had called upon the assistance of God on the morning of the battle and this, coupled with his own obvious military skill, appears to have ensured that the Goudhurst Band of Militia were triumphant. However, the villagers must have had a particularly anxious moment when the gang's leader, George Kingsmill, had shouted to them that he had been at the killing of fifty of His Majesty's officers and soldiers and swore that he would be damned if he did not broil four of the peoples' hearts in the flames of the town and eat them for his supper. This dreadful imprecation must have made Kingsmill a marked man, for during the ensuing 'long dispute' (Sturt had ordered his men to receive the first fire) he was shot dead along with another, Bernard or Barnet Woollet of Cranbrook. The parish register at Goudhurst, of which George Kingsmill and his brother Thomas were, ironically enough, natives, records his death. After the date is written in Latin *Dux scelerum glands plumbi emisso cecidit*, which translated reads: 'leader of the scoundrels fell, killed by the discharge of a lead bullet'.

In the Cranbrook register the death of Woollet is recorded and after his name is written 'a smuggler, shot in Goudhurst churchyard'. In the case of Kingsmill there was considerable local debate as to whether he should be accorded a Christian burial in consecrated ground. Probably, being a murderer, he was buried in an unmarked grave in the corner of the churchyard.

The inhabitants of Goudhurst, by standing up to the smugglers and by force of arms, had secured for themselves a certain freedom from the unwelcome visitations of the Hawkhurst Gang. However, as their petition testifies, they still considered it prudent to mount guard on their town as the smugglers had sworn revenge:

> Since they have sworn revenge on us Your Lordships' Most Humble Servants and Petitioners threatening us in the most inhuman death they could think of and the said Town with fire and sword, which to defend we have set a strict watch and have pursued them several times to the great loss and hindrance of our several employments and who are chiefly tradesman and have nothing to depend on but our industry for our livelihood, and we do at all times on occasions kindly and cheerfully join His Majesty's Officers both of Custom and Excise in order to prevent their illegal and pernicious practice of running and landing of goods liable to pay duties to His Majesty's Customs and Excise which through the blessing of God and our small endeavours that had so good effect that it hath drove them from their wicked practices.

The petition goes on to claim for the inhabitants a reward of £100 for George Kingsmill, who was concerned with a number of others in retaking some tea from a party of Customs officers and dragoons at Hurst Green, Sussex, on 26 December 1744. During this affray a Customs officer, Thomas Carswell, was shot dead and the Commissioners of Custom offered a reward for the capture of anyone involved. The Goudhurst Militia later on assisted in apprehending two other persons suspected of this murder and they were convicted and hanged following the Lewes Assizes in July 1749. They also claimed a £50 reward for both Woollet and Kingsmill, who were outlawed by Acts of Parliament on 24 June 1736. There is, as already stated, no evidence that this petition was in fact presented, probably because the two men were shot and not brought to trial.

However, the bravery of the Goudhurst folk was publicised in the *Gentleman's Magazine*, which devoted six short lines to the skirmish and mentioned the fatal shooting of two of 'these desperadoes, who rob and plunder and live upon the spoils'. Two months later, on Saturday 6 June, an 'Order Against Smugglers' was issued by the government as a direct result of the Goudhurst affair. 'All His Majesty's subjects civil and military, magistrates, officers and private persons may meet force with force in bringing armed and assembled persons to law for which it is their duty.' Other voluntary associations were now formed. One such association was referred to in a letter written by John Collier, who was Surveyor General of the Riding officers in Kent from 1733 to 1756. He tells the Custom's Solicitor, Mr Simon, that on 21 October 1747 the 'Cranbrook Associators' had apprehended William Gray of Hawkhurst, one of the 'gang of smugglers who have so many years triumphed over the officers of the Revenue and struck terror into the country for so many years'.

It appears, however, that Gray was released by the local Justice of the Peace for lack of evidence of any offence 'and has become more insolent than ever'. The inference again is obvious. Gray was taken once more early the next year, 1748, and committed to Newgate Gaol but managed to escape. One of his friends and also a well-known member of the Hawkhurst Gang was a certain Thomas Potter, who was later hanged on Penenden Heath, Maidstone, in 1749 for stealing a horse. Potter, in the company of three others, effected Gray's escape by ringing the bell at the press-yard door. The turnkey came to let them in, and on his opening the door Potter immediately knocked him down with a horse pistol. Gray and a fellow smuggler named Thomas Kemp made good their escape; the former had so arranged his irons as to let them fall when he pleased, while Kemp had no leg-irons on. Three other prisoners got away at the same time – but, having their irons on, were soon recaptured. Gray's freedom was short-lived; he had been recaptured by June and was brought to trial on 22 June 1748. He was sentenced to seven years' transportation. At the time he was reputed to be worth £10,000, a considerable sum in those days, and to own a large house that he had had built at Seacox Heath near Hawkhurst, Kent.

The grateful folk of Goudhurst showed their esteem for Sturt by making him master of the local workhouse and, as Sprange recounts, 'Which place he holds at this time (1780) and where no workhouse in the kingdom is better regulated; every department of it being kept in such regular and nice order, with a display of industry throughout; such as constitutes the manager fit for an undertaking of that kind.' Sturt's military discipline was still evident, as indeed was his love of beer, for a writer of the *Gentleman's Magazine* in 1785 informs the reader that 'he himself [Sturt] is still alive and has a soldier-like regard to the strong beer of Old England, of which, for the credit of the place, I hope he is not in want'. Despite Sturt's stout defence of Goudhurst and the severe and bloody lesson he had dealt the Hawkhurst Gang, subsequent events show that their insolence and barbarity continued unabated. In fact, many more violent deeds were perpetrated and the gang's reign of terror was not brought to an end until three of the most vile and sadistic murders ever committed had greatly shocked the general public. The perpetrators of these deeds were no longer free traders in the romantic sense; they had deteriorated into common murderers who well deserved the epithet 'death's ministers'.

9

The Poole
Custom House Robbery

'The most unheard of act of villainy and impudence ever known'
'This gallant expedition'

In October 1747 an incident took place which was described eighteen months later by Messrs Bankes and Smythe, two of His Majesty's prosecuting counsel at the Old Bailey, as 'the most unheard of act of villainy and impudence ever known'. In the dock were five men standing trial for their lives, accused on 7 October 1747 of 'being concerned, with others, to the number of thirty persons, in breaking the King's Custom House at Poole, and stealing out thence thirty hundred weight of tea, value £500 and upwards'. It was this trial in April 1749 that finally completed the work that had been started two years earlier by William Sturt of Goudhurst and his militia men, for in the dock were the following members of the Hawkhurst Gang: Thomas Lillewhite, Richard Glover, Richard Perrin alias Pain alias Carpenter, and the most notorious pair of all, Thomas Kingsmill alias Staymaker and William Fairall alias Shepherd. The authorities had caught up with an infamous gang that had considered itself above the law and had for years intimidated, abused, cut, maimed, tortured and even murdered.

The prisoners had been brought the short distance from Newgate Gaol to the Old Bailey on the morning of Friday 7 April 1749 and it is a measure of their notoriety that the guard was unusually heavy and included footsoldiers. The usual formalities were observed, with the accused being asked if they objected to any of the members of the jury. They were reminded that they could object without reason to as many as twenty jurors but if they objected to any more than that number then they had to explain why. No objections were made and the prisoners, who were all tried together, were asked how they pleaded to the indictment. 'Not guilty' was the unanimous reply. Lillewhite, Glover and Perrin had engaged legal counsel to prepare their defence but Fairall and Kingsmill, tough and arrogant as ever, offered no defence and occupied their time in 'behaving very insolently: or more properly ignorantly, laughing all the time at the witnesses while they were giving their evidence'. Fairall went even further and, as a contemporary account records,

'At his trial seemed to show the utmost daringness and unconcern; even showing tokens of threats to a witness, as he was giving his evidence to court, and standing all the while in the bar with a smile or rather a sneer upon his countenance.'

The Crown Prosecution's case rested primarily on the evidence of two members of another smuggling gang who had been involved, not only in this Poole affair, but also in the vile murders of William Galley and Daniel Chater that had taken place in February 1748. Presumably the informers had turned King's evidence to escape the death penalty. No doubt their action was made easier by the £200 reward offered by the Commissioners of Custom after the incident at Poole for each offender brought to justice. Whatever their actual reasons, it was largely because of the evidence of John Race and William Steele together with that of William Fogden, who was also involved in the Poole incident, that the prosecution successfully proved the indictment. The jury at the Old Bailey that Friday morning listened to a bold and daring tale of sea chases; the seizure of a quantity of rum, brandy and tea; heated arguments between desperate men ending with an audacious resolution; forced marches through the night and the brazen breaking open of a locked public building in the early hours of an autumn morning. The incredible facts presented to the court were the unembellished, sworn testimonies of people who were actually present at the crime. The transcript of the trial is still extant.

Before discussing the evidence presented to the court, it is as well to set the scene. Richard Perrin, a native of Chichester, was an important member of the South Coast smuggling fraternity, for it was he who in September 1747, with money subscribed by several free traders from the Hawkhurst and the Chichester areas, sailed to Guernsey to purchase a quantity of both 'wet' and 'dry' goods. He bought thirty-nine casks of rum and brandy in 4- or 8-gallon casks but his main purchase was a quantity of tea. The trial records are not exact as to the specific quantity; the indictment mentions 30 hundredweights, 37 hundredweights, 2 tons, and 41 hundredweights. However, what is certain is that the tea accounted for a considerable financial outlay, in the region of £500. Perrin, as a contemporary account describes him, 'was esteemed a very honest man, and therefore was often entrusted by others to go over the water to buy goods, and for himself'. This trading was now his full-time business, whereas formerly he had been a carpenter 'and had pretty good business till the use of his right hand being in a great measure taken away on being subject to the rheumatism'.

In the Channel Islands, he picked his way from merchant to merchant in the prosperous and bustling St Peter Port bartering for the ankers of brandy and rum, and for the tea already done up in oilskin bags of about 27 pounds, a safe and convenient way to run them ashore on the English coast. Perrin also bought a small bag of coffee. His dealings completed and paid for, he arranged for his goods to be put on board a cutter named the *Three Brothers* and, after some refreshment and when the tide was right, he went aboard himself and the ship set sail, heading up the Channel toward the pre-arranged landing place on the Sussex coast. No doubt it was a journey everyone on board had made several times before, and the running and distribution of the goods were expected to be the usual formality. But on this occasion the *Three Brothers* met its match in the shape of a privateer Revenue cutter, aptly named *Swift*, captained by William Johnson, who was called as the prosecution's first witness.

On oath in the witness box Captain Johnson told the court precisely what had happened that September day:

> I have a deputation from the Customs to seize prohibited goods. On the 22 September 1747 I was stationed out of Stainham Bay, just by Poole. I was under the north shore. I examined a cutter I suspected to be a smuggler; after quitting her I had sight of the *Three Brothers*. I discovered her to the eastward; after discovering her she put before the wind at N.N.W. I gave chase with all the sail I could make. I chased her from before five in the afternoon till about eleven at night. After firing several shots at her, brought her to, and took charge of her.

The Customs Service at this time was desperately short of Revenue cutters, particularly in a year when England was at war with both Spain and France; the government therefore had allowed enterprising ship owners to take out 'deputations' from the Commissioners of Custom and Excise licensing them to pursue smugglers and seize them in the King's name. 'Letters of marque' were also given to trading vessels to carry out the same function on the enemy's shipping. For the privateer with the necessary deputation the incentive was the permission to keep and sell a proportion of all seizures of run goods. The system was open to abuses and it was at times difficult to ascertain which vessel was involved in which operation – in other words whether a vessel was preventing smuggling or was engaged in the clandestine traffic itself.

With such a determined chase it was quite clear that the *Swift* was on official anti-smuggling duty. The captain makes no mention of the *Three Brothers* returning his fire, which might mean that the vessel was unarmed or, more probably, that the crew realised the hopelessness of trying to shake off the pursuer, despite the fact that it was now dark. The smugglers hove to and gave up without a fight. The six members of the crew and the rheumatic Perrin must have got into a smaller boat, which was lowered over the side and they disappeared into the dark cursing and damning their ill-luck at losing such a valuable cargo. Johnson and his crew were more interested in the cargo than in searching for a small boat in the dark Channel. No doubt vastly pleased with an excellent evening's work, Johnson ordered the *Swift* and the *Three Brothers* to be brought about and to sail for Poole. There they tied up at the quay, and the rum, brandy and tea and the small bag of coffee were taken out of the hold and delivered into the charge of William Milner, the Collector of the Customs. He saw to the stowing of the goods in the Custom House just across the quay; the tea was taken upstairs to the upper store to await the normal process of legal condemnation as smuggled goods, before being sold by public auction. Captain Johnson would receive a percentage of the money raised at the auction and would then divide the prize money among his crew.

Within a few days Perrin was back among his smuggling friends in Kent. The tale he recounted cannot have been very well received by the likes of Kingsmill and Fairall, who were both involved financially in the venture. This coming of the setback only five months after the Goudhurst debacle must have inflamed their passions and one can imagine that Perrin was subjected to a very torrid cross-examination as to why the crew had not forcibly resisted the privateer.

The post-mortem must have produced some very heated accusation and recrimination, for not only had they lost their goods but they had also received a further blow to their pride. The fact that their goods were under lock and key in an official government storehouse many miles away did not deter them. They resolved to get them back and despatched Perrin to consult with the Chichester smugglers to see how best this could be done.

The Chichester Gang had already heard about the loss and according to the evidence of William Steele 'a great many of us' met at the Centre Tree in the middle of Charlton Forest, owned by the Duke of Richmond, on or about 3 October. Perrin was present at this meeting when the band resolved to break open the Custom House by force and recover their goods. Also present at this meeting was a man called Edmund Richards, described by a law-abiding contemporary as 'that notorious wicked fellow' and as a man of 'cruel and enormous crimes'. It was he who insisted that they keep their word by making all present put their names to a piece of paper. The smugglers dispersed, agreeing to meet again at a hamlet called Rowland's Castle three miles north of Havant on the Sunday. This time they would be armed.

About twenty-three of the Chichester folk arrived at the appointed meeting place. The party, all mounted and armed with blunderbusses, carbines and pistols, moved off westward into the Forest of Bere sometime before sunset on the Monday. At 'a lone place' in the forest they made their first stop and awaited the arrival of the 'East country people'. Seven of the Hawkhurst Gang arrived, including Fairall, Kingsmill, and John and Richard Miller; their arms were carried on a little horse 'that would follow a grey horse one of them rode on'. The whole party had now assembled and they continued their journey westward, riding through the night. They skirted the head of Southampton Water and did not stop again until the early hours of Tuesday morning by which time they were at Lyndhurst in the New Forest. All day Tuesday they rested and then 'in the glimpse of the evening' they began the final part of their journey to Poole. As Steele testified, before leaving Lyndhurst 'we all look'd to our firearms, to see if they were primed', and just before reaching Poole the Hawkhurst men took their arms from the little horse and slung their long rifles over their shoulders. By eleven o'clock that evening they were on the outskirts of Poole. Thus a company of thirty men visibly armed had ridden nearly fifty miles through Hampshire without any attempt by the authorities to stop them or enquire of their business.

Apart from these thirty men there were, as the anonymous author of a contemporary account relates, other men deployed about the town of Poole 'placed as scouts upon different roads, to watch the motions of the officers and the soldiers, and to be ready to assist or alarm the main body, in case any opposition should be made'. It seems unlikely that the officers and soldiers of the neighbourhood did not know of the plans; they probably assumed that even the infamous Hawkhurst Gang would not have the audacity to break open the King's warehouse. Or maybe they considered that 'watching the wall' was the better part of valour. Whatever the case, Poole that night was quiet and everything was going according to plan until Thomas Willis and Thomas Stringer, two of the smugglers, who had been sent ahead to see if all was clear, met the company and relayed bad news.

Willis reported that it would be impossible to break open the Custom House as a large sloop was tied up at the quay and 'she'll plant her guns to the Custom House door, and tear us to pieces'. This indeed was serious, and the immediate reaction of most of the company was to consider turning around and riding away. But not so the Hawkhurst men, who had travelled well over a hundred miles to reclaim their goods and would not be put off so easily. All seven of the Kent men unanimously declared that, even if the others pulled out, they would go ahead themselves and break into the Custom House on their own. The Hawkhurst men refused to countenance the idea that they were going into a well-laid trap and were about to ride forward when a horse was heard coming through the streets of the town towards them. The conversation stopped, fingers instinctively went to cock their firing pieces and their eyes strove to make out in the blackness who the rider was. Their alarm was short-lived, for it was Stringer returning to report that the tide had gone down and that the sloop's guns could no longer be brought to bear on the Custom House. It was now safe to go ahead with the plan. The fact that the sloop might land a party of men does not seem to have been considered a threat.

Their fears allayed by Stringer's report, the Chichester men went forward with the Hawkhurst Gang, keeping to the eastern outskirts of Poole by riding down a narrow back lane that led to the water's edge. Here was a patch of open common land along one side of which was a rail, where they hitched their horses after dismounting. Thomas Lillewhite (an unfortunate name for a smuggler), who was a lad of only seventeen, and the rheumatic Perrin, who was little use in wielding axes and crowbars and humping heavy bags of tea, were left in charge of the steeds, while the main party walked the few hundred yards to the Custom House. Before reaching their objective they stumbled upon a young lad who was going about his legitimate job of fishing; they overpowered the surprised youth, tied him up and took him prisoner. He had no option but to watch them as they prised the stout staples away from the door posts, to which the door was padlocked, and broke open the inner doors with axes.

While the Custom House was being broken open, William Steele and another man were keeping watch on the quay. But there was no movement in the sloop. Inside the Custom House two nightwatchmen, cowering and terrified as the great oaken door was broken down, were taken prisoner. All three hostages must have thanked the Lord that their only injuries from that eventful night were sore wrists and ankles.

The smugglers went to work in a single-minded way; they had broken into the King's warehouse and the sooner they had completed their business and got away the better. Ignoring the brandy and rum, they forced their way upstairs to where the tea was stored and began carrying it out to a 'gravelly place' ready to be slung onto the horses. The little lane was too cramped for loading so the horses were brought to where the tea had been dumped. The tea was packed into 'horse-sacks', two of which were tied together and slung over the horse's back. The little horse that had carried the Hawkhurst armament had his share too 'but not so much as the other horses had on them'. Then the gang left the town and headed towards Fordingbridge, where they stopped for breakfast and to water and feed the horses. At Brook the gang acquired two pairs of steelyards which they used to divide the tea up more exactly. They now had equal shares which came to five quartern bags each.

William Milner takes up the story: 'On the 7 October, between two and three in the morning, I had advice brought me, by one of the officers that the Custom house had been broken open.' He immediately went down to the quay and could scarce believe what he saw. The outer door had been smashed in and, inside, his lamp picked out three trussed hostages, more broken doors and tea scattered over the floor. The smugglers had opened each sack to see if the tea was in good condition and must have spilt some in their haste to carry it out. There is no evidence to suggest that there was any attempt to follow the smugglers.

As already mentioned, three of the men on trial had engaged counsel to defend them. Kingsmill and Fairall, however, said (when asked to make their defence) they had nothing to say, only that they knew nothing of the matter. John Perrin had persuaded two brothers to testify to the court as to his character. First to be called was John Gray, who stated, 'I have known Perrin almost twenty years; he is a carpenter, and always bore a very good character among his neighbours. I never heard he neglected his business.' William Gray was more categorical: 'I have known him these fifteen or sixteen years, he always bore a very good character. I never heard in my life of his neglecting his business and going smuggling.' Perrin seems to have had a good friend here but the prosecution were not impressed by this statement, because this witness was asked, no doubt with the appropriate legal intonation implying disbelief, 'Did you never hear he was a smuggler?' Gray was on the defensive; all he could say was, 'No, never but by hearsay, as folks talk.'

Glover was next in the witness box and it appears that he was one of the more faint-hearted members of the gang who were involved in the incident. He pleaded his case under oath: 'I was forced into it by my brother-in-law [Edmund Richards], who threatened to shoot me, if I would not go along with them.' This evidence appears not to be the desperate pleading of a man under sentence of death, for William Tapling was called to corroborate this statement: 'I know his brother-in-law Richards; and that Glover was about two months with him. Richards is a notorious wicked swearing man, and reputed a great smuggler; and I can't help thinking he was the occasion of Glover's acting in this.' Six other witnesses were called to testify to his good character, including a parson, a lawyer and the Superintendent of Deptford Naval Dockyard. Henry Hounsel told the court how Glover had lived with his father until the latter's death in 1744. In June 1747 he had gone to 'that wicked brother-in-law's house' for two months, and after that to be a servant for the Revd Blackden at Slindon and from there he became an apprentice to a shipwright in Deptford. While working for the shipwright he was arrested by the authorities. Glover certainly does not seem to be in the same rough class as Richards, Fairall and Kingmill, for all the witnesses referred to his good behaviour, sobriety and aversion to swearing. One witness, Woodruff Drinkwater, thought he could never be a smuggler because 'his temper is not formed for it at all'.

Thomas Lillewhite next gave his account as to how he became involved in the crime. 'I was down in that country, and a person desired me to take a ride with him. I agreed upon it not knowing where they were going. I had no firearms nor was anyway concerned.' If this evidence seems a little implausible it must be remembered that Lillewhite was only seventeen at the time and probably anxious to join this swaggering, daring band in their journey through the night. His naivety was probably matched by his excitement at being in the company of the dreaded Hawkhurst Gang.

Lillewhite lived on Parham estate, which was owned by Sir Cecil Bishop, who in fact travelled to London to testify on Lillewhite's behalf. In the February before the trial took place, Sir Cecil had been in written communication with the Duke of Richmond informing him of why he was going to testify. The letter affords an interesting insight into the differing views held by the gentry on smuggling. Sir Cecil argues that Lillewhite only attended the horses and did not take any part in the breaking open the Custom House or removing the tea. He argues, 'He at the time of this gallant expedition, for as such it was esteemed by most of this neighbourhood, was but seventeen years old.' The Duke's reply was firm and very much to the point. He said that the crime had such an effect upon his mind that he was shocked at an application for a smuggler. He went on, 'I have often heard you say, and with great truth that the common people of this country have no notion that smuggling is a crime, what then can a Government do to show them their error but punish the guilty.' He further pointed out that holding the horses was as great an act of crime as committing the actual offence. He concluded with a stern reprimand: 'This shows the necessity of examples, without which Sir Cecil, neither you nor I, nor any good subject can live in tolerable security in this country.'

After the Baronet's testimony, Judge Sir Thomas Abney summed up the whole case 'in a very impartial manner'. He reminded the jury that if they thought that the case against Lillewhite 'was not quite full' in view of the fact that he was unarmed and that he appeared to have been pressed into joining the smuggling band, then they may acquit him. The jury retired and they were ominously quick in coming to a decision. Within a quarter of an hour they were back in court. They had returned the following verdicts: Thomas Kingsmill – guilty; William Fairall

– guilty; Richard Perrin – guilty; Richard Glover – guilty, but recommended to mercy by the jury. Thomas Lillewhite was found not guilty and, being acquitted, was immediately discharged. Fairall's impudence and ready wit were not defeated even now. At the solemn moment when the death sentence had been pronounced and the Recorder Richard Adams had said 'and the Lord have mercy on your souls', Fairall quipped in a bold voice heard by all the court, 'If the Lord has not more mercy on our souls than the jury had on our bodies, I do not know what will become of them.'

The four condemned prisoners were returned to Newgate Gaol, the infamous, over-crowded and filthy prison just near the Old Bailey. However, it was possible by bribery to secure reasonably tolerable conditions like the removal of leg-irons and permission for friends to bring in food, tobacco and drink. Glover and Perrin were composed after the verdict and resigned themselves to their lot; they constantly prayed and sang psalms, continuing, as the contemporary record reports, most of the night. Fairall and Kingsmill, however, continued to show off their recklessness to the delight and amusement of their fellow prisoners and friends among the general public. Their philosophy was expressed by the irrepressible Fairall: 'Let's have a pipe and some tobacco, and a bottle of wine, for as I'm not to live long I am determined to live well the short time I have to be in this world.'

The four prisoners were fortunate in one sense in that they escaped the putrid fevers which were common in the prisons and which took a large death toll. These fevers, not identified at the time, in fact included typhus and smallpox. Dr Johnson claimed, 'All the complicated horrors of a prison put an end every year to the life of one in four of those that are shut up from the common comforts of human life.' The worst outbreak of jail fever ever recorded happened in May the following year, at the aptly named 'Black Sessions'. A hundred Newgate prisoners had come up for trial at the Old Bailey. As a result of the infections they spread in the court, four of the six judges died, as well as forty jury men and minor officials. People were terrified. After that, Newgate prisoners had to be purified by being washed from head to foot in vinegar before being exposed to the public.

As said, the smugglers were lucky to escape both prison fever and the indignity of purification by vinegar. The Recorder on Thursday 20 April 1749, two weeks after the trial began, sent a report of the four found guilty of breaking open the Poole Custom House to His Majesty King George II. The reply came back the same day. Glover was pardoned 'several favourable circumstances appearing in his favour'; Kingsmill, Fairall and Perrin were to be hanged at Tyburn on 26 April.

The death warrant appeared to strike home for Kingsmill and Fairall, as the contemporary account states:

> They began to consider their unhappy circumstances more than they had done before, and always attending divine service at chapel and prayed very devoutly but retained (despite the fact that any hope of a reprieve or of transmutation of sentence was now gone) their former behaviour of boldness and intrepidity showing no fear

and frequently saying that they did not think they had been guilty of any crime in smuggling or breaking open the Custom House as the property of the goods they went for was not Captain Johnson's or anybody else's but of the persons who sent their money over to Guernsey for them.

It was decreed that both Kingsmill and Fairall be hanged in chains. Perrin, on hearing this, lamented their fate but the defiant Fairall remarked with poetic irony, 'We shall be hanging in the sweet air when you are rotting in your grave.'

After his brother George's violent death at Goudhurst in April 1747, Thomas Kingsmill appears to have assumed the leadership of the Hawkhurst Gang. Contemporary sources state that he was a native of Goudhurst and had been a husbandman, 'But having joined the smugglers, was distinguished and daring enough to become captain of the gang, an honour of which he was so proud that he sought every opportunity of exhibiting specimens of his courage, and putting himself foremost in every service of danger.' But now he was languishing in Newgate Gaol with the shadow of Tyburn Tree hanging over him.

The Ordinary of the prison gave the following account of him:

Aged 28, born at Goudhurst, a young fellow of enterprising spirit, and for some years past employed by the chiefs of the smugglers, the moneyed men or merchants, as they are usually amongst themselves called, in any dangerous exploits. As his character in general among his countrymen was that of a bold, resolute man, undaunted, and fit for the wicked purposes of smuggling and never intimidated, in case of any suspicion of betraying their secrets, ready to oppose King's officers in their duty, and being concerned in rescues of any sort or kind, so he wanted not business, but was made a companion for the greatest of them all and was always at their service when wanted and called upon.

Bold and resolute he might have been but now, with the prospect of jerking and kicking on the end of a rope, he appears to have had at least an inkling that his past 'dangerous exploits' were not only 'exhibiting specimens of his courage' but they were also against the law. The contemporary record reports, 'He acknowledged he was present at the breaking open of the Custom House, and that he had a share of the tea; and said what was sworn at the trial and all truth; but that they must be bad men to turn evidence to take away other people's lives.' Steel, Race and Fogden had incurred the wrath of the leader of the Hawkhurst Gang but these three were to escape his terrible vengeance, for the hard core of the gang, Kingsmill, Fairall and Perrin, choked away their short lives to the jeers and cheers of a crowd that had gathered that spring morning in 1749. With the last twitch of their bodies, the fear instilled by the brutality and intimidation of the Hawkhurst Gang had finally come to an end.

On the night before their execution the three men were parted from their friends for the last time. When the time came for leave-taking the reluctant

Fairall remarked, 'Why in such a hurry, cannot you let me stay a little longer and drink with my friends? I shall not be able to drink with them tomorrow night.' At midnight the bellman from the Church of the Holy Sepulchre without Newgate came and rang 'twelve solemn towles with double strokes' outside the condemned cell and delivered 'with an audible voice':

> All you that in the condemned hole do lie,
> Prepare you, for tomorrow you shall die.
> Watch all, and pray: the hour is drawing near
> That you before the Mighty must appear.
> Examine well yourselves, in time repent
> That you may not to eternal flames be sent,
> And when St Sepulchre's Bell in the morning tolls
> The Lord above have mercy on your souls.
> Past twelve o'clock.

At nine o'clock the next morning, Fairall and Kingsmill were put in an open cart, and Perrin in a mourning coach, and were taken under a strong guard of soldiers, both horse and foot, to Tyburn. It was traditional for nosegays to be given to the condemned men as they passed St Sepulchre's churchyard and it can be imagined that Fairall and Kingsmill insisted on receiving theirs. At the George and Blue Boar in High Holborn, the boisterous procession stopped again for the doomed men to have their last drink and make the traditional quip, 'I'll pay for it on the return journey.' After about half an hour they reached the place of execution near present-day Marble Arch, where a three-sided triangular frame was capable of 'turning off' twenty-four people at a time. The executioner fitted the nooses round their necks, and the clamour of the crowd rose to a baying crescendo of excitement as they prepared to witness the last moments of a human being. Henry Fielding describes one such scene:

> The day appointed by law for the thief's shame is the day of glory in his own opinion and that of his friends. His procession to Tyburn and his last moments there are all triumphant, attended with the compassion of the meek and tender-hearted, and with the applause, admiration and envy of all the bold and hardened. His conduct in his present condition (not the crime, how atrocious so-ever, which brought him to it) is the subject of universal contemplation.

The dramatic exit of Perrin, Kingsmill and Fairall from this world was not over yet. Perrin's body was delivered to his friends, who put him in a coffin and buried him, but the bodies of Kingsmill and Fairall were carried to a smith's shop in Fetter Lane, Holborn, for the last grisly fitting of body irons. Their fettered bodies were taken into Kent and hung up 'in the sweet air', where they were left to rot slowly away. Kingsmill was gibbeted at Goudhurst Gore, a little hamlet close to Goudhurst, and Fairall in his native village of Horsendown Green.

10

The Chater and Galley Murders

'Those horrible deeds of darkness'

If the reader still entertains a romantic concept of the daring smuggler, eye patch, anker of brandy and all, then consideration of the Chater and Galley murders will clearly show that the men involved in smuggling were also capable of deeds utterly lacking in romance, for the murders of the old shoemaker from Fordingbridge and the tidewaiter from Southampton in 1748 must rank among the vilest ever committed. These murders involved calculated and sadistic torture by a group of evil men who subjected their unfortunate victims to a brutal succession of whipping, kicking and cutting until their battered bodies could take no more. The story is not a pleasant one but it must be looked at in full as it is of crucial importance in the history of smuggling. Nothing so bad had happened before in the smuggling fraternity, and the revelations made in the course of the subsequent trials gave public and official complacency such a shock that nothing like them was allowed to happen again.

The train of events began with the breaking open of the Poole Custom House on 7 October 1747 and then the gang of smugglers rode in triumph through the New Forest with their bags of tea. They breakfasted at Fordingbridge and when the time came for them to move off quite a crowd had gathered to view the impressive cavalcade of armed riders. There was no question of 'watching the wall' as the smugglers were quite open about the fact that they had broken into the King's warehouse and, no doubt flushed with gin as well as the success of the operation, they bragged and enjoyed the awed respect and congratulations of the crowd.

Among the company who mounted up after breakfasting was John Diamond, also variously known as Dymer, or sometimes simply as the Shepherd. He had taken part in the events of the previous night and also, according to the contemporary account, had gone over to Guernsey with Perrin to buy the tea. As they rode out of Fordingbridge, acknowledging the cheers of the crowd, Diamond noticed an old friend, Daniel Chater, with whom he used to work at harvest time.

Reaching down from his horse the smuggler shook hands with the cobbler and they exchanged words. Before riding off Diamond threw him a bag of tea, which, if it was one of the 27-pound bags already mentioned, was indeed a handsome gift. Probably Diamond's generosity was directly related to the amount of ale and gin that he had drunk during the past few hours. Anyway, the old man had not only talked to one of the daring and distinguished smugglers, a personal friend of his, but had also been given a large amount of tea. Unfortunately this chance meeting and gift was too good a tale to keep to himself and he foolishly began to brag about how he knew one of the men on the 'gallant expedition'.

Eventually the knowledge of the conversation and the gift reached the ears of the authorities. How this came about must be left to conjecture. The Commissioners of the Customs had offered a substantial reward soon after the Poole affair in the hope that it would persuade someone to turn King's evidence. Chater may have been informed on by a person seeking this reward, or maybe the gossip was simply passed on and a Riding officer got to hear of it. Whatever the real reason, the fact remained that the authorities knew that Chater had seen Diamond on 7 October in Fordingbridge, armed and carrying tea. This would be very useful evidence if Diamond was apprehended. And in February 1748 that happened.

On 6 February 1748, Mr Till, the Collector of Chichester, told the Board of Customs that John Diamond, alias Dymer, one of the persons concerned in the Poole affair, had been apprehended and committed to gaol. The Commissioners instructed Mr Till to find Daniel Chater and have him sent to East Marden, near Chichester, to be examined about the events of 7 October by Mr Battine, a Justice of the Peace and Surveyor General of Sussex, who was arranging for Diamond's committal. The authorities had to have a cast-iron case against Diamond. It was well known that local magistrates were loath to find people guilty of smuggling, as they feared reprisals, but breaking open the Custom House had been such insolence that the authorities wanted to prosecute the culprits and make an example of them. Chater's evidence was vital to a successful prosecution and, moreover, when faced with the prospect of a rope around his neck, Diamond might be persuaded to turn King's evidence and name his accomplices.

The old shoemaker was in a tricky position. Because of his vainglorious gossip he had become a vital Crown witness against a friend who, by his evidence, was going to be found guilty of a hanging offence. Without realising it, he had become an informer, and as such, a hated enemy of the smuggling fraternity. He could not say to the authorities that he had not seen Diamond that day because half of Hampshire knew that he had; if he refused to give evidence he himself could be prosecuted for receiving goods knowing them to be uncustomed, which would involve a heavy fine or a period of transportation. Chater must have rued the day that he shook hands with Diamond and accepted the bag of tea.

The contemporary writer of *Sussex Smuggling* paints an ominously black picture of the state of affairs at the time:

The smugglers had reigned a long time uncontrolled; the officers of the customs were too few to encounter them, they rode in troops to fetch their goods, and carried them off in triumph by day light; nay so audacious were they grown, that they were not afraid of regular troops, that were sent into the country to keep them in awe; of which we had several instances. If any of them happened to be taken, and the proof ever so clear against him, no magistrate in the country durst commit him to gaol; if he did he was sure to have his house or barns set on fire, or some other mischief done him, if he was so happy to escape with his life, which has been the occasion of their being brought to London to be committed. But for a man to inform against them, the most cruel death was his undoubted portion.

This terrible prophecy came true for the unfortunate Chater.

In pursuance of the Commissioners' instructions Mr Till wrote to his opposite number in Southampton, Mr Shearer, informing him that Daniel Chater was required to be questioned by Mr Battine. Chater can hardly have been surprised by the summons to go to Southampton and he duly presented himself at the Custom House, where he was told by Shearer that William Galley, a tidewaiter of that port, was to accompany him to Mr Battine's, presumably to ensure that he did carry out his instructions rather than to protect him. With them went a letter addressed to Mr Battine explaining why Chater had made the journey from Fordingbridge. Thus on St Valentine's Day 1748 the two men set out on their fateful journey. William Galley, on a hired grey horse, was wearing 'a blue great coat, with brass buttons covered with blue, a close bodied coat, of a light brown colour, lined with blue, with waistcoat and breeches of the same' and Daniel Chater was wearing 'a light surtout coat, with red breeches and a belt round him' and rode upon a brown horse. When their bodies were found seven months later, positive identification was only made possible by the son of William Galley identifying his father's clothes and Mrs Chater recognising her late husband's belt with a particular mark on it. In view of the importance of the letter they carried, it would seem madness to send these two without an armed guard through country with a notorious smuggling reputation. But off they went on a mission which, as it turned out, proved to be their death warrant.

They first broke their journey at Havant, where Chater persuaded Galley to stop off so that he could visit a good friend of his, Edward Holton. Chater went inside and chatted away rather self importantly, airily mentioning that he was going to Chichester 'upon a little business'. To prove his point he went outside and asked Galley to give him the letter with the imposing address on it, which he did and Chater in turn showed it to his friend. Before leaving Havant, Chater asked the best way to get to East Marden and Holton directed them to go north through Stanstead, near Rowland's Castle. The two remounted and, telling Holton they would drop in on the way back next day, rode off.

They were obviously not in a hurry as it was not yet midday and they had made good time from Southampton. No doubt both Chater and Galley were beginning to enjoy the ride, which was quite an event in their dull lives. Anyway, before leaving the parish of Havant they stopped at a public house called the New Inn in the hamlet of Leigh. In order to strike up a conversation with the other people present the two travellers asked the way again. William Galley felt into his blue great coat and for the second time showed off the letter. George Austen was drinking in the pub and, noticing that the letter was addressed to a Mr Battine at East Marden, said for some strange reason that the two were going ten miles out of their way. This was an exaggeration of course, but it is common enough, when asking directions, to get different answers. However, George Austen was anxious to help the strangers and told them that he and his brother Thomas and their brother-in-law Robert Jenkes were going in their general direction and would travel with them for part of the way and then put them on the right road. The five drank up and left.

A couple of miles further on and only five from their destination of East Marden, the party stopped about noon at another public house, the White Hart, owned by a widowed woman called Paine. They obviously meant to spend some time there as they stabled their horses. To drive out the February cold Chater and Galley called for rum and the five of them settled down to a convivial drink in front of the open fire. As the warmth from the fire and the rum gradually seeped into their bodies they must have felt pleasantly contented, having virtually reached their destination and with the prospect of a couple of hours spent chatting with their friendly fellow travellers. But the friendliness was not shared by the woman of the house, widow Paine. She was suspicious of the two strangers and called George Austen, whom she obviously knew, aside and asked him who they were and what they were about. He told her that they were going to Mr Battine's and that they would show them the way.

The name of Battine must have increased her suspicions, for not only was he a high-ranking Customs official but also a Justice of the Peace. She questioned Austen further, telling him that she thought the strangers were going to do some harm to the smugglers. He replied that they were simply taking a letter to Mr Battine and although he did not know what was in it he imagined it was only about some common and unimportant business. But the seed of suspicion had been sown in the widow's mind and this honest appraisal did nothing to dispel it. She asked Austen straight out to misdirect the strangers but this he refused to do and returned to the group drinking in front of the fire. Thereupon the widow Paine secretly dispatched her sons, William and Edmund, to summon the local smugglers.

Within a short space of time the urgent summons to go to the White Hart was received. The message was ominously clear; there were two strangers come to swear against the Shepherd. Without actually seeing the letter, the widow Paine correctly deduced the purpose of the two men's journey. Diamond was a local man and the smuggling fraternity were very anxious about what might happen to him; they did not discount the possibility that he would turn King's evidence and reveal the names of many local men to the authorities. That Diamond's imprisonment greatly worried his fellow smugglers is demonstrated by the following confession to the vicar of Donnington, Simon Hughs, in the condemned cell after the subsequent trial:

> Both Charter and Tapner a few hours before their execution, confessed to me, that they with several others, assembled together, with a design to rescue Diamond out of Chichester jail; that the only person amongst them, who had arms, was Edmund Richards, but that being disappointed by a number of persons, who had promised to join them from the East [the Hawkhurst Gang again], their scheme was frustrated, and their purpose carried no farther into execution; that one Stringer was at the head of this confederacy, but not present with them at the time of assembling together.

The smugglers' anxiety on hearing the news can be imagined and fed their desperation as they spurred their horses towards the White Hart, where the two loathsome informers were still quietly drinking. Meanwhile the landlady had dealt successfully with a minor crisis. The two strangers had got up to leave, whereupon she had told them that the stable lad had locked up the stables and gone home, taking the key with him, but would be back presently. Chater and Galley appear to have accepted this fabrication willingly and settled down for more drink.

One of the first smugglers to arrive was William Jackson, 'one of the most notorious smugglers living in his time', who entered the pub with his wife and called for a mug of 'hot' (gin and beer mixed) and listened anxiously as the widow Paine repeated in private that she thought the two strangers were informers. In ones and twos the gang assembled: William Carter, with his wife; Edmund Richards; William Steele; Henry Sheerman, known as Little Harry; Samuel Howard, alias Bowner, known as Little Sam; and John Race. They all began to drink freely and to exchange sociable chat with the two strangers. The landlady moved among them generously replenishing their glasses with rum and hot. But the two Austens and Jenkes were beginning to feel uneasy despite the amount of drink they had had. Carter and Jackson were notorious smugglers and had a certain reputation which commanded a feared respect; it was not their habit to chat sociably in a pub on a Sunday afternoon with two travellers. The Austens and Jenkes sensed a darker motive and must have wondered how the copious drinking was to end.

By this time the smugglers had manoeuvred Galley and Chater into a smaller side room to get them away from the other drinkers in the bar. Jackson wanted to get rid of their travelling companions, the Austens and Robert Jenkes, and made it menacingly clear to Jenkes that he did not want him to go through into the little room where Chater and Galley were. Jenkes said at the trial that Jackson told him, 'If I had a mind to go I might go through the garden to the back part of the house, where I found my horse although I hadn't asked for it to be brought there.' That had got rid of one possible witness. The widow's potent drink had taken care of Thomas Austen, for he was in a drunken stupor. This left his brother George, and the landlady called him aside and said that his brother-in-law wanted to speak to him outside. When he got outside he found that his horse had been brought as well. However, he was sober enough to remember that he had promised to put Chater and Galley on the right road for East Marden and to warn them that the sooner they left the company of Jackson, Carter and friends the better for them. So he went back into the pub, where he was headed off by the landlady, who advised him to go home and said that the two men would be directed on their way. Reluctantly he heeded this advice and rode off, leaving the tidewaiter and the shoemaker in the company of people 'not having the fear of God before their eyes, but being moved and seduced by the instigation of the Devil'.

It was now gone two o'clock and for the next hour or so the scene inside the White Hart remained that of a country inn on a cold February afternoon. But the alcohol was not only loosening the tongues of the innocent travellers; it was also turning the brain of Jackson, whose loathing for informers was increasing with every mug of hot. He saw an opportunity to get Chater away from Galley for a few moments and, clapping an arm round the old shoemaker, suggested with mock *bonhomie* that they get a breath of fresh air outside in the yard. Once outside he casually asked Chater where his friend Diamond was. Chater, with the trust and honesty of a man who hopes that his questioner has had as much to drink as he, replied that Diamond was in custody and that he was going to give evidence against him. He regretted having to do it, but it could not be helped.

Whether Jackson still intended to try some friendly persuasion even at this late stage will never be known, for at that very moment Galley, sensing that Jackson must be trying to influence his witness, came out into the yard and called Chater to come back inside. Jackson's restraint finally snapped; with a violent oath he punched Galley in the face with a blow that laid him out on the cobbles, cutting his mouth and left cheek. The fracas was heard inside and to prevent any of the casual drinkers from going to see what happened Edmund Richards pulled out a pistol; pointing it in turn at the startled country labourers, he ominously warned, 'Whoever discovers anything that passes at this house today, I will blow his brains out.'

The three came back in from outside and it was plain to see that Galley had been hit, for he was holding a bloody handkerchief to the left side of his face and his wig was off. In an attempt to cool the hothead who had struck him and to assert his official position, he pulled out his deputation from the Commissioners of Custom, and in front of several witnesses declared, 'I am a King's Officer, and I will take notice of you that struck me' and wrote Jackson's name down on a piece of paper with all the authority of one resorting to a last desperate move. On hearing that not only an informer but a King's officer was present, Jackson erupted once again into a drunken rage, shouting that for a quartern of gin he would hit him again. Before this could take place both of the widow's sons ran forward and restrained him and told him not to be such a fool. Galley and Chater made an attempt to go but again, incredibly, were persuaded to stay by Jackson, of all people, who begged Galley not to part as enemies, with a hollow pretence at pleading for forgiveness and excusing his actions as that of a drunken man. The inherent naivety of the two stupid men must have been raised to new heights by the copious draughts of the widow's rum, for stay they did to drink themselves into a drunken slumber so that at about four o'clock they were carried into a back room and laid on a bed. On going through the pockets of Galley, the smugglers found the incriminating letter.

The contents left the smugglers in no doubt that Chater could not possibly be allowed to testify against Diamond. They spent two or three hours debating in a singularly callous way what should be done to the two sleeping off their drink in the other room. One suggestion was to put them on a boat for France with whom Britain was then at war. The French authorities tolerated English smuggling vessels all through the times of war, for they bought goods with gold guineas and also provided information on movements of the Royal Navy and other useful facts. Not all the information was correct, some was deliberately misleading, and the British authorities, it is known, used the smugglers to acquire information about French activities. If Chater and Galley were taken to France then they would probably be arrested as spies and imprisoned or put to death. However, this expedient was rejected as not being sufficiently permanent or certain. 'There was the possibility of them coming over again, and then they [the smugglers] should all be known.'

Straightforward murder was discussed: the bodies could be disposed of in a well in a horse pasture half a mile from Rowland's Castle, 'But it was thought not convenient to put them into a well so near, for fear of discovery.' No doubt the widow Paine was against this expedient as several casual drinkers that Sunday afternoon had seen her ply the two strangers with drink. Her public house could be used for plotting murder but not for the execution of it.

A third suggestion was made, which, coming from a drunken and enraged group, appears uncharacteristically moderate and almost humane. 'It was then proposed to join, and each men to allow them three pence a week, and to keep them in some secret place till they saw what became of Dymer, and as Dymer was served, so these two people [Chater and Galley] were to be served.' This proposal was discussed and set aside. The group did not come to any common conclusion, but the general feeling was expressed by the two wives. According to Steele's evidence, 'While they were talking these things, the wives of Carter and Jackson said it was no matter what became of them or what was done to them; they ought to be hanged, for they were come to ruin them, meaning the smugglers.'

Thus after two or three hours of drunken discussion they had agreed, rather vaguely, that the two strangers should be hanged. However, as events proved, the murders that took place were not carried out by men with any common plan or any definite leader.

At about seven o'clock that evening the meeting broke up and Carter and Jackson went into the side room to wake Galley and Chater. This they did by jumping on the bed where the two were stretched out and viciously drawing the spurs on their riding boots across the faces of their sleeping victims. They proceeded to kick and horsewhip the fuddled two into semi-consciousness, and then pitched them out of the room into the main parlour. Again William Paine had to restrain Jackson, who was about to strike one of them in front of the other drinkers in the bar. He meekly accepted this second rebuke and the whole party went outside, but not before Richards had once again threatened the startled drinkers left in the bar with certain death if they as much as murmured to anyone else what they had seen. Before they rode off, Jackson returned with a pistol in a vain attempt to save a little face and demanded a belt or strap or a piece of string. Nobody moved or said a thing, struck dumb by the astonishing events of the past few minutes, and Jackson left the public house. Outside, one of the party had found some rope and the two prisoners were forced to get up on one horse; their legs were tied underneath the animal's belly and the four legs were lashed together. Then the cavalcade moved off, all except for the wives and John Race, who, perhaps sensing the enormity of what was about to happen, made the excuse that he did not have a horse and so could not join them.

They had not gone a hundred yards down the road when Jackson called out, 'Whip them, cut them, slash them, damn them', and immediately they began to lash their victims with their horsewhips, all except Steele, who was leading the captives' horse. They continued this merciless assault for half a mile, 'Lashing and cutting them over the head, face, eyes and shoulders, till the poor men, unable any longer to bear the anguish of their repeated blows, rolled from side to side, and at last fell together with their heads under the horses belly; in which posture every step the horse made, he struck one or other of their heads with his feet.' The cavalcade stopped and recharged their sadistic batteries by more spirits and 'when their cruel tormentors saw the dismal effects of their barbarity, and that the poor creatures had fallen under it, they sat them upright again in the same position as they were before and continued whipping them in the most cruel manner'.

After another half-mile of this cruel treatment the victims fell again and eventually Galley was put up behind Steele, and Chater behind Little Sam. However, the whipping did not stop and Galley's blue greatcoat was ripped off so that their lashes could take better effect. The smugglers were so incensed that the tips of their whips were snapping over the tops of their victims' shoulders and hitting Steele and Little Sam, who naturally called for them to desist, which they did.

They had now arrived at the village of Dean and Jackson pulled out a pistol as they rode through and vowed that if anyone made a noise he would blow their brains out. Once outside the village the six smugglers agreed among themselves to go to Lady Holt Park, owned by John Caryll Esquire, and to murder Galley there and throw him down Harris's Well. On hearing this, 'The poor unhappy man desired them to dispatch him at once, or even throw him down the well, to put an end to his misery.' This despairing plea for a quick end heralded another flurry of lashes from Jackson's horsewhip and, being unable to endure any more, Galley slumped off his horse onto the ground.

A contemporary historian describes the sordid scene: 'Could the devil himself have furnished a more execrable invention to punish the wretched victims of his malice, than to grant them life only to prolong their torments!' But Jackson and Carter had not done with this poor unfortunate man; they picked him up and spread him sideways across the saddle 'as a butcher does a calf' and Richards got up behind him and held him there for another mile or so until he tired of holding him in place and let him fall again. Again it was Jackson and Carter who picked him up and this time placed him on the grey horse that Steele had been riding so that he slumped forward over the horse's mane; Jackson got up behind him and proceeded to squeeze and twist his private parts for another half-mile, paying no heed to the poor man's cries of 'Barbarous usage! Barbarous usage! For God's sake shoot me through the head.'

Eventually Little Harry took Galley up behind him on his horse and tied him there with a rope. The horrific journey continued until the informer Galley called out desperately that he was about to fall, whereupon Little Harry gave him a shove and said, 'Fall and be damned.' Galley toppled off the horse head-first and with a sickening crunch hit the ground. Supposing that he had broken his neck, they laid him across a horse and with two holding him in place and a third leading the horse they made their way to a nearby house owned by a noted fellow smuggler called Pescod and knocked on the door. Pescod's daughter came down and opened the door. The smugglers, on hearing that Pescod was ill in bed, persuaded her to go upstairs and get permission from him to bring the two men inside. This she did but came back and said that her father was so ill and, sensing that they were on some 'villainous expedition, resolved to have no hand it in, or have his name brought in question on that account'. Accepting this rebuff, they decided to go to a nearby public house, the Red Lion at Rake, where they hammered on the door and eventually persuaded the landlord, Scardefield by name, to come down and open up, which he did, and after lighting a fire in the parlour went off to draw some liquor. It was now about two o'clock on Monday morning.

The smugglers told the landlord that they had had an engagement with some Revenue officers and that they had lost their goods and that some of their number were dead and others wounded. Scardefield did not seem unduly worried about this revelation, for he went to the brewhouse, where he saw something lying on the ground. Two or three smugglers told him that it was a dead man. The landlord hurried back to the parlour with gin and beer; but although Richards tried to prevent him coming in, Scardefield noticed that one of the men standing there had a bloody face and one eye was swollen a great deal. This of course was Chater. There were considerable comings and goings in the early hours of that morning. After three mugs of hot had been drunk, Chater was taken by Little Harry and Jackson to Old Mill's house at Trotton, where he was chained by the legs in an outhouse called a skillin, which was used for storing turf. Little Harry remained to guard Chater while Jackson returned to the inn. Rum and brandy were called for; while Scardefield was in the cellar getting this, the smugglers mounted up again with the limp body of Galley thrown over a horse's saddle. One of the company asked the landlord if he knew the place where they had stored some goods a year and half ago. Sensing that he had done more than enough for the smugglers that night, Scardefield wisely refused to go with them and show them where it was, whereupon Richards 'fell in a passion because he refused to go along with them'. His fellow smugglers calmed him and the cavalcade with their grisly cargo went off into the night with a lantern to light their way down the dark, narrow lanes.

In the evidence (in the trial transcript), Scardefield makes no reference to being present when the body of Galley was finally buried, but a contemporary historian records that the landlord was present and in fact helped to dig the hole as it was such a cold night. In view of the fact that helping in the disposal of the body of a victim would make one an accessory after the fact and therefore, if found guilty, liable to be hanged, it seems likely that the Crown, in order to get Scardefield to testify against the smugglers, agreed not to press charges if he would appear as a prosecution witness.

Irrespective of Scardefield's whereabouts, there were at least four other people present when Galley's body was put in an excavated foxes' earth near Hasting Combe, about a mile from the Red Lion; they were Carter, Steele, Richards, and Little Sam. Jackson had not returned from taking Chater to Trotton. By the flickering light of their lamp a rough grave was dug in the sand and the body dumped in. The smugglers assumed that Galley had broken his neck on falling off the horse and was dead but it seems likely that when the sand was thrown on top of him he was still alive, for when the body was discovered some months later his hands were up around his face, probably in a last desperate attempt to keep out the choking sand from his nose and mouth, and he was standing almost upright.

The burial party returned to the Red Lion in the early hours of Monday morning, where they met Jackson, who told them that Chater was well secured. They relaxed in the only manner they knew how: by drinking mugs of hot and other spirits. They spent all Monday carousing, bragging and drinking in a veritable orgy of drunkenness. During the course of the day Richard Mills junior came in and, hearing them mention how they had treated the informer Chater and that they had ridden along the top of a steep cliff some thirty feet high, he casually remarked that if he had been present then he would have called a council of war and thrown him down headlong. Despite their drunkenness they realised that they had been away from their homes now some thirty-six hours and that it would be expedient if they returned that night so that they could show themselves the next day (Tuesday) to prevent neighbours and possible informers wondering where they had been. They also considered that the six of them present (albeit that Little Harry was at Trotton guarding Chater) had performed a valuable service on behalf of the far greater local smuggling community; therefore it was decided that the rest of the smuggling gang should do their share of the dirty work and to this end all should be summoned to meet at the Red Lion on Wednesday evening, when the shoemaker's fate would be decided. Then, when it was dark, the party of five broke up and rode to their separate homes.

That Wednesday evening under cover of darkness, the whole smuggling gang assembled, dropping in at the Red Lion in discrete ones and twos. Apart from the six already mentioned, there arrived John Cobby; William Hammond; Benjamin Tapner; Thomas Stringer, a cordwainer from Chichester; Thomas Willis, commonly called the Coachman of Selbourne in Hampshire (both of the latter two had been involved in breaking open the Poole Custom House); Daniel Perryer, otherwise known as Little Daniel of Norton; Richard and John Mills (old Major Mills's sons); and John Race, who had been present at the original gathering at the White Hart at Rowland's Castle and had now got a horse and ridden the fifteen miles from Chichester. Richard Mills senior and Henry Sheerman were at Trotton guarding Chater.

The discussion centred on how best to murder the informer with least likelihood of discovery. As was usual with these discussions, there was little agreement. Richard Mills proposed an ingenious method calculated to fit the necessary requirements. As Chater was already chained by his leg to a beam, Mills proposed that they should place a gun loaded with two or three bullets on a stand levelled at the informer's head and that a string be tied to the trigger and that all of them should take hold of the string and pull it simultaneously: 'Thus we shall be all equally guilty of his death, and it will be impossible for anyone of us to charge the rest with his murder, without accusing himself of the same crime; and none can pretend to lessen or mitigate their guilt by saying they were only accessories, since all will be principals.' But this method was objected to by some 'more infernally barbarous than the rest' as being too expeditious and they resolved that he should suffer as much and as long as they could make his life last 'as a terror for all such informing rogues for the future'.

Rejecting Mills's proposal, they eventually agreed to take Chater back to Harris's Well in Lady Holt Park (where Galley had so nearly met his death) and murder him there and throw him down the well, which was dry and so no longer used. The body would remain there undetected as no one had cause to visit the spot. With the plan agreed upon, they saddled up and rode to Trotton to enact the gruesome finale.

The unfortunate Chater had been chained up for the past two days. He had been given a little bread and water, and once some pease porridge, but he was in such a bad physical condition from internal injuries that he vomited the food and drink back up in pools of blood. The past two days had seen the beatings continue and the people guarding him took the opportunity to 'swear and upbraid him in the vilest terms and most scurrilous language that their tongues could utter'.

On reaching Trotton, a group of the smugglers burst into the outhouse and Tapner, more incensed and drunk than the rest, pulled out a clasp knife and threatened Chater in the most horrible manner. 'God damn your blood, down on your knees and go to prayers, for with the knife I will be your butcher.' The terrified shoemaker knelt in prayer but even this act of communion with his Maker was interrupted by a vicious kick in the back from Cobby. The poor man asked what had become of his companion Galley, to which Tapner replied, 'Damn you, we have killed him, and we will do so by you' and then without more ado slashed his knife over Chater's eyes and nose with such violence that he 'almost cut both his eyes out, and the gristle of his nose quite through'. Not content with this, he inflicted another terrible gash across the victim's forehead, which prompted Old Mills to intervene. 'Take him away, and do not murder him here, but murder him somewhere else.' They picked up their bloody victim and sat him on a horse to take him to Harris's Well. All went except Mills and his two sons, who made the excuse that their horses were out in the pasture and would be difficult to catch in the dark – and, besides, there were enough of them to kill one man and Harris's Well was on their way home anyway.

Tapner, more cruel (if possible) than the rest, proceeded to make Chater's cuts bleed more by whipping him as they rode along, and swore that if Chater blooded his saddle (for it seems Chater was on his horse) then he would 'destroy him that moment and send his soul to Hell'.

Some distance before they got to the well, Carter and Jackson told the other gang members not involved in the Galley murder – namely Cobby, Tapner, Hammond, Race, Perryer, Willis and Stringer – that they had done their part and now it was up to them to do theirs. They gave directions how to get to the well and there the smugglers split into two parties, with Carter, Jackson, Steele, Richards, Little Sam and Little Harry going off in the direction of Rowland's Castle, leaving the remainder to dispose of Chater. When the latter group arrived at the well they pulled Chater from his horse and Tapner took a cord out of his pocket and tied it in a noose around their victim's neck. The well was protected by a paling fence designed to prevent cattle falling in it and the smugglers told Chater to climb over it. He noticed, however, that there was a gap where a couple or three palings had been broken and he attempted to crawl through this 'but that was a favour too great to be allowed to so heinous an offender' and he was forced to struggle over the top. Tapner tied the end of the rope to the fence and then they all got over and pushed Chater into the well.

Because they were drunk, they could not even hang the old man properly. The cord was so short that he was left half dangling over the edge of the well slowly choking and spluttering. They waited a quarter of an hour before realising that the shoemaker was going to take an inordinately long time to die. Stringer, with the assistance of Cobby and Hammond, pulled him back from the edge and, after Tapner had untied the cord from the fence, they held the shoemaker by his legs and pitched him head-first into the well. They waited in the cold February air, straining to hear any signs of life from the depths of the well. They were just about to go, having thought that their task had been completed, when low moanings were heard. Incredibly Chater was not dead yet. In a fury of consternation they went to a nearby cottage owned by a gardener called William Combleach and told him that one of their companions had fallen down the well and they wanted to borrow a ladder and rope to get him out. Without asking what people were doing at this lonely place in the middle of the night, or more likely knowing them to be smugglers, Combleach lent them a long ladder.

They carried the ladder back to the well in the valley bottom but were so drunk or so confused and disturbed by Chater's refusal to die that they could not lift the ladder over the palings surrounding the well. They struggled and sweated and swore and then threw it down in disgust and went back to listen at the well top. Chater was still groaning thirty feet below at the foot of the black hole. They desperately discussed how to finish him off and spent some time scouting round for large pieces of flint and two logs which had been gate posts and these they hurled down onto the old man, who was still groaning. On listening again, they could hear nothing from him and so concluded that he was finally dead. They remounted and rode off to their respective houses.

William Galley had been brutally whipped and abused for ten hours and buried most probably before he was dead; the shoemaker from Fordingbridge, Daniel Chater, had been cruelly treated for three and a half days and life was finally battered out of him by stones and logs as he lay horribly mutilated at the foot of a well. The vile and loathsome murders were perpetrated by a group of people which – if we include Jackson's and Carter's wives, widow Paine and her two sons, and Scardefield of the Red Lion – numbered at least twenty-two persons. Not one of them had shown any vestige of humanity or compassion. All deeply involved in the smuggling trade, their warped and gin-sodden minds were seduced into thinking that the foul acts would safeguard their livelihoods. 'But such is the depravity of human nature, that when a man once abandons himself to all manner of wickedness, he sets no bounds to his passions, his conscience is seared, every tender sentiment is lost, reason is no more, and he has nothing left him of the man but the form.' The bold free traders had been reduced to the level of depraved beasts. Because of the very enormity of these crimes, designed to protect the smuggling trade and instil fear into its opponents, they could not go unpunished.

The next few months provided a classic confrontation between public terror on the one hand and a Christian conscience with its wish for law and order, and justice, on the other. And as it proved, the latter triumphed, for eventually an anonymous informer provided the clues the authorities were hoping for.

11

The Chichester Trial

'Yet the eye of Providence was not asleep'

As recorded earlier, on Sunday 14 February 1747, Daniel Chater accompanied by William Galley had set off to ride to East Marden near Chichester, so that the old shoemaker could give his evidence to the authorities following the Poole Custom House robbery. They broke their journey in Havant, where Chater wanted to see an old friend, Edward Holton; they told him, on parting, that they would call on him again the next day on their way back to Southampton. No doubt Holton was disappointed at not seeing his old friend on the Monday but was not unduly worried as the two riders could have changed their plans and decided against making the detour to Havant on their way home. The families of both Galley and Chater were anxious for the two travellers when they failed to show up on the Monday night but probably assumed that the men's official business had delayed them or that the roads had been so bad that they had been forced to stay overnight at some wayside inn. Their anxiety gave way to a nagging fear as the days went by and still the men did not return. The two travellers had disappeared completely, and it was feared that they had fallen into the hands of the smugglers. Perhaps the two had been sent across to France to prevent Chater testifying against Diamond, or maybe a more permanent and irrevocable method of prevention had been carried out. The worst fears of both families and employers must have been confirmed when, on 25 February, a blood-stained blue greatcoat was found on the road between Rowland's Castle and Rake. In one of the pockets was Galley's deputation, dated 1 April 1731, appointing him to be a tidesman in the Port of Southampton. This evidence was taken to Mr Battine, who produced it in court at the subsequent trial.

With the continued absence of the two men from their homes and jobs, the Customs Commissioners were duly notified and they immediately issued a proclamation offering a substantial reward to anyone who should discover what had become of them, with His Majesty's pardon to such a person. As the authorities incorporated a pardon into the wording of the proclamation, it appears that they too feared the worst. The proclamation did not have the desired effect and a sullen, impenetrable silence greeted all official enquiries. Even a considerable sum of money and a pardon were not sufficient inducement to turn King's evidence, as no informer was safe from the terrible visitations of the smugglers. Without doubt there were many in Sussex and Hampshire who knew the fate of Galley and Chater, but none dared challenge the smugglers' authority.

The Crown already possessed an important piece of evidence in the form of the blood-stained greatcoat belonging to Galley. Several days later a second important clue came trotting forward when the brown horse hired or borrowed by Chater was found wandering and was returned to its owner. Before the shoemaker was finally murdered at Harris's Well, the smugglers realised that there were two witnesses still alive 'which, though dumb, would certainly render them suspected, if suffered to survive their masters'. They had a hurried consultation of what to do with the two horses that Chater and Galley had been riding. Some favoured letting them free in a large wood so that it would be a long time before they were caught and identified. Others thought the best way to prevent possible identification and association with the two missing persons would be to put them on a boat for France; this, however, was objected to as 'liable to some miscarriage and therefore, after much debate, it was unanimously agreed to knock them on the head at once, and take their skins off'. Accordingly they killed Galley's horse, skinned it and chopped both body and hide into small pieces and scattered them in the undergrowth. The vicinity of Harris's Well was indeed a scene of horrific butchery that night. But when they came to do the same to Chater's horse, they found that the knot tying the reins to a tree had come undone and the horse had prudently disappeared into the dark. A contemporary historian records, 'But the grey which Mr Shearer of Southampton had hired for Mr Galley and which they had now killed, he was obliged to pay for.'

All concerned in the murders must have been very anxious as the drama unfolded. As soon as their hangovers cleared, the fact remained that they had murdered a Customs officer and an old shoemaker, and were not certain that their reputation would ensure public silence, nor that the bodies would not be discovered. As the weeks passed, their anxiety gave way to complacency and probably to bragging of how they had dealt with their enemies.

> But as providence seldom suffers such atrocious crimes to go undiscovered or unpunished even in this world, so in this case, though the Divine Justice seemed dormant for a while, yet the eye of Providence was not asleep, but was still watching their motions and taking the necessary steps to bring to light these horrible deeds of darkness, and to punish the perpetrators of such abominable wickedness in the most exemplary manner.

The 'necessary steps' taken by Providence came in the form of an anonymous letter to a person of distinction, possibly one of the Pelhams or the Duke of Richmond.

It is not known whether this action was prompted by the possibility of a reward or whether the writer's conscience would not allow him to remain silent. The informant was 'one of the persons who had been a witness to some of the transactions of this bloody tragedy, and knew of the death of either Galley or Chater, and where one was buried, though he was no way concerned in the murder'. Perhaps he was the son of the landlady of the White Hart who had restrained Jackson on two occasions from hitting Galley and who could have overheard in subsequent conversation between Carter and Richards where they had buried his body. Or again it might have been a person who frequented Scardefield's inn at Rake.

Whoever wrote the letter provided the clue that the authorities required. A party was despatched to find Galley's burial place near Rake and after a short search they uncovered the grisly remains. The body must have begun to decompose, for it had been interred in February and the date was now September. Soon, a second letter was received naming William Steele alias Hardware as one concerned with the murder of the man found in the sand and stating also Steele's present abode. The authorities immediately issued a warrant for his arrest and accordingly took him into custody. Steele promptly offered himself as evidence for the King and agreed to 'make a full discovery and disclosure of the whole wicked transaction, and of all the persons concerned therein'. This was what the authorities had been hoping for as a confession by one of the people involved in the murders would secure conviction of the remainder.

The first disclosure that Steele made was the whereabouts of Chater's body and another party of men were sent to Harris's Well in Lady Holt Park on 16 or 17 September. At the bottom of the well, underneath logs and stones, they found the remains of a man. The local coroner's assistant, a Mr Brackstone, hurried to the scene to supervise the exhumation. The body was brought out with the rope still around its neck; one of Chater's legs had been severed and was brought up separately. The boots and belt were removed and allowed for the shoemaker's widow to make a positive identification.

While Steele was making these disclosures another of the participants came forward; John Race had lost his nerve and offered himself as King's evidence too. With this new witness, the Crown had enough evidence to issue warrants for the arrest of the others involved, and the round-up began. John Hammond was taken into custody at the beginning of October and on 18 October John Cobby was arrested. On 16 November Chater's cruelest persecutor, Benjamin Tapner, was also taken and joined the other two in Horsham Gaol. Tapner's employer, a Chichester shoemaker by trade, told the authorities of the wanted man's whereabouts. His employer probably took this action more to clear himself from possible accusation of harbouring a murderer than out of the hope to get a reward.

When Steele and Race had named everyone involved, the authorities realised that they already had one of the Mills brothers in custody; this was Richard, who had been taken in Sussex on 16 August along with George Spencer, Richard Payne and Thomas Reoff – all outlawed smugglers. In order to stand any chance of getting a conviction, the four had been taken to Southwark and had appeared before Justice Hammond accused of being concerned with others, armed, in running uncustomed goods and in not surrendering themselves within twenty-eight days after their names had appeared as outlawed smugglers in the *London Gazette*. They had been committed to Surrey Gaol, where on 5 October Richard Mills junior was further indicted for the murder of Chater and Galley. On 14 November William Jackson and William Carter were apprehended near Godalming in Surrey, some twenty-five miles from their usual haunts; they probably were running goods to London as three days later they were taken before Justice Poulson at Covent Garden and committed to Newgate on the general charge of running uncustomed goods and not surrendering themselves.

In addition to Race and Steel, the authorities now had six smugglers behind bars. Warrants were also issued for the arrests of Henry Sheerman (Little Harry), labourer; Edmund Richards, labourer; Thomas Stringer, cordwainer; Daniel Ferryer (Little Daniel), labourer; John Mills, labourer; Thomas Mills (the Coachman) and Samuel Howard (Little Sam), labourer. Surprisingly there is no evidence in the chief contemporary account of the trial to suggest that the widow Paine and her two sons were taken into custody, although Lord Teignmouth and Charles Harper mention in their book *The Smugglers* that the three were taken on 19 December and committed to Winchester Gaol and charged with being accomplices to the murder. This seems to be the only reference regarding the fate of the Paines; as they were now in custody it seems surprising that they were not tried at the special assize held in January 1749 at Chichester for the main body of the gang. Only three days before the Paines were arrested, the same fate befell Richard Mills senior, who had made no attempt to escape to France or to lie low for a while despite the arrests and warrants of the past few months. As far as he was concerned, he knew nothing about the Galley murder, and asserted that the Chater murder did not take place in his house, nor was he present at Harris's Well. However, the Attorney General, on studying the case in depth, decided that Mills senior was an accessory to murder, having allowed the shoemaker to be chained in his outhouse and being present when Chater was cut and abused there; accordingly he was arrested five days before Christmas 1748.

So thorough was the purge of smugglers that even Combleach, the gardener from whom Chater's murder party had borrowed the ladder, was examined by the authorities as he foolishly made it known that some of the persons in custody had told him they had murdered two informers. When Combleach was brought before the magistrates he made things much worse for himself by refusing to give satisfactory answers to the questions asked 'and idly and obstinately denied all that was sworn against him'. The authorities took a dim view of his uncooperative attitude and promptly committed him to Horsham Gaol on suspicion of being involved in the murder of Chater.

By the end of 1748 there were seven of the guilty men behind bars, plus Combleach for good measure. It was decided that the men in gaol should be tried, and the remainder not yet taken should stand trial as and when they became available. The persons concerned with law and order in Sussex were 'desirous of making public examples of such horrible offenders and to terrify others from committing the same crimes'. The noblemen and gentlemen therefore requested His Majesty to grant a special commission to hold an assize to try the offenders. It was suggested that Chichester was a sufficiently large city to accommodate the judges and all their train, and as 'it was contiguous to the place where the murders were committed, they thought it the most proper place for the assize to be held'. The government had finally been goaded into action by the events of the past few months. Now the law would have to be seen to be working in protecting the reasonably honest citizen from corrupt and depraved men, for the smugglers had reached such a degree of audacity that the authorities were seriously worried for the peace of the land.

His Majesty was pleased to agree to the request from Sussex; accordingly a commission passed the seals to hold a special Assize of Oyer and Terminer beginning in Chichester on 16 January 1749. The seven were to be tried for their terrible deeds committed almost a year ago. The charges against Combleach were set aside but he was remanded in custody and appeared in the trial as a Crown witness. At the next Horsham assizes he was acquitted of being an accessory after the fact and released. It seemed from the elaborate precautions taken that the authorities wanted to make this trial a public example of British justice or hatred of injustice.

On the morning of Monday 9 January, Jackson and Carter were taken from their Newgate cell, told to strip and forced to wash all over with vinegar as a precaution against the spread of possible infection caught in gaol. They were then lent a new set of clothes especially for their trial. The two of them were put in an open cart and taken under strong guard to Horsham, on the way collecting Richard Mills junior at Surrey Gaol. At Horsham they were joined in the cart by the other five, Combleach included, and thence were trundled off under heavy guard to Chichester, where they arrived, ominously enough, on Friday the 13th. On arrival they were all confined in one room except for Jackson, who was so ill that the authorities thought there was great danger of him not surviving to be hanged and so had him put in a separate cell where 'all imaginable care was taken of him in order to keep him alive'.

Despite their dire position the confined smugglers were in good spirits, no doubt gaining courage from their close companionship and keeping up their tradition of arrogance and indifference. 'They behaved very bold and resolute, and not so decent as became people in their circumstances.' They certainly had not lost their appetites, for 'they ate their breakfast, dinner and supper regularly without any seeming concern, and talked and behaved freely to everybody that came to see them'. Meanwhile the three judges assigned to hold this special assize were leaving London with their numerous servants and attendants as outriders. The judges, counsellors and principal officers filled six coaches, each pulled by six horses, an impressive and cumbersome legal cavalcade. The judges were the Hon. Sir Michael Foster, Kt, a judge of the King's Bench; the Hon. Edward Clive, a baron of His Majesty's Court of Exchequer; and the Hon. Sir Thomas Birch, a judge at the Court of Common Pleas. They spent the night of 13 January at the Duke of Richmond's house at Godalming. The next day the Duke entertained them for lunch at his hunting lodge in Charlton Forest, not far from the 'Centre Tree', where the smugglers had had their first council meeting before the raid on Poole.

On the Sunday before the trial was due to begin, the three judges went to the cathedral, accompanied by the Duke of Richmond, as well as the Mayor and Aldermen of the Corporation, to hear 'an excellent sermon, suitable to the occasion', preached by the Dean of Chichester, the Reverend Mr William Ashburnham. He chose as his text three rather obscure verses from the Book of Job, chapter 29:

> I put on righteousness, and it clothed me: my
> Judgment was as a robe and diadem,
> I was eye to the blind, and feet was I to the lame.
> I was father to the poor: and the cause which I
> knew not I searched out.

By the time he left the pulpit his congregation, however, was left in no doubt as to the purpose of his choice. The Dean disclosed to his congregation that Job was a man of great eminence because of his birth and the high positions that he held. Not only did he hold 'the supreme rule and government', he was also 'a principal magistrate of the place he dwelt in' and the integrity of his conduct was a pattern worthy of imitation. The Dean's eyes fell on the assembled judges in the front pews as he told the congregation of Job's great love of justice and his pleasure in exercising it. Many must have inwardly squirmed as he continued:

> So that if we wilfully connive at, if we suffer or neglect to correct abuses in the public, we do what in us lies to lessen our own security, and insensibly promote the ruin of our private interest and prosperity … Everyman … is both in justice and charity obliged to use his best endeavours of protecting the innocent from injuries and securing them from the oppression of bloodthirsty and deceitful men … It is our duty for everyone to exert the utmost of his strength to deliver the oppressed, and it is extremely criminal to be weary or faint in our minds for fear of the oppressors, or forbear to deliver those who are ready to be slain.

If the prisoners had been present to hear this sermon, even their uneducated minds would have told them that the likelihood of escaping the hangman's noose was extremely remote.

The Dean drove home this concept that God had given man the right to carry out justice by pointing out that the original end of government itself was that all persons should 'enjoy unmolested the fruits of their own industry and lead peaceable and quiet lives, in all godliness and honesty'. He continued by drawing attention to the miserable condition mankind would be in if there were no laws to protect society. Direct reference was made to the seven who were to stand trial the next day:

> The behaviour of some dissolute and abandoned persons which we have lately seen … may serve as a kind of specimen, to teach us what savage creatures they would be without it; what havoc and devastation they would make upon the earth were they set wholly free from the restraint of laws, and left to follow the imaginations of their own evil hearts without hindrance or control.

People in positions of authority were set there by God Himself,

> So that the peace and prosperity of nations is owing principally, under God, to the wise care and conduct of their rulers, and the prudent administration of government therein. Without this all those intolerable mischiefs must ensue, which men's unrestrained appetites and passions would produce, and which unavoidably break the bands, and are the sure destruction of all society.

And so the sermon went on.

Later the Dean's gaze and words once again fell directly on the state's representatives when he expounded that the scriptures informed them that magistrates were appointed to be 'the guardians of the public quiet' and that they had the sword of justice put in their hands for this very purpose 'to execute wrath upon him that doeth evil'. The Dean skilfully returned attention to the present day:

> It is a melancholy truth, which I can only publish and lament, that never was the vigilance and courage of the civil magistrate more necessary than in these evil days into which we are fallen: when to say nothing of the private vices that abound amongst us, an almost general licentiousness is practised throughout the Kingdom, against both the common reason and the common interest of mankind, and in defiance of all authority, whether sacred or civil.

This unhappy state of affairs was, in his view, the 'unavoidable consequence of that contempt of religion which is so prevalent in this degenerate age'.

Thus the Dean of Chichester encouraged and exhorted the judges to engage on the public's behalf and with the blessing of God 'if not to correct all the abuses of these daring and outrageous people, at least give check to their insolence, and keep them within modest bounds'. He concluded by leading the congregation in prayers which were ostensibly a humble request to God, who having created a peace and allowed a freedom from fear from England's enemies abroad should now turn His divine attention to 'repressing our disorders at home'.

The following morning between eleven and twelve o'clock, the three judges left the Bishop's Palace preceded by the High Sheriff of the County and made their way in a dignified procession to the Guildhall, where they were met by the Duke of Richmond and other members of the gentry and nobility of Sussex who had petitioned King George for the special assize. A grand jury of twenty-seven was sworn in and among them was William Battine, to whose house at East Marden Galley and Chater had set out almost a year before.

When the grand jury had taken their seats in the Guildhall, the audience of nobility, gentry, lawyers, clerks, labourers and townsmen in the public gallery, and the seven prisoners in the dock, all fell silent as the Honourable Sir Michael Foster rose to deliver a 'most learned and judicious charge'. He began by saying that this special commission was confined to enquiring into murders, manslaughters and felonies committed in the county of Sussex alone. Later on, when all hope for the prisoners seemed lost, their counsel Mr Staniford tried to gain an acquittal of the indictment by claiming that the place where Galley had died was not in the county of Sussex but in the county of Southampton. This ingenious legal quibble was dealt with by the prosecution, first by recalling the ever-obliging Steele to the witness box. Unfortunately he could not assist this time, for 'he had never heard, as he remembered, what county that place was in' where Galley had been pushed off his horse and presumed to have broken his neck.

Undaunted, the Crown produced another witness, John Aslett, one of the men who had exhumed the tidewaiter's body; he then proved that he was with Steele and some dragoons on Friday last and that Steele pointed down to the ground with a stick, and said,

> 'There the man died' that he [the witness] took particular notice of that place, and is sure it was in the parish of Harting in Sussex; that he now lives at Harting, and was born and bred just by, and had lived there ever since he was a lad, and served the office of surveyor and constable.

There was no way the smugglers, even with the assistance of legal pedantries, were going to escape the rope.

But to return to his Lordship's opening address, he drew the grand jury's attention to the fact that smuggling was not a modern evil:

> Dangerous confederacies … had been formed for many years past in Sussex and its neighbouring counties, for very unwarrantable, very wicked purposes; even for robbing the public of that revenue which is absolutely necessary to its support and for defeating the fair trader in his just expectations of profit … and this wicked practice had been supported by an armed force and acting in open daylight, in defiance of all the law, to the terror of his Majesty's peaceable subjects; and had gone so far in some late instances, as deliberate murders, attended with circumstances of great aggravation, in consequence of those unlawful combinations.

So the Hon. Sir Michael Foster went on, inexorably and eloquently implanting in the jurors' minds the only possible verdict of guilty. 'These things loudly call for the animadversion of the public.' Lest anyone in the dock had the faintest hope of reprieve because he was not actually present at the scene of a murder, as was the case with the two Mills, father and son, the judge made it perfectly clear that the prosecution wanted all seven to be turned off.

> When we say that the presence of a person at the commission of a felony will involve him in the guilt of the rest, we must not confine ourselves to a strict, actual presence, such a presence as would make him an eye or an ear witness of what passes. For an accomplice may be involved in the guilt of the rest, though he may happen to be so far distant from the scene of action, as to be utterly out of sight or hearing of what passes.

He went on to show how when armed parties assembled to run contraband and came up against the King's officers, an affray occurs and invariably serious injury or even death results. He concluded,

> I am very sensible, gentlemen, that I have been something longer than I needed to have been, if I had spoken barely for your information. But in this place, and upon this occasion, I thought it not improper to enlarge on some points. That people may see, and consider in time, the infinite hazard they run by engaging in the wicked combinations I have mentioned; and how suddenly and fatally they may, being so engaged, be involved in the guilt of murder itself, while perhaps their principal view might fall very far short of that crime.

With that the judge resumed his seat.

The two bills of indictment were then presented to the jury, one for the murder of Galley and one for the murder of Chater. Then the twenty Crown witnesses, including Steele, Race and Scardefield, were sworn in and went immediately to give their evidence before the jury, who had retired to the council chambers in North Street to study the bills of indictment. Eventually, the court was adjourned until nine o'clock the next morning. On reassembling on the following day, the jury, after the fashion of the time, returned the bills of indictment to court and the prisoners were duly charged. Six of them were put to the bar and Jackson, who was so ill that he was carried into the court sitting on a chair, was allowed to remain seated throughout the trial. The prosecutor arraigned Tapner, Cobby and Hammond as principals for the murder of Chater, and Carter, Jackson and the two Mills as accessories before the fact.

The massive indictment was full of imposing phrases designed to strike terror into the hearts of the accused:

> That Benjamin Tapner, John Cobby and John Hammond, together with Thomas Stringer and Daniel Perryer, not yet taken, not having the fear of God before their

eyes, but being moved and seduced by the instigation of the Devil, upon the 19th day of February, in the 21st year of his present Majesty's reign, with force and arms at the parish of Harting, in the county of Sussex, in and upon one Daniel Chater, being then and there in the Peace of God, and his said Majesty, feloniously, wilfully, and out of his malice aforethought …

And so it went on, finishing with a marvellous flurry of tongue-twisting invective:

The felony and murder aforesaid, in manner and form aforesaid, feloniously, wilfully, maliciously, and out of their malice aforethought, to do, perpetrate, and commit, feloniously, wilfully, and out of malice aforethought, did incite, move, instigate, stir up, counsel, persuade and procure, against his Majesty's peace, his Crown and Dignity.

To which indictment they separately pleaded not guilty. Jackson and Carter were further indicted in like manner for the murder of Galley, together with Little Sam, Little Harry and Edmund Richards, who were not yet taken. Their long-winded indictment ran to well over a thousand words.

After the indictment had been read to them, the prisoners were informed that they could challenge twenty of the panel of jurists, without showing cause; but if they challenged more, they must show a reasonable cause. No challenges were forthcoming and a petty jury consisting of twelve men was sworn in. The prisoners, after a consultation, agreed to be tried jointly in the Chater case, and the formidable legal battery of seven lawyers engaged by the Crown began their assault. The Recorder of Chichester, Mr Steele, opened the indictment and then Mr Henry Banks 'very judiciously and learnedly laid down the facts attending the murder'. Banks began by saying that he intended to prove that all seven were guilty of the charge and therefore all seven would be liable to the same judgment and punishment. He virtually demanded a verdict of guilty,

When I come to mention those aggravating circumstance of cruelty and barbarity, in the course of this trial; I doubt not but they will have all that effect upon the Gentlemen of the Jury, which they ought to have; to awaken and fix your attention to every part of this bloody transaction; and to balance that compassion which you feel for the prisoners, though they felt none for others. The effect I mean these circumstances should and ought to have, is, to clear the way for that justice, which the Nation expects and calls for from your determination and verdict.

Banks took the opportunity to make some general comments about smuggling:

Smuggling is not only highly injurious to trade, a violation of the laws, and the disturber of the peace and quiet of all the maritime countries in the Kingdom; but is a nursery of all sorts of vice and wickedness; a temptation to commit offences at first unthought of; an encouragement to perpetrate the blackest of crimes without provocation or remorse, and is in general productive of cruelty, robbery and murder.

It is greatly to be wished, both for the sake of smugglers themselves and for the peace of this country, that the dangerous and armed manner now used of running uncustomed goods, was less known, and less practised here.

It is a melancholy consideration to observe, that the best and wisest measures of Government, calculated to put a stop to this growing mischief, have been perverted and abused to the worst of purposes. Every expedient of lenity and mercy was at first made use of, to reclaim this abandoned set of men. His Majesty by repeated proclamations of pardon invited them to their duty and to their own safety. But instead of laying hold of so gracious an offer, they have set the laws of defiance, have made the execution of justice dangerous in the hands of magistracy, and have become almost a terror to Government itself.

Next, with painstaking attention to the horrific details, Banks revealed to the jurors how Chater was made drunk in the White Hart, whipped and abused when taken to Rake, chained in Mills's turf house at Trotton and finally taken to Lady Holt Park and thrown down the well. The following witnesses were called, who pieced together the whole bloody picture of the events of the previous February: Edward Holton of Havant, the Austin brothers, Robert Jenkes and five of the widow Paine's customers on that fateful Sunday. The seven accused, for the most part, kept silent, not questioning or contradicting the damning evidence.

When the witnesses had finished giving their evidence, the Crown rested its case. Mr Justice Foster told the prisoners it was now their turn to offer what they could in their own defence. He summarised for each the particular facts the evidence had charged them with and asked each separately what he had to say to clear himself. Tapner pleaded that he did not know they were going to kill the man and that Jackson and Richards threatened to kill him if he would not go with them; he denied that he had ever cut Chater's face. The judge, not waiting for the prosecution counsel to cross-examine, dismissed this weak defence himself by telling Tapner,

> Supposing he was threatened in the manner he insisted on, yet that could be no legal defence in the present case; and that in every possible view of the case, it was infinitely more eligible for a man to die by the hands of wicked men, than to go to his grave with the guilt of innocent blood on his own head.

Each of the others made similar desperate and pathetic pleas of ignorance of what was going on. Finally, in case there was still any legal doubt, the judge reiterated his remarks about the equal guilt of an accessory before the fact. With this final reminder, the jury retired.

'After some little consideration', they returned to give their verdict: Tapner, Cobby and Hammond were guilty of the murder, as laid out in the indictment, and Richard Mills senior, Richard Mills junior, Jackson and Carter were guilty as accessories before the fact.

All seven were returned to the gaol that afternoon and the next morning, 18 January, were told that a further appearance in court was required of them. Jackson and Carter were to be tried for their part, this time as principals, in the murder of Galley; and all were to receive judgment in the Chater case. The Crown prosecution counsel were anxious to convict Jackson and Carter as principals in the Galley murder, otherwise the accessories to that murder not already captured could not be convicted. The gruesome details of the previous day's evidence were reiterated and the same jury had no difficulty in arriving at a similar verdict. Thus Edmund Richards, Little Harry and Little Sam would be assured of a hempen cravat if and when they were apprehended.

There now remained the delivery of judgment. The prisoners were again brought before the bar and the judge asked them why judgment of death should not be passed on them. They did not reply. As if to wring every possible vestige of condemnation out of the case, the judge embarked on a further grim resume of their crimes:

> Deliberate murder is most justly ranked among the highest crimes human nature is capable of; but those you have respectively been convicted of, have been attended with circumstances of very high and uncommon aggravation.
>
> I hope your hearts have been long since softened to a proper degree of contrition for these things; and that you have already made a due preparation for the sentence I am about to pass upon you.
>
> If you have not, pray lose not one moment more. Let not company, or the habit of drinking, or the hopes of life divert you from it; for Christian charity obliges me to tell you, that your time in this world will be very short.

Then with chilling finality, Mr Justice Foster delivered the following words:

> Nothing now remains but that I pass that sentence upon you which the law of your country, in conformity to the law of God, and to the practice of all ages and nations, had already pronounced upon the crime you have been guilty of. This Court doth therefore award that you Benjamin Tapner, William Carter, John Hammond, John Cobby, Richard Mills the Elder, Richard Mills the Younger, and William Jackson, and each of you shall be conveyed from hence to the prison from whence you came, and thence you shall be led to the place of execution, where you shall be severally hanged by the neck, until you shall be dead, and the Lord have mercy on your souls.

The execution of the sentence was fixed for the following day. Jackson, Carter, Cobby, Hammond and Tapner were to be hanged in chains afterwards and on the Wednesday afternoon when they had returned from the court a person came to measure them in jail. The five were thrown in great confusion by this grisly measuring, but the two Mills seemed to be 'mightily pleased' that they were not going to be hung up afterwards to slowly rot away in the air and 'were contented to be hung only as common malefactors'. Jackson was still very ill and no doubt the fitting hastened his end, for he was so consumed with horror that he died within two hours of it.

Anti-Catholic feeling ran very high at this time, only four years after the Young Pretender Charles Edward Stuart had tried to seize the throne of England, and it must have been of some interest to the average Anglican reader of *Sussex Smugglers* to learn that Jackson

> professed the Romish religion some years before his death and that he died a Roman Catholic may very reasonably be presumed from a printed paper which was found carefully sewed up in a linen purse in his waistcoat pocket, immediately after his death, supposed to be a Popish relique, and containing the following words (in Latin and French) which translated read: Ye Three Holy Kings, Gasper, Melchior, Balthasar. These papers have touched the three heads of the Holy Kings at Cologne. They are to preserve travellers from accidents on the road, headaches, falling sickness, fevers, witchcraft, all kinds of mischief and sudden death.

During their last few hours the other condemned men were visited by several members of the Anglican clergy, who noted down their penitent last words. John Smyth, curate of St Pancras, Chichester, went to them at ten o'clock on Wednesday evening to give them the Holy Sacrament 'and during the whole time of my performing that office, they all behaved with great decency and devotion, especially Carter and Jackson'. Benjamin Tapner, aged twenty-seven 'before he was turned off; owned the justice of his sentence, and desired all young persons to take warning by his untimely end and avoid bad company which was his ruin'. John Cobby, a thirty-year-old carpenter, appeared to be very much dejected, and said little in gaol and nothing at the gallows, nor did John Hammond, a forty-year-old farm labourer.

On Thursday 19 January 1749, a great crowd collected on the Broyle, about a mile out of Chichester on the Midhurst road. The procession of condemned men under heavy guard was slow and solemn as they made their last journey on this earth. The time set for the mass turning off was two o'clock in the afternoon. As the hangman fitted the ropes, the men exchanged words among themselves and with the crowd. Carter cautioned the crowd against those courses which had brought him to such a shameful end. Tapner and Carter shook hands just before the cart pulled away. Richard Mills senior was unrepentant and protested his innocence to the crowd while his son seemed to be as little moved 'as the most unconcerned spectator' at what he was about to suffer. Old Mills managed to joke with the hangman to the jeers and cheers of the crowd. The halter used for the old man was so short that he was obliged to stand on tiptoe to reach it; and several times while his neck was being fitted into the noose he was heard to say, 'Don't hang me by inches.' Just before the whip came down on the horse's back and the cart jerked away, the two Mills seemed to offer up a prayer.

When the kicking and twitching had ceased, the bodies were cut down. Carter's was taken to Rake to be hung at the side of the Portsmouth road; Tapner's was taken to Rook's Hill, near Chichester; Cobby's and Hammond's were taken to the coast and hung up on the beach near Selsey Bill, 'where they are seen at a great distance both East and West'. The bodies of the Mills, father and son, having neither friend nor relation to take them away, were thrown into a hole for the purpose just by the gallows, and Jackson's corpse was tossed in as well.

The authorities erected a stone with the words:

> Near this place was buried the body of William Jackson, a proscribed smuggler, who, upon special Commission of Oyer and Terminer held at Chichester, on 16th day of January 1748–9 was, with William Carter, attainted for the murder of William Galley, a Customhouse Officer; and who likewise was, together with Benjamin Tapner, John Cobby, John Hammond, Richard Mills the Younger, his son, attainted for the murder of Daniel Chater; but dying a few hours after sentence of death was pronounced upon him, he thereby escaped the punishment which the heinousness of his complicated crimes deserved, and which was the next day most justly inflicted on his accomplices. As a memorial to posterity and a warning to this and succeeding generations – This stone is erected A.D. 1749

This sensational trial and the chained bodies on the gibbets had the desired effect. People were shocked out of their apathy and all classes were forced to consider the bitter harvest that years of tolerance, corruption and collusion had yielded. Even the genteel circles of high society at Bath were shaken by the murders, as John Collier, Surveyor General for the Riding officers of Kent, reported. He had gone there for the sake of his health and wrote to the Solicitor of Customs congratulating him on the successful outcome of a very difficult task:

> I well know the fatigue you have undergone in the prosecution and bringing to Justice the villains at Chichester … The trials thereon shocked everybody, and was the subject of discourse for some time in the public rooms, coffee houses and parade.

12

Further Murders and Trials

'He was turned off, crying to the Lord to receive his soul'

Early in 1748 a cruel and callous murder was perpetrated by the smugglers. It occurred on 28 January, seventeen days before Chater and Galley left Southampton on St Valentine's Day to ride to Mr Battine's at East Marden. But it was not until March 1749, two months after the Chichester trials, that one of the persons involved stood trial at East Grinstead Assizes indicted for the murder of Richard Hawkins of Yapton by 'violently assaulting, sticking, beating, whipping, kicking, him, the said Richard Hawkins over the face, head, arms belly and private parts of which wounds, bruises, kicks and stripes he instantly died'. The man in the dock was John Mills, son of Mills the Elder of Trotton. Within the space of twenty days he was to take part in two more killings of equal barbarity for, as we have seen, all three of the Mills family were involved in Chater's murder.

In the dock with John Mills was the landlord of the Dog and Partridge at Slindon Common, as well as a certain John Reynolds, who was accused 'of aiding, assisting, comforting and abetting the said John Mills, alias Smoker, and Jeremiah Curtis, alias Butler, Pollard, and Richard Rowland, alias Robb known as Little Fat Back (both not yet taken) in the murder of the said Richard Hawkins'.

The facts of the case demonstrate the inhuman way in which the smugglers secured fear and respect from the populace. Hawkins was murdered on suspicion of having stolen two bags of tea from a cache of run goods hidden near his workplace. As it turned out, he was probably innocent of the charge, for the anonymous historian of *Sussex Smugglers* reveals that when the smugglers checked again there was no tea missing. However, the story begins with a typically brazen public warning. Jeremiah Curtis and two others were sitting in a Yapton public house owned by a man called Cockrel, the brother-in-law of the man later murdered. As Henry Murril related to the jury at the East Grinstead Assizes over a year later, 'Curtis was very angry and said some rogues had stolen two bags of tea from him, and damn him, he would find out, and severally punish those concerned therein for, damn him, he had whipped many a rogue and washed his hands in their blood.'

The smugglers' fearsome reputation would ensure that this threat of vengeance would spread around the district in a matter of hours. To further encourage the discovery of the culprit, Curtis offered Murril five guineas if he could get the tea back or find out who had it. If money could not do the trick, Curtis declared that he himself would come sword in hand and find out the culprit.

The smugglers' suspicions fell on Richard Hawkins, who worked with Henry Titcomb, another farm labourer, in a barn near where the cache of run goods had been hidden. Fear must have gripped the two labourers when the door of the barn opened and in walked the dreaded smugglers, Jerry Curtis and John Mills. Curtis called Hawkins out to speak with him and, after exchanging words, the three of them rode away, leaving Titcomb fearful for his workmate yet relieved that he had not been questioned.

The three rode to Hawkins's father-in-law's inn at Walberton, where they drank together and talked. The conversation must have worried the suspect, for Mr Cockrel's servant, John Saxby, remembered, 'At going away, Mills bid Hawkins get up behind him which he at first refused, saying he would not, without making a sure bargain, they bid him get up for they would satisfy him, which Hawkins did.' His workmate Titcomb saw Hawkins riding in this fashion, pillion to Mills, along the road from Walberton toward Slindon.

At the Dog and Partridge earlier in the day, Curtis had been drinking with Thomas Winter alias Coachman. They had been talking business, presumably about run goods, and Curtis had gone off to get some money that he owed him. Winter remained all day at the inn imbibing spirits. In the late afternoon Little Fat Back, a servant of Curtis, arrived and asked if his master was there, and, as he was not, he settled down with Winter to await his arrival.

After dark, Curtis and Mills arrived with the unsuspecting suspect and apparently as soon as they had dismounted the mood changed, for Curtis called for his servant Robb and announced that they had a prisoner. The three of them, with the aid of Winter, took Hawkins into the parlour and began interrogating him again about the tea. Once again their accusations were strenuously denied. Curtis lost his temper and began swearing and issuing threats, at which point the landlord, Reynolds, came in and, sensing matters were about to get out of hand, advised Hawkins, whom he obviously knew quite well as he called him Dick, to confess as it would be better for him. Doggedly, Hawkins replied, 'I know nothing of it.' Reynolds left the room, not wanting to be party to any ugly incident.

The patience of the accusers was spent and Robb punched the unfortunate Hawkins full in the face, making his nose bleed, and threatened to whip him to death. Mills took sadistic delight in this and bayed his approval and again threatened the man. Even in this dire position Hawkins protested his innocence: 'If you whip me to death I know nothing of it.' Such infuriating stoicism prompted Mills and Robb to strip their victim, except for his thin undershirt, and then to whip him over the face, arms and body until they were out of breath, whereupon they took off their coats and whipped him again until he fell down. The unfortunate Hawkins writhed and cried out between each lash that he was innocent and 'begged them, for God's sake, and Christ's sake, to spare his life for the sake of his wife and child'. But his desperate cries simply served to goad them to greater cruelty. When they whipped him across his belly he instinctively pulled up his legs to protect himself and in so doing uncovered his genitals, 'Then they took aim thereat and whipped him so that he roared most grievously.' Not content with this, they began kicking him both in the genitals and belly. During this final agonising ordeal he called out the names of his father and son-in-law, the two Cockrels. Whether they were the true culprits or accomplices and his resolve to protect them had finally been broken, or whether these were simply the names that came to him in the hope of stopping the rain of lashes, no one will ever know. But on hearing these names the two incensed and drunken torturers rode off to get their next victims, leaving Winter and Robb to slump the bloody Hawkins into a chair.

After a while Winter and Robb saw that Hawkins had stopped breathing, whereupon Robb locked the parlour door and put the key in his pocket. Then he and Winter rode off to tell the other two what had happened.

At about ten o'clock that night Mills arrived at John Cockrel's public house at Yapton and upon entering called for some ale and ordered his horse to be stabled. The landlord took the horse round to the stables and there was confronted by Curtis, who demanded their two bags of tea which Hawkins had confessed that his brother-in-law had. Cockrel denied all knowledge of the tea's whereabouts and the denial had the effect of sending Curtis into a violent rage and 'he beat him with an oak stick till he was tired'. After this attack they made Cockrel get up behind one of them on a horse and they rode back to Walberton, where their victim's father kept a pub. They forced the elder Cockrel to join them and the four were riding toward Slindon when, about a mile before they reached the Dog and Partridge, they were met by Winter and Robb. They all dismounted and, out of earshot of the Cockrels, Robb and Hinter told the smugglers that Hawkins was dead. All except Curtis were thrown into confusion by the news. After a hurried conversation, the others persuaded Curtis that it would be best if the Cockrels were released. Curtis told the terrified pair that they could go home and added darkly that when they wanted them they would fetch them.

When the smugglers got back to the Dog and Partridge they found Reynolds, the landlord, highly agitated. He complained bitterly that they had ruined him; a corpse was now propped up in a chair in his parlour and what were they going to do about it. Curtis calmed him by vaguely suggesting that they would 'make amends'. The immediate problem was disposal of the body and the first place considered was a nearby well in a park belonging to a Mr Kemp. Once it had been thrown in they would spread the rumour locally that Hawkins had been taken across to France. Reynolds objected because the well was near his public house, so they carried the victim some twelve miles to Parham Park, which belonged to Sir Cecil Bishop. There in the dead of night they weighted the body with stones and threw it into Woodmills Pond, about a thousand yards from the big house.

The body remained submerged until the ropes tying the stones to the legs and arms rotted and the corpse floated to the surface three months later in April. It was discovered by one of the estate workers and Sir Cecil Bishop must have had more than an inkling of whom it was, for he immediately sent for John Cockrel the Elder to see if he could identify it. The body was mangled in a most terrible manner, having a hole in the skull, but he identified it as his son-in-law by 'the finger next to the little finger of his right hand being bent down to his hand', a peculiar and distinctive little deformity.

For a whole year there was a silence of terror throughout Sussex. No one was prepared to risk death from the smugglers by informing the authorities of what they knew, and undoubtedly there were many who knew something about the happenings on 28 January at the Dog and Partridge. However, the special Chichester Assizes of January 1749 demonstrated to the public that law and order had come to Sussex and that the authorities meant to crush the smuggling gangs. The public trial and subsequent hangings were visible proof of the authorities' determination and must have encouraged someone in the know to disclose anonymously that John Mills was one of the persons involved in the murder of Hawkins. On 31 January 1749 a proclamation was issued 'for the apprehending of several notorious smugglers that were concerned with the murder of Richard Hawkins of Yapton'. It promised His Majesty's pardon to anyone who should apprehend or give information about any of the offenders, even if such an informer was an outlawed smuggler, provided he was not concerned in any murder, or in breaking open His Majesty's warehouse at Poole. This proclamation was sufficient temptation for one such outlawed smuggler to risk the wrath of his desperate fellows in order to save his own neck. Not only did Jacob (also called William) Pring decide to inform the authorities, but he also agreed to deliver the notorious offender himself. If he saw him delivered safely to the authorities he would be sure that the betrayed could not take vengeance. For now it was clear that once the authorities had Mills in custody he would in due course be hanged.

Again a contemporary account is responsible for telling us how Mills came to be in the dock. Pring, although an outlawed smuggler, had not taken part in the Poole raid nor had he committed murder, so he contacted 'a great man in power' informing him that he knew Mills and that if he could be assured of his own pardon he would endeavour to take him, for he was pretty certain to find him either at Bristol or Bath, where he knew he had gone to sell some run goods. Obviously, Mills was back at his old business selling contraband, and it is interesting to note that although he lived in Sussex his wide-ranging business connections stretched as far west as the port of Bristol. Pring, having struck his bargain with the authorities, set off for the West Country on his mission of betrayal.

In Bristol he visited the haunts of the smugglers, the taverns and inns of the quayside, and eventually tracked down Mills, who was in the company of two other notorious smugglers, the Kemp brothers, members of the same gang and natives of the Hawkhurst district in Kent. As described earlier, Thomas Kemp was wanted by the authorities for escaping from Newgate. Lawrence was an outlawed smuggler, and both were wanted for being concerned in robbing a farmer called Richard Havendon in November 1748 at Heathfield in Sussex. It must be now all too clear that smugglers were not averse to other criminal activities such as highway robbery and armed burglary, particularly when, for one reason or another, there were few cargoes of contraband to run or sell. Mills had been involved in the same robbery along with Francis Doe, who later turned King's evidence and was instrumental in securing the death sentence for the two brothers at the same East Grinstead Assizes in March 1749. The Kemps were found guilty of taking Havendon's loose change of eleven shillings and sixpence, and afterwards, with violence, seizing and carrying away from his dwelling house £35, two silver spoons, three gold rings, a two-handled silver cup and a silver watch in a tortoiseshell case.

Having no reason to suspect Pring, who was a fellow outlawed smuggler, the three welcomed him into their company and began drinking and discussing their future plans in view of the fact that all of them were wanted for capital offences. Pring, as a friend, offered his advice; as they were all in the same boat, why not go back with him to his house in Beckenham in Kent, where they could lie low for a while? Then when things had quietened down, they could keep themselves busy at housebreaking and highway robbery. The plan met with the others' approval and, being so duped, they set out on the road for London.

Riding along they talked and bragged about their various crimes and by the time they reached Beckenham were in high spirits. Being outlawed men they had become wary and watchful; here in Pring's house they could drink, eat, rest and make future plans in complete safety. Quite unsuspecting, they allowed Pring to go off on his own while they remained and enjoyed his hospitality. He told them that if they were going to carry out robberies then he would go into town and fetch his other horse, a mare which was a very good one in comparison with the one he was riding at present which 'might bring him into danger in the case of pursuit'. He had played his part so well that the three left in the house had no idea of his true motives. Once out of earshot, the betrayer spurred his horse through the night towards Horsham.

He must have already made some sort of plan with the anonymous 'great man in authority' to be able to get assistance from the authorities if desired, for he rode straight to the house of an Excise officer called Rackster, who, with unusual alacrity, organised a posse of seven or eight armed men. Then they all set out for Beckenham, where they arrived in the dead of night. The unsuspecting smugglers were just about to demolish 'a fine breast of veal' when the posse burst in. The startled Kemps were quickly bound up but Mills put up some resistance and refused to be bound 'and being very refractory, they were forced to cut him with one of their hangers, before he would submit'. All three were taken to the county gaol, where also Robert Fuller and Jockey Brown were confined for alleged smuggling activities and other crimes. A writ of habeas corpus was secured, giving the authorities permission to take the five to East Grinstead to be tried.

Mills must have been in little doubt as to the verdict of the jury, for testifying against him was none other than Thomas Winter, alias Coachman, who had witnessed the horrible whipping session in the parlour of the Dog and Partridge. Winter had turned King's evidence sometime after the January proclamation, a move that must have been something of a gamble, for although not actually involved in the whipping, he most certainly was an accessory like the Mills family had been in the Chater case.

Among others who testified were the two Cockrels and the obliging Pring, who told the jury that, riding back from Bristol, Mills had told him how they had whipped Hawkins and had thrown the body in the pond in Parham Park. Mills's only defence was that when he and Curtis had left Hawkins he was alive and in the care of Robb and Winter and 'how Hawkins come by his death he could not tell'.

Counsel for Reynolds, the landlord of the Dog and Partridge accused of aiding and abetting, rose to defend his client. Counsel pointed out that Reynolds was 'no ways privy to or concerned in the said murder' and to confirm this, two witnesses were produced, William Bulmar and William Rowe, who were at the inn on 28 January 1748. They testified that Reynolds was with them all evening, 'excepting for when he went to draw beer for his customers in the kitchen'.

The judge summed up by reminding the jury that the facts were that clear against the prisoner Mills, who did not call any witnesses to disprove the Crown's case, that he must be guilty. As for Reynolds, the witnesses called on his behalf, if their testimony is to be believed, must surely prove that the defendant was not in the party that committed the murder, but that he was 'at home at peace in his own house when this transaction happened'. These seem incredible words from the judge, as it is more than probable that Hawkins's screams and the sickening cracks of the horsewhips must have been heard throughout the inn. However, the jury accepted the direction of the learned judge and without retiring found Mills guilty and acquitted Reynolds.

So John Mills was going to swing for the murder of Hawkins; he had also been indicted earlier for the Chater murder but had not been caught and now would only have been tried for that offence if he had been acquitted of the murder of Hawkins. As for Jeremiah Curtis, it was reported that he escaped to France and enlisted with the Irish Brigade at Gravelines. This was a mercenary band of soldiers, mainly Irish, who originally had fled from Ireland after William of Orange had defeated James II at the Battle of the Boyne; they fought in several wars on the Continent and by joining them Curtis added treason to his many other crimes. There is no record what became of him except that he escaped the rope of British justice.

As for Winter, he appears to have saved his neck by turning King's evidence, and Little Fat Back Robb was not yet taken, although presumably he had not followed his master abroad, for he had been seen and spoken to at the end of the previous January on East Grinstead common.

While awaiting his execution, Mills was asked to confirm the rumour that had been spread back in January that he had been on Hind Heath when the judges were coming from London to try his brother and father at the special Chichester Assizes, and that he and other smuggling associates were going to kidnap the judges and hold them ransom in exchange for those in Chichester Gaol. The authorities knew about this rumour but took pains to stress that not even the Hawkhurst Gang would dare to pervert the course of justice in this manner and denied that the judges were protected by a 'large party of horse, both thither and back again'. Mills admitted that he was on Hind Heath at the time in question with two companions but they were upon 'other business' and, in fact, committed three robberies that afternoon and evening. He and his companions had no intention of interfering with the judges, and so it appears that the rumour was false though the fact that it arose at all and spread so widely is symptomatic of the troubled times.

Mills refused to give the names of his companions that day on Hind Heath and remained loyal also to his other partners in crime. His opinion of Pring and Winter was very low.

He complained of the witnesses, that is, such of them as had been smugglers and had turned evidences, and said, that they had acted contrary to the solemn oaths and engagements they had made and sworn to among themselves, and therefore wished they might all come to the same end, and be hanged like him, and damned afterwards.

He was pressed hard to make an 'ingenuous confession' of all the crimes he had been guilty of, but he refused; he said he would tell them about the crimes that the authorities knew of but would reveal nothing else.

He acknowledged that if Winter and Robb had not met Curtis and himself on the road on 28 January and told them that Hawkins had died, then they would have 'beated the Cockrels well' if they had got them to the Dog and Partridge. So Hawkins's unexpectedly quick death saved the lives of his in-laws. Mills also admitted the murder of Hawkins but repeated that when he and Curtis left to get the Cockrels he did not think the man was so near death.

He acknowledged being present at Scardefield's when Daniel Chater's murder was discussed and also being in the gang that broke open the Poole Custom House; and also he was concerned with the two Kemps in going with 'crape over their faces' and robbing farmer Havendon of Heathfield in Sussex. Not only did he refuse to disclose the names of his friends involved in his many crimes, but on the gallows he put in a good word for Robb whom, he said, was a servant of Curtis and as such had been ordered by him to whip Hawkins. At this place of execution on a gibbet constructed specially on Slindon Common near the scene of the murder, Mills

> behaved himself much more sedate than he had done before, during the small time he had left under condemnation and prayed very devoutly … just before he was turned off, he declared he was sorry for his ill-spent life, and desired all young people to take warning by his untimely end … for the cruelties [of whipping Hawkins] and the murder of Chater, and all other wicked actions of his life, he hoped God would forgive him; declaring he died in peace with all mankind, and therefore hoped for forgiveness.

Whereupon the cart pulled forward and he was left to dance the hempen jig. Unlike his father and brother, he was hanged in chains and his decomposing body reminded passing travellers and labourers, in simple yet grisly terms, of the wages of sin.

At the same assizes at East Grinstead in March 1749, four other smugglers were tried for highway robbery and burglary offences. John Mills, as we have seen, was condemned for the murder of Hawkins while the landlord of the Dog and Partridge was acquitted. However, the latter did not escape justice completely as a footnote in the contemporary account reveals:

> Not-withstanding James Reynolds was acquitted of the murder, yet as it appeared very plain that he concealed the murder, by knowing the same had been committed by the prisoner and the others who stand indicted for the same, as being present at the consultation for concealing the murder, and of burying the dead body, and advising therein, and his wife also being present, they are both indicted for the same, and are to be tried at the next assizes.

Little Harry Sheerman was arraigned for the Galley murder; Jockey Brown for assault and robbery; Lawrence and Thomas Kemp for the Heathfield robbery; Robert Fuller for assault and robbery, and Richard Savage for robbery.

These six were smugglers by inclination but had been forced to turn to other means of late to earn a dishonest penny. Sheerman, it will be remembered, was a servant of Jackson and no doubt had been leading a fugitive's life since his master was taken back into custody in November 1748. His trial was a formality and the verdict of guilty was returned; he, it seemed, had had a vestige of compassion for their unfortunate victims, for when he shared round the nips of spirits on their first stop after leaving the White Hart at Rowland's Castle he was going to give Chater and Galley one apiece, but he testified that Richards, Carter and Jackson all swore they would blow his brains out if he did. Sheerman at his trial 'behaved with reservedness, but no way audacious, as some of the others were … he said he was never concerned in many robberies as numbers of the smugglers had been, and what gave him most uneasiness was the vexation he had brought on his wife and family'. He blamed Jackson for leading him away from his honest employment and was 'turned off, crying to the Lord Jesus Christ to receive his soul' at Rake on 20 March 1749, and afterwards his body was hung in chains.

Jockey Brown, the brothers Kemp, and Robert Fuller were all sentenced to death, whereas Savage, although sentenced to transportation, was ordered to be detained in order to be tried at the next assizes 'for another fact'. A contemporary recorder, with great thoroughness, gives an account of the behaviour and last words of all that were to be hanged. His description of one of these condemned prisoners shows clearly how the official action against smuggling in recent months had affected their lives:

> John or Jockey Brown, about 33 years of age, was born of honest parents in the county of Sussex, who gave him a tolerable education, but he had followed smuggling for many years, and being apprehensive of being taken up for that crime, he absconded from his home and lurked about; and being acquainted with Winter, commonly called the Coachmen … Fuller, and the two Kemps, his fellow sufferers, and many more smugglers, many of whom were outlawed, they all agreed to rob on the highway, and break open houses, in order to support themselves, being afraid to go a-smuggling, but they did sometimes when they could get anybody they could trust to take the goods.

Another assize was held in March 1749, this time at Rochester in Kent and similar charges of robbery were laid against four other smugglers who had resorted to a different crime during the last few months. Stephen Diprose, James Bartlet, William Priggs and Thomas Potter (the smuggler who had helped spring Gray and Thomas Kemp from Newgate) were all found guilty and sentenced to be hanged on Penenden Heath in Maidstone on 30 March. Again the damning evidence against them was supplied largely by informers, their erstwhile partners in crime. Thus the authorities maintained the anti-smuggling impetus initiated by the January Chichester trials. Potter, born in the infamous smuggling village of Hawkhurst, must have had little chance of following honest employment; he was only twenty-eight years old when he confessed that he

> had been a very wicked sinner, and that he had been guilty of all manner of crimes except murder; which he declared he never was; though he confessed he did design to murder the turnkey at Newgate, when he went to get Gray and Kemp out of gaol, but that he was glad it happened no worse than it did, and that he often prayed the man might recover of the wounds he gave him, and that when he heard he was well again, he said it gave him great satisfaction.

It is surprising what Christian and compassionate thoughts appear in the confession of a condemned man.

James Bartlet was probably present when an Excise officer, Mr Castle, was shot on Silhurst Common by a gang of smugglers when he and other officers had seized some run goods. As the accused would not give a positive answer 'there were some grounds to think he was concerned'. Stephen Diprose made the familiar confession: he had never entertained a thought of smuggling being a crime until now, and was sincerely sorry for all his past iniquities. He, like Priggs, blamed evil company for his downfall, and applying somewhat confused logic 'verily believed that the reason why so many notorious villainies and murders had been committed by the smugglers was owing to their not being safe in appearing publicly'.

As already seen, in April 1749 Kingsmill, Fairall and Perrin were capitally convicted at the Old Bailey Sessions for breaking open the Poole Customs House, thanks largely to the evidence of Steele and Race, who had, ever obligingly in the securing of their freedom, appeared as key Crown witnesses at three trials in the space of four months. Sometime before August of the same year, the authorities picked up Edmund Richards, an outlawed smuggler and a principal in the Galley murder, and at the Lewes Assizes, held towards the end of July, he too was capitally convicted. He was hanged on 9 August and afterwards gibbeted on Hambrook Common. Among the accounts of the Horsham gaoler Charles Cooper is a record of expenses, 'For carrying Edmund Richards to his execution at Hambrook Common, horse hire and guards, four days ... £4.0s.0d.' At the same assizes, John Geering, William Trower and Thomas Holman were also capitally convicted for being concerned with others in a smuggling affray at Goring in Sussex in which a dragoon named Bath was killed; John Blew, who actually fired the fatal bullet, escaped. In addition, Richard Double and George Chapman were brought to justice by a Riding officer called Drury from Robertsbridge, with the help of the Goudhurst Militia. They had been indicted for the murder of Thomas Carswell in 1744, a Riding officer, and for carrying off 2,000 lb of tea that he had seized from them. Both were hanged.

Thus in the space of eight months the vast smuggling organisation along the South Coast from Kent to Hampshire had been greatly depleted. At least twenty-three of their number had been capitally convicted and twenty-two had been hanged; Jackson, it will be recalled, died in gaol the night before he was due to be turned off. No doubt the remaining smugglers went in fear of their lives not only from the Custom and Excise officers, but mostly from the fear of being betrayed by one of their number. Law and order had confronted squarely the smuggling fraternity and delivered it many hard blows, but, although down, it definitely was not out, and other men gradually and cautiously took over where the Hawkhurst Gang had left off, because the financial incentive was still there. But none of the events of the succeeding years of open smuggling rivalled the bloody outrages of 1747 and 1748.

13

The Preventive Services

'Our sailors are in high spirits and full of money'

The descriptions of the smugglers and their activities must be seen against the background of the services engaged in thwarting them. Up to the middle of the eighteenth century, only a few Revenue cutters were owned and maintained wholly by the Customs Board; the majority were provided by outside contractors in exchange for a share of the profits arising from the seizures. Thus a cargo of a ton or two of tea with a market value of four shillings a pound provided ample incentive for the crews. Seized good were taken, along with the vessels, to the nearest port. There the cargo would be lodged in the Custom House until sold at auction. Half of the proceeds went to the Exchequer, the so-called King's moiety, and the other half was divided between the contractor and the crew of the Revenue cutter according to rank.

The goods seized were lodged mainly at Rye and Shoreham but the Custom Houses at Hastings, Eastbourne, Newhaven, Arundel, and Chichester were also used. The auctions were held periodically and within a couple of days, if the seized goods were perishable. In 1777, 80,000 lb of tea and 24,000 gallons of spirits were sold in this way at the abovementioned Custom Houses as well as enormous quantities of dry goods, including tobacco, currants, coffee, chocolate, gloves, lace, silks, nankeen cloth, striped cotton, muslin, calico, ribbon, neck cloths, counterpanes, caps and lappets, headdresses, hats, human hair, leather, ivory, wire fans, combs, ties, earthenware, muskets, pistols and sometimes the smuggling vessels themselves. The contract system was open to abuse, particularly by some of the cutter commanders who never failed to claim a share of the seizures even though they might not have been present when they were made. In 1787 a disciplinary inquiry involving one such absent commander led to the ending of the system in the following year. Thereafter, until the Royal Navy took over in 1831, the Revenue fleet was both owned and administered by the Board of Customs.

The Revenue vessels were constructed specifically for the job; they had to be fast in order to catch up with the smuggling vessels, and strong because they were expected to cruise in all weathers. For the most part they were cutters, sloop-rigged and clinker-built (using overlapping planks, which provided stoutness but at the expense of a few knots of speed). The typical cutter had a single mast with two headsails and a long bowsprit which could be run in and out. This long bowsprit made possible a great spread of jib-sails and was known as the 'illegal bowsprit' because the fitting of such was forbidden by law to any but a Revenue craft or a man-of-war. The smugglers, with no shortage of funds for building, also favoured the sloop-rig cutter and often their superb boats were carvel-built (with planks laid edge to edge to provide a smooth outer surface) as the smooth hull reduced the water resistance and gave a couple of knots of extra speed. The smuggling vessels could time their runs according to the weather and so it was a reasonable gamble to sacrifice stoutness for speed as the extra knots could make the difference between escape and capture. The pros and cons for each type of vessel produced some close and exciting sea chases as Captain Johnson of the Revenue cutter *Swift* related to the Old Bailey jury at the trial of the Poole Custom House smugglers, when he described how he overhauled the *Three Brothers* with its consignment of tea.

The crew of a typical Revenue cutter consisted of a commander, a mate (or two in the bigger craft), and a number of mariners, depending on its size. The commander and the mates held commissions as Customs officers by virtue of their posts. In addition, one or two of the crew would be similarly appointed as 'deputed mariners'. Much preventive work was carried out in open rowing boats away from the parent vessel and it was necessary that there should always be one member of a boat's crew who was authorised to act as an officer of Customs, in order legally to detain and search vessels, and to seize contraband. It was not until 1807 that the power to seize contraband goods was extended to soldiers and members of a militia.

The Revenue cutters were the one sector of the Preventive service that was never short of recruits, particularly after 1808 when provisions were made for the payment of compensation for injuries received on duty. If a mariner lost a limb he was paid £10 per annum in compensation and in addition the Crown undertook to pay the bill when the services of a surgeon were necessary. In the same year pensions were also introduced for the widows and orphans of men killed in action against smugglers. Pay and conditions for Revenue work afloat compared favourably with those in the merchant service, especially as large sums could sometimes be earned in seizure rewards. Another considerable inducement was the exemption from impressment into the Royal Navy, in the form of a written protection carried at all times whether ashore or afloat.

During the American War of Independence and the Revolutionary and Napoleonic Wars with France, the Admiralty often had to resort to press-ganging to man the ships of the Fleet. Other inducements were also tried. In 1782 a Bill was passed in Parliament offering a free pardon to all smugglers who voluntarily entered themselves as sailors on board any ship belonging to the Royal Navy, providing the penalty to which such persons were liable did not exceed £500.

The greater the penalty to which a smuggler was liable, the more men he had to provide to secure his pardon; for example, if the penalty exceeded £500 but was less than £2,000 he had to provide two able-bodied seamen and two landsmen. It must have been a difficult task to persuade friends and acquaintances to secure your pardon by enlisting in the Royal Navy with all its rigours and hardships. Another measure much hated by the smugglers was introduced in 1807. Rewards on a sliding scale, beginning with £500 for the first and going down to £200 for the third, were offered to the commanders of Revenue cruisers who in the course of the year ending 1 October 1808 had secured and delivered over to His Majesty's Naval Service the greatest number of smugglers. These rewards were additional to the normal £200 a head for each smuggler pressed into the Navy. The smugglers referred to this monetary offer as 'bloody money' and it served further to increase their hatred of the Revenue men.

During time of war, the government encouraged private adventurers to fit out ships on their own account and to capture enemy shipping, a particularly commendable idea as this harassed the enemy and cost the state nothing. The necessary funds were raised by London merchants who clubbed together to fit out a fleet of privateers, by contributing £10 shares by open subscription. In November 1755, when war with France was once again imminent, proposals were made by a group of merchants that if they could raise £1 million they could fit out 300 privateers of 300 tons each, which if stationed in squadrons would block up all the Western ports and the gut of Gibraltar thereby preventing France from communicating with her North American territories and leaving the Royal Navy at liberty to operate other schemes without interruption. The merchants argued that trade would continue and even expand and thus keep British manufacturers at work during the course of the war.

Although the sum subscribed was only £300,000, many new privateers with their necessary 'Letter of Marque' were introduced. They were authorised to board and seize any vessel under enemy colours encountered on the high seas and, more importantly from their point of view, they were entitled to prize money for doing so. Revenue cutters themselves had this same facility, but the Board of Customs was not enthusiastic on giving them 'Letters of Marque' as they feared that the Revenue work would take second place to the quest for prize money. The Board said they would not contribute to the cost of repairing any damage sustained in taking prizes of war (as opposed to smugglers); any such damage was to be made good by the commanders themselves. Rather optimistically they urged the commanders not to neglect their preventive duties, nor to leave their stations 'under pretence of looking for captures, it being our resolution to recall the permission hereby granted as soon as it shall be discovered in any instance to be prejudicial to our service'.

When a Revenue cutter or a privateer captured an enemy ship it was brought into harbour; the crew were put in prison and the vessel, together with its cargo, was sold to the highest bidder. The amount realised, plus a sum of 'head money' for each enemy alien in the captured crew, formed the basis of the prize money. After a small percentage had been deducted for expenses, the balance was paid over to the commander and crew. The share-out was in the following proportions, as laid down by a Royal Warrant dated 11 June 1795:

The Commander	14/32nds
The Mate	7/32nds
Deputed Mariner	3/32nds (exclusive of his share as Mariner)
Other Mariners	8/32nds

With these considerable prizes at stake, it was small wonder that Revenue cutters were anxious to get their share. If a smuggling vessel were taken the same procedure was followed but the prize money was less as the King's moiety had to be paid. Thus during wartime the position for the smuggler was further complicated; Revenue cutters still cruised, but they would get a greater reward for an enemy merchant ship than for a smuggling vessel. Privateers, both French and British, were another possible source of interference, thus the British smuggler had to run the gauntlet of both privateers and Revenue vessels.

The sailors of the time knew how to enjoy themselves on a run ashore when they returned to port with a prize. A letter from a writer in Bristol in the *Gentleman's Magazine* of 1744 relates,

> How nothing is to be seen here but rejoicings for the number of prizes brought into this port. Our sailors are in high spirits and full of money, and while on shore spend their whole time in carousing, visiting their mistresses, going to plays, serenading etc. dressed out with lace hats, tassels, swords with sword knots and every other jovial way of spending their money.

During the Seven Years' War, the French King published an edict to encourage his own privateers. The captors of any prize could claim the whole value of the cargo and vessel except one tenth which went to the French Admiralty. Bounties (between 100 and 225 livres) were also paid on guns according to bore and whether taken from a merchant vessel or a privateer or man-of-war. A bounty of 30 to 50 livres was also paid for each enemy prisoner; and privateers were exempted from all taxes on duties on provisions, artillery, ammunition and all other necessaries for their construction, victualling and armament. At the same time the French authorities received English smuggling vessels into their ports, where business was done with the smugglers who used British gold to purchase their cargoes. These exchanges went on during all the wars with France. Dr Barry O'Meara in his *Napoleon at St Helena* quotes the Emperor:

> They [the smugglers] have courage and ability to do anything for money. They took from France annually forty or fifty millions' worth of silks and brandy … During the

war they had a part of Dunkirk allotted to them, to which they were restricted, but as they latterly went out of their limits, committed riots, and insulted everybody I ordered Gravelines to be prepared for their reception, where they had a little camp for their accommodation. At one time there were upwards of five hundred of them in Dunkirk.

Napoleon's name is linked with a notable English smuggler whose exploits make exciting reading. Although some of his adventures seem to come straight out of an adventure tale for boys, Teignmouth and Harper in *The Smugglers* accord him considerable space. His name was Thomas Johnson and in 1798 he was captured and imprisoned for being a convicted smuggler. However, he escaped and despite a reward of £500 remained free until the following year, when he offered his services as pilot to the British forces sent to Holland. Being a smuggler, Johnson had an intimate knowledge of the coast on the other side of the Channel, and acquitted himself so well that the commander of the force, Sir Ralph Abercromby, procured a pardon for him.

This extraordinary character then plunged into extravagant living and soon was so heavily in debt that he resolved to go smuggling again. He managed to elude the Revenue forces but the bailiffs caught him and he was flung in the Fleet prison in London. One exceptionally dark night at the end of November 1802, he escaped once more and made his way to Brighton, where he crossed to Calais and went thence to Flushing. He was promptly flung in prison by the agents of Napoleon. Up to this point Johnson's patriotism had varied with his circumstances. Latterly he had been involved in gold smuggling as a guinea in France was worth a good deal more than on the English side of the Channel, particularly as the French needed gold to buy war supplies from neutral countries. Eight- and ten-oared galleys were used for the traffic, usually out of Deal in Kent. The money was slung in long leather purses around the oarsmen's bodies and anything up to £50,000 was carried. Despite assisting France's war effort in this way, Johnson is reputed to have refused Napoleon's offer of a very large reward if he would consent to pilot his invasion force. Johnson replied with suitable British indignation, 'I'm a smuggler, but a true lover of my country and no traitor.'

Again he escaped and, unaware that there was a pardon for him in England, he fled to America. On returning from that 'land of the brave and the free', he offered his services to the Fleet again as pilot, and was also involved in secret work. Lord St Vincent, the commander of the Fleet stationed off Brest, wrote in a letter dated 8 August 1806, 'The vigilance of the enemy prevented Tom Johnson from doing what he professed.'

Johnson soon seems to have returned to his original profession of smuggling, for in 1809, when the unhappy Walcheren expedition was about to be dispatched, he once more offered his services as pilot and once again were accepted, with the promise of another pardon for lately accrued offences. He duly piloted the expedition, to the entire satisfaction of the government, and received his pardon and a pension of £100 a year. The next episode in his eventful life was as commander of a Revenue cutter, but perhaps his greatest claim to notoriety came when he was approached by the powerful friends of Napoleon, exiled at St Helena, to assist them in springing the banished Emperor from his open prison. It was said they offered him the sum of £40,000 as down payment, and a further large sum if the attempt was successful. Johnson's patriotism seemed directly related to the size of the payment, for this time he accepted the offer and was working on the construction of a submarine (possibly it was this invention that Lord St Vincent was referring to in his letter of 1806) when the Emperor, somewhat inconsiderately, died. The enigmatic Johnson continued his submarine experiments, building one to the order of the Spanish government and conducting underwater trials in it between London Bridge and Blackwall, once coming very close to death when the craft caught in the cable of a vessel lying in the Pool. 'Captain' Johnson, as he was generally styled, died at the age of sixty-seven, not by the hand of an enemy agent nor suffocated in his prototype submarine, but peacefully in bed in his house in Vauxhall Bridge Road.

But what about anti-smuggling activities inland? Ashore the Preventive service was still battling to suppress the contraband trade which, after a lull following the official successes in 1749, was now beginning to increase again. This resurgence is reflected in a report from Arundel in Sussex sent to the *Gentleman's Magazine* in 1757. It tells of a 'sharp skirmish' between a gang of smugglers and Customs men aided by dragoons in which one of the soldiers died and several were wounded. The smugglers were moving three or four tons of tea, and lost about a quarter of it. The writer comments that this was 'the first material resistance since six were hanged by the special commission some years ago'.

Pay in the Preventive service was still poor, but during the middle years of the century several schemes were put forward to provide compensation for injury or death while on duty. One writer wanted 3*d* in the pound to be deducted out of officers' pay for a fund for their widows, while another argued that the pay should be increased and that the bachelors in the service would be more likely to get a wife if she was assured of £10 per annum in the event of widowhood. By the 1780s pay and conditions had improved in the service and compensation for an injury and all medical expenses were paid for. In addition, a pension was payable to the widow of an officer killed on active service.

Around 1781 there began the career of another interesting character, who earned for himself not only a reputation for courage and originality but also a considerable fortune. He was Mr Walter, the Chief Revenue officer at Horsham in Sussex. His zeal and activities extended over the greater part of Sussex and Surrey, and under him he had two equally dedicated and industrious officers in Hubbard and Jenden, and sometimes the assistance of twenty dragoons. He had also a network of paid spies and informers who kept him supplied with information about where and when runs were to take place. These latter were known as 'bush officers'. Walter enjoyed a brilliant run of successes, and around 1783 he organised and trained his own troop of men, all properly mounted, accoutred and armed. Dressed in a 'handsome uniform of blue and silver, with round laced hats', this civilian force was known as 'Walter's men' and became hated and feared by the smugglers in Sussex.

Large seizures, mainly of contraband tea and brandy, were made every month by Walter's men, but it is significant that very few smugglers were taken and committed to gaol. The inference is that the success of Walter and his troop had implanted in their minds a regard for the old saying that 'you never bite the hand that feeds you'. Walters himself was reputed to be making between £4,000 and £5,000 a year, a colossal sum for those days. The seizures were taken to his home at Horsham and were sometimes disposed of there, but most of the goods were usually sent to the authorities in London. The 'fair trade' price of tea at this time was from 6s to 10s a pound according to the grade, and the profit involved can be understood when it is remembered that Walter dispatched sometimes as much as 200 bags of tea (about two tons) in a month.

But it must not be overlooked that these ample rewards were not achieved without enduring many defeats and taking great risks, for in addition to the direct antagonism of the smugglers there was the opposition of a large number of people who dealt in or received free trade goods, including some members of the landed gentry. At the Horsham Assizes, 22 July 1782, an action for trespassing was brought against Walter by a tradesman at Hurstpierpoint. The Customs officer had forcibly entered the tradesman's house and seized some smuggled tea, and his action was defended on the ground that it was his duty to seize all smuggled goods and it was legal to do so by any means, but the jury found otherwise and gave a verdict for the plaintiff for £25 plus costs.

Walter's subordinate officer Jenden was also a very courageous officer. On 7 June 1787 with some of Walter's men he tackled a large gang of smugglers on the beach near Hove and charged them sword in hand. One of the smugglers, called Bonny, was killed by Jenden, who slashed his broadsword across his head and split it open. Three other smugglers were wounded. This bold and bloody affray resulted in 167 casks of spirits in the King's warehouse, and Jenden in the dock, accused of wilful murder, for at Bonny's inquest the jury, consisting of pro-smugglers, decided that the officer should be put on trial at the next assizes at Lewes. Here Jenden was found guilty of murder and sentenced to be hanged at Horsham on 3 August and his body to be dissected and anatomised.

An observer at the trial wrote that Jenden did not seem to be much affected by his death sentence. His composure is explained by the fact that such a verdict had been anticipated by the authorities, who produced in court a respite during the King's pleasure. On 10 September a free pardon arrived and Jenden was set free.

Walter's men and the methods they employed did not commend themselves to everyone, as we have seen; even people in authority had mixed feelings about them. In June 1784 the Earl of Surrey (later Charles, the 11th Duke of Newcastle) and Mr Beckford, both of whom had just been elected Members of Parliament for Arundel, came through Horsham on their way to London. It was said that the Earl, having heard so much of the doings and successes of Mr Walter and his men, sent a polite message that he would like to see them mounted and accoutred at Horsham, and they were accordingly drawn up on parade for that purpose. His lordship duly inspected the troop, appeared much pleased with what he saw and was said to have expressed his entire approval of Mr Walter's plans. Afterwards he inspected the stock of seizures and presented the men with something handsome to drink his health. This was the story going about Horsham among the townspeople, who took pride in Walter's daring deeds.

However, their pride was somewhat dented afterwards when his Lordship denied that he had sent a request to see Walter's men. A contemporary account puts the record straight:

> The fact is that Mr Walter's men being mounted and accoutred, the Earl of Surrey was desired to look at them which his Lordship did from the same motive which would have induced him to look at a collection of wild beasts had his Lordship been requested so to do by their keeper. His Lordship did not express his entire approbation of Mr Walter's plan, but he did express to his friend Mr Beckford, his apprehension of the use which might be made of a body of armed men under no regular and legal discipline.

Mr Walter and his 'wild beasts', despite the Earl of Surrey's apprehension, continued to operate until about 1790, much to the chagrin of the smugglers, who looked upon themselves as the aggrieved party and the Preventive men as interlopers and thieves.

Despite the efforts by the authorities to combat the trade in duty-free goods, the fact remained that the duties were such that it remained profitable to evade the payment of them. Even though the Preventive service was becoming increasingly efficient and attracting a better standard of personnel, the incentive to smuggle remained strong; the potential profit was so great that it was worth the risk of being caught. Even when the smuggler was apprehended and his goods seized, there was often so much money involved that the smugglers invariably tried to recapture the contraband.

One such incident occurred in February 1780. Joseph Nicholson, Supervisor of Excise at Canterbury, with a number of men made a large seizure of geneva at Whitstable. He decided to take the goods to Canterbury and lodge them in the King's warehouse until they could be condemned and auctioned. In order to protect the contraband, he arranged for a corporal and eight dragoons of the 4th Regiment of Foot to accompany him on his journey out of Whitstable. Unfortunately he was followed by a 'very numerous body of smugglers, upwards of fifty of whom had firearms, who, without demanding the goods, fired upon the party, by which two dragoons were killed upon the spot, and two more dangerously wounded'. The geneva was recaptured by the smugglers, who made off leaving the bloody soldiers in the road.

The authorities issued the usual promise of a pardon to any person who would come forward and name his accomplices and a reward of £100 was offered by the Commissioners of Excise and another £50 by Lieutenant Colonel Hugonia of the 4th Regiment of Foot. Only one of the culprits seems to have been caught; he was John Knight, a dredger, who was apprehended soon after in Whitstable. He was tried and convicted at Maidstone Assizes, hanged on Penenden Heath, and gibbeted afterwards on Borstal Hill, where the incident took place.

Whitstable was by no means the most notorious smuggling port. Deal probably far excelled it for iniquity. In the days of sail, Deal was a bustling seaport as the Downs between the shore and the Goodwin Sands provided a comparatively safe anchorage from all winds except a southerly gale. The town was a vast storehouse for the sailor in which he might buy anything from anchors and cables down to 'salthorse' and ships biscuits. It was also a Mecca for smugglers. William Cobbett described it 'as a most villainous place. It is full of filthy looking people … I was glad to hurry along through it, and to leave its inns and public houses to be occupied by the tarred and trousered, and blue and buff crew whose vicinage I always detest.' The town had achieved notoriety at the beginning of the eighteenth century when on the night of 26 November 1703 a terrible gale swept thirteen men-of-war, containing Admiral Beaumont and 1,200 officers and men, onto the Goodwin Sands. Most were drowned as the Deal boatmen, formerly noted for their courage and fearlessness, were more concerned with booty and plunder from the smashed ships than rescuing many of the sailors who had taken refuge on the sands as it was low tide. Daniel Defoe wrote a poem entitled 'The Storm' which begins:

> Those sons of plunder are below my pen,
> Because they are below the names of men.

And he indicts them for leaving the sailors to drown with the next tide. He concludes:

> And if I had any satire left to write,
> Could I wish suited spleen indite,
> My verse should blast that fatal town,
> And drowned sailors pull it down.
> No footsteps of it should appear,
> And ships no more cast anchor there,
> The barbarous hated name of Deal shou'd die,
> Or be a term of infamy.
> And till that's done, the town will stand
> A just reproach to all the land.

Thomas Powell was the Mayor of Deal and offered 'these callous wretches', the Deal boatmen, five shillings per head and then he and his mercenaries took the

Customs boats by force and managed to rescue two hundred of the shipwrecked sailors. Powell looked after them, paying for their food and lodging out of his own pocket; he buried the dead and gave the survivors their travelling expenses. A writ of libel was issued by the townspeople of Deal against Defoe because of his poem, but there is no record of what became of it.

Deal's dubious reputation continued throughout the century and in 1783, just before the Peace of Versailles, the town once again was in the news. The authorities received information that 1,500 casks of smuggled spirits were being harboured in the town's warehouses and the Excise officers of Canterbury decided to raid the town and condemn the spirit. They were supported by forty-seven light dragoons under Captain Perryman of the 38th Regiment of Foot. On the evening of 8 February, the small army of soldiers and Revenue men arrived on the outskirts of the town, but the smugglers had been tipped off and they fired on the interlopers. In order to harass the soldiers, cables were pulled across the streets and in the darkness their horses stumbled and shied; the soldiers and Revenue men were forced to retreat. But not before they had broken open one warehouse and seized a quantity of brandy, geneva and raw coffee. The casualties of this incredible sniping battle in the dark between the forces of law and order and the smugglers were two dragoons wounded and one horse, which had to be destroyed. The casualties among the smugglers were not known. The usual pardon was offered as well as a £100 reward but there is no record of anyone turning informer.

In the report on smuggling presented to Parliament later in the year 1783, George Bishop wrote, 'The town of Deal at present is a free port for this pernicious trade.' Pitt was determined to make an example of the smugglers in Kent and, mindful of the insolent rebuff the dragoons and Revenue men had experienced there, he chose to vent his spleen on the East Kent town. The opportunity arose in January 1788 when a series of heavy gales forced the Deal men to pull their boats up on the shore. A whole regiment of dragoons was drafted into the town and the sneering looks of the inhabitants turned to frustrated disbelief as the troops proceeded to pour pitch over all the boats in sight and set light to them. Because the military force was so great 'the inhabitants were obliged to remain silent spectators, and dared not attempt a rescue'.

Not all the incidents between smugglers and Preventive men were brutal and unpleasant. The stories may now have passed into folklore but their beginnings contained an element of truth. The first story closely resembles that of the Wiltshire moonrakers. Tubs were sometimes weighted down and sunk in ponds as a convenient hiding place with a view to them being collected at a later date. One moonlit night some smugglers were raking a pond to recover their contraband when they were discovered by an Excise officer. They immediately pretended to be simpletons and told him they were trying to rake to the side the great cheese that was floating in the pond. On another occasion a Riding officer on the coast, who was much disliked for his overzealous activity, was captured by a gang of smugglers who blindfolded him and made out they would throw him over the cliff.

They left him holding on by his fingertips (reminiscent of the blinded Gloucester in *King Lear* on the cliffs at Dover) and he remained like this for over an hour, in agonies of terror screaming for help and straining every sinew to maintain his hold, till at length the blood in his arms seemed to solidify to lead; his strength failed, his brain reeled at the thought of the rocks many feet below, and he was on the point of letting go in despair when, as a last effort, he released one hand, tore the bandana from his eyes, turned his head with horror and beheld … the bottom of a chalk pit within a yard of his feet! It is interesting to note that in both stories the Preventive man is duped and the folk heroes are the smugglers.

As recorded, Pitt made determined efforts to combat smuggling during the short peace that existed between signing the Treaty of Versailles in 1783 and the declaration of war by Revolutionary France ten years later. His suppression of smuggling would have had a more lasting effect if political events had not forced him to increase the tax on tea and other commodities once again. For virtually the whole period between 1793 and Napoleon's final defeat at Waterloo (the Peace of Amiens was very short-lived), Britain was at war with France, and the Preventive services both ashore and afloat were stretched to the limits. However, in 1809, despite the pressures of war, the waterguard was reorganised. The coast of England and Wales was divided into three districts, each of which was placed under an inspecting commander. The districts and complements were as follows: London to Land's End, 23 cruisers and 42 Preventive boats; Land's End to Carlisle, 10 cruisers and 13 Preventive boats; and London to Berwick, 4 cruisers and 13 Preventive boats.

This new force, called the Preventive Waterguard, helped to close the gap in the overall efficiency between the sea- and land-based Preventive service, but the prohibitions and heavy taxes consequent upon the war meant that smuggling remained profitable and it was not until after peace had come to Europe that the British government made another determined effort to suppress the infamous traffick.

14

The Coast Blockade

'The men … are driven like slaves to their duty with the cat at their backs'

The defeat of Napoleon at Waterloo meant that, in the succeeding weeks and months, thousands of servicemen began returning to Britain to be discharged. In the Navy alone, nearly 150,000 men had been persuaded or press-ganged to join up in order to blockade the French continental ports and defeat the French fleet. A great number of these sailors left the service at the end of hostilities to return to a way of life that promised drudgery if they were fortunate enough to get a job, and poverty and destitution if they were not. It was not surprising that many emigrated and it is recorded that by May 1816, 5,000 ex-sailors had gone to America. Many others reverted or drifted into smuggling, for a dishonestly earned shilling was good enough to buy bread. The authorities, although thankful that a long and costly war had ended, were disturbed by the numbers of idle ex-servicemen who, according to a Treasury minute of 1816, 'will be the ready instruments of those desperate persons who have a little capital and are hardy enough to engage in the traffick of smuggling'. What is more, the authorities now had the time to deal with internal abuses. So the fifteen years from 1815 to 1830 saw the bloody end of open and large-scale smuggling operations. The year of Waterloo was the critical turning point in the history of open smuggling in Britain; for slowly thereafter, ingenuity, concealment and deception began to replace force, boldness and corruption.

Smuggling had continued all through the war with France but with the cessation of hostilities a dramatic increase occurred. The existing Preventive service was woefully inadequate and any attempt to interfere with the activities of the smugglers, many of whom were hardened in the school of war, met with abuse and, at worst, injury or death. The Riding officers particularly were reduced to their not unfamiliar role of merely observing the runs, being impotent to do anything about them. The government, under Robert Banks Jenkinson, Earl of Liverpool, realised that now was the time for determined action to suppress the trade, and he made the third major attempt – Walpole and Pitt had both tried in the past – to end the smuggling on such a massive scale.

In view of their successful operations against the French, the Admiralty put forward a plan suggested by Captain McCulloch of HMS *Ganymede* to establish a blockade off the coast between Dungeness and the North Foreland. Not only would this expedient put down smuggling, but it would also prevent a number of sailors from being discharged. The plan was adopted and Captain McCulloch was assigned a force under the orders of the Admiralty which was to take the place of the Preventive service in that area. At the same time, the Treasury decided that the efficiency of the Revenue cruisers would be greatly increased if they too were placed under the Royal Navy's watchfulness and discipline. Accordingly, HMS *Ramillies*, of seventy-four guns, was stationed in the Downs while HMS *Hyperion*, of forty-two guns, was stationed at Newhaven. The former ship had last seen service in the American war under the command of Sir Thomas Masterman Hardy, during which the ship narrowly escaped destruction by torpedoes on two occasions. Later, this force at the east end of the Channel was augmented by the frigate HMS *Severn*. Some of their crews were landed and split up into detachments or 'boats', each boat's crew being allocated to a particular station under the command of a Naval lieutenant. The men were frequently quartered in the Martello towers recently built for coastal defence, and each station was responsible for a 'rolling guard' on its sector of the coast, and for a shore patrol in bad weather. Before long the Coast Blockade was extended to Hampshire and Dorset.

The placing of the Revenue cruisers under Admiralty control did not prove successful. In 1821 a Commission of Inquiry expressed the opinion that the efficiency of the vessels protecting the Revenue was by no means proportionate to the expense of maintaining them. It recommended that the number be greatly reduced, and that they, as well as the Preventive Waterguard, be again placed under the control of the Customs, as 'such a course would not only tend to efficiency by placing all the different forces employed for the prevention of smuggling under one authority, but would also render it possible to make considerable reductions and effect substantial savings'. Other suggestions were that the title of Preventive Waterguard be changed to 'Coastguard', and that this body should form the principal force for the prevention of smuggling; and that the land force consisting of Riding officers should be renamed the Preventive Mounted Guard and should be auxiliary of the Coastguard. The Treasury accepted all these recommendations and by a minute of 15 January 1822 the whole of the Preventive staff of Great Britain was placed under the Board of Customs, with the exception of the Coast Blockade. By this same minute new appointments were to be made to the Preventive Mounted Guard only from cavalry regiments, numbers were to be increased and the officers were to take orders from the captain of the nearest boat. At that time the staff, excluding the men on the naval vessels, consisted of 157 Riding officers, 1,738 officers and men of the Preventive Waterguard, 1,650 officers and men on the cruisers, and 1,276 officers and men on the Coast Blockade, a total of 4,821. There were 59 Revenue cruisers assigned to the coasts of England, Wales and Scotland, and 11 to the coast of Ireland.

The Coast Blockade, as might be imagined, was not a popular service. The people of the South Coast detested the way that a brutal force of outsiders was being used to suppress their trade. The blockade service attracted men of the lowest type, ignorant, uncouth and fond of drink, but who proved ideal for working unsocial hours in unpleasant weather and in meeting force with force, for the one thing they respected when on duty was the cat-o'-nine-tails.

Recruitment was difficult because of the bad reputation the force had acquired.

> The role is thus filled, for the most part, if by blue-jackets, by 'waisters' [the least intelligent of ship's crew], or which is more frequent, by unskilled, though hardy, Irish landsmen, whose estrangement from the sentiments, habits and religion of those placed under their surveillance seems to point them out as peculiarly adapted for a service whose basis consists in an insidious watchfulness over others, and a hostile segregation from their fellow men.

McCulloch, the commanding officer, was nicknamed 'Flogging Joey' by his men because for the slightest offence they would be sent off to the ship for a 'dusting down'.

The brutality that existed in the service is described in a letter of June 1821 sent to the *Sussex Advertiser* from an eyewitness:

> Sir, I cannot resist the impulse of human nature in communicating to you, for the benefit of the poor suffering men, deeds fit for the barbarous countries of Africa only in their savage state. The Coast Blockade on the Kent and Sussex coast had been made the subject of the observations and the animadversions of several members of Parliament … with a view to the entire abolition of such scandals; but success had not attended these efforts because it had been very evident to Government that the system has in a great measure checked smuggling on this part of the coast, although at an enormous expense. The men who compose the great body are driven like slaves to their duty with the cat at their backs, and for the least deviation from the strict line of duty are thrown into the hold, ironed, and kept there until the pleasure of the Commander be known. Would you believe it. There were no less than twenty-six of these poor creatures tied up yesterday and flogged on board the ——. Their cries were piercing and reached Rye … They are human beings; but if brutally governed they themselves become brutal.

This letter prompted an indignant reply wherein the writer stigmatised it as an attempt to prejudice public opinion against the Coast Blockade with a view to its abolition, which, according to the editorial comments thereon, 'would indeed be a day of Jubilee for the smugglers'. The reply further pointed out, in disproof of the accusations of inhumanity, that the officer commanding the vessel where the barbarities were alleged to have taken place was of 'tried character and humane disposition'. However, there seems little doubt that although some of the accusations against the Blockade were exaggerated, the system of discipline at this time in both the Blockade and the Royal Navy was very harsh. Some of the men wounded themselves in an attempt to procure their discharge, as Captain Mingaye of HMS *Hyperion* reported in November 1826.

But undoubtedly the Coast Blockade was proving an effective force despite its many hardships and setbacks. Their success forced the smugglers to resort to either organising fewer, but larger, groups of men, each section of which had an appointed job, or else employing methods that did not rely on the use of force and superior numbers. These so-called 'scientific' methods of smuggling were rarely successful for very long because as soon as a new method had been detected by the authorities, details of it were sent to London and all outports were notified in due course. The ingenuity of the smugglers was matched by the perspicacity of the Customs officer.

A directive from Custom House dated 17 January 1820 describes the cutter *Lavant* of Chichester recently seized

> by means of her having been fitted with an entire additional bottom outside of and under the old bottom … leaving a space of about two feet for the reception of goods … which concealment was detected by laying the cutter on shore, when she appeared much deeper outside than inside … observing that if any vessel of the afore-going description should be met with at sea, the discovery of similar concealments would be most likely to be made by trying the depth of the pump, which of course goes down to the lowest bottom.

Tobacco from Guernsey was discovered concealed in flour bags, while shops in Flushing were offering for sale tobacco made up into ropes 'from the size of a hawser down to ties for sails and which upon being slightly washed with rum has every appearance of being hempen rope'. Other methods of concealment employed were rocks apparently on board as ballast, but in fact were found to be hollowed out and inside were barrels of spirits. Bandana handkerchiefs were discovered in the false bottom of cabin bunks and one enterprising smuggler endeavoured to bring in silks concealed within two hams.

> The meat and bones thereof were scooped out very clean, except at the knuckle and the extremity of the thick end, the skin was then lined with calico, the silk packed very hard in paper and oil, silk deposited within it and the vacancies between the packages stuffed with rags to plump them out, the orifice was then very neatly closed and the whole rubbed with dirt and sawdust, so as effectually to conceal the aperture.

This painstaking method was discovered in 1822 and, notwithstanding its detection, showed that there was still sufficient profit to be made on small quantities of silk.

Another practice which became commonplace with the increased vigilance and efficiency of the Preventive service was that of weighting the tubs with sinking-stones, dumping them overboard when approaching the shore and leaving them attached to a recovery line tied to a buoy on or close to the surface. In this operation, known as 'sowing the crop', the tubs were harvested later at an opportune time with the aid of a grapnel or 'creeping iron' dragged along the seabed. The Preventive boats took to rowing offshore in likely spots and dragging a grapnel in the hope of hooking a recovery rope. Sometimes this was not necessary because in rough weather the 'crop' might be spewed up on the beach, where invariably it was the local coastguard who spotted it first. Usually the barrels gave adequate protection from the seawater and the spirit could remain submerged for several days without being tainted by the salty water. However, if the barrel was faulty or the 'crop' left too long, the spirit became infected and the resultant 'stinkibus' was not fit to drink.

The increasing success of the Preventive service in reducing the scale of open smuggling was further assisted by a network of paid informers who kept watch in all the Continental ports used by British shipping, and they were in constant communication with Custom House in London. If the information supplied by the European contact contributed to the apprehending of the vessel once it arrived in British waters, then the informer expected his share of the reward. The Board of Commissioners received a letter from Amsterdam dated 17 March 1817 informing them,

> A vessel is charting from this city loaded with 600 tubs of gin and in order to conceal the gin, she is loaded with timber even upon deck. The secret entrance is in the forecastle to the hold … Also on board is a great quantity of French silk and bandannas, and 500 lbs weight of snuff.

Another letter was received from Jersey telling the Board that a small schooner named the *Diamond* from that island, ostensibly laden with potatoes, was also carrying considerable quantities of tea, tobacco and silk. This ship and others like her would hang around in a South Coast port supposedly waiting for a favourable market price but in reality dispersing its smuggled goods.

A strict watch was still kept at the ports for people trying to take machinery or trained workers out of the country. The Customs officers were not always successful in preventing this. An informer at Calais reported in 1819 that four lace machines had arrived in France, smuggled across the Channel from Leicester by a man named Paine. The informer warned of the dire consequences of this: 'as soon as the machinery arrives in this place, it is to be conveyed to Lyon and then goodbye to the trade of your town for the people at Lyon work almost for nothing'.

Harper and Teignmouth in *The Smugglers* record the exploits of one gang which operated in Kent during the 1820s; known as the North Kent Gang, members were recruited for the most part from Ickham, Wingham, Wye, Canterbury and the Isle of Thanet and their particular stretch of coastline was that between Whitstable and Dover.

Between 1820 and 1821 this gang was involved in a number of forced runs which followed a familiar pattern. The smugglers, numbering up to 150, would assemble near the point where the smuggling vessel was expected and divide into three groups, two of which were armed. Once communication had been made with the vessel by flashing a prearranged signal with unloaded guns or with a special lamp, the three groups came down to the beach to work the boat. The unarmed tubmen waded into the surf to collect the barrels and carry them up the beach to the waiting carts. They were flanked on either side by the armed batmen, who kept the Blockade men at bay by firing volley after volley in their general direction. Once the boat was unloaded the smugglers withdrew with the unhurried efficiency of a military retreat until the barrels of spirits had been safely stowed away in their respective hiding places.

In June 1820, a clash took place on the shore between Herne Bay and Reculver when the Coast Blockade men, under Lieutenant Douglas, engaged the smugglers. There were casualties on both sides and a midshipman and several sailors had to be treated for cuts and bullet wounds. The next month, the Blockade men intercepted another run and this time succeeded in securing a cart laden with tubs of spirits and five smugglers, who were committed to Dover Gaol.

Undaunted by this setback, the smugglers continued their forced runs but matters came to a head in the following April when Sydney Sydenham Snow, midshipman of the *Severn* in charge of a small party of Blockade men, was shot dead. The gang involved had assembled the evening before at a country fair at Herne Street in order to avoid suspicion and many of them arrived quite drunk on the beach near the Ship Inn at Herne Bay. The contraband cargo was successfully run ashore and Snow was shot when he rushed forward in an attempt to seize the boat. A contemporary report describes how the unfortunate man lingered on for a while in great agony, before he expired, 'lamenting that his life had not been yielded in open battle with the enemies of his country, instead of being sacrificed in a vile midnight encounter with a gang of outlaws'. In the sequel to this incident five men were indicted at Bow Street on 10 May, charged with being concerned in the outrage of 24 April. They were remanded in custody and tried on 9 June but the jury, after retiring for half an hour, returned a verdict of not guilty. An officer of the Blockade described the acquittal as a lamentable miscarriage of justice. It was apparently achieved by a legal technicality, or 'some slight deficiency of evidence; and according to a report written some years later the actual assassin was living in 1839, and boasting of his exploit, in a parish near Herne Bay'.

The summer of 1821 seems to have passed off quite quietly, with no reports of violent clashes between the North Kent Gang and the Blockade men. However, the gang was still operating, for in September a bloody clash occurred one cloudy night at Marsh Bay near Margate. A Blockade sentinel had discovered a six-oared galley trying to run a cargo of spirits. The alarm was immediately given and Mr Washington Carr, a lieutenant with four men, hastened to the spot. The Blockade men rushed straight in and in the ensuing confusion men swore, fired their pistols and hacked wildly at fellow men on the dark beach. The smugglers sensed that they were being attacked by a far bigger force than was actually the case and after about a quarter of an hour they hurriedly dispersed into the darkness taking the tubs with them. The boat that had brought the contraband pushed off into the surf. The blood on the pebbles testified to the casualties on both sides but this time none of the Blockade men had been killed, although Lieutenant Carr had received a nasty wound inflicted by a smuggler who had wrenched the Blockade man's sword out of his hand and slashed at him in the dark. The Blockade men succeeded in capturing no more than a musket dropped by one of the fleeing smugglers, the stock and lock of another, two hats, a handkerchief and several large bludgeons.

But during the affray a seaman had recognised one of the smugglers as they grappled desperately on the beach, and this information was immediately conveyed to Lieutenant Barton of the *Severn*, 'one of the most zealous, able, persevering and honourable officers in the service'. He immediately realised the necessity of secrecy and speed, and the following morning applied privately for a warrant against the offender from the Revd Bailey, vicar and Justice of the Peace, at Margate. The lieutenant's zealousness was rewarded, for that same day, a certain Taylor was in custody and had turned King's evidence against his fellow gang members. The proceedings were then transferred to John Boys, a solicitor of Margate, who employed a Bow Street Runner called Bond to arrest several of the gang. From the gang members already in custody it was elicited that sixty persons were concerned in the affray, and that fifteen of them had carried firearms. At the same time a notice was inserted in the *London Gazette* of 11 September signifying that a free pardon was offered by His Majesty's Government to an accomplice, with a reward of £500 by the Lords Commissioner of the Admiralty, for 'the discovery of the persons concerned in the felonious affray at Marsh Bay'.

Taylor's arrest greatly perturbed his fellow smugglers, and their fears were increased when on 26 September James Rolfe was arrested at his house in Ivy Lane, Canterbury, by the Bow Street Runner Bond and was charged with a capital felony under a warrant backed by the Mayor. The immediate effect was to drive the other members of the gang into hiding.

Rolfe was taken to the county gaol at Maidstone and committed for trial at the next assize. The *Kentish Gazette* of 28 September 1821 takes up the story:

We are informed that the prisoner showed some signs of contrition, and was willing to make every atonement and disclosures of accomplices might afford; but the solicitor for the prosecution being already in possession (from a variety of good private information) of the names of most of the principal offenders, and finding the prisoner's name to stand amongst the list of those who made use of firearms in the attack, refused to admit him to become evidence for the Crown and especially, as he had made no offer to impeach his accomplices until he was apprehended.

The diligent Bond, with good detective work, had himself managed to arrest six out of the eleven smugglers who were in custody by the end of the year. One of the wanted men was Daniel Fagg, a noted ruffian, who had already escaped from constables who were pursuing him, by swimming a river, and had been heard to declare that he would not be taken alive. The redoubtable Bond managed to lay even him by the heels. The *Kentish Chronicle* of 28 December 1821 recorded:

Last Monday evening Bond received private information that Daniel Fagg was in a house at St Mildred's, in Canterbury, where he repaired accompanied by two able assistants, aware that he should meet with a desperate resistance and to guard against an escape, one of these he stationed at the front door, and the other at the rear. Bond contrived to gain admittance to the house, but not without a considerable degree of management and manoeuvring and proceeded with all speed to search the house, having no doubt that Daniel Fagg was in it. In the lower part of the house he heard a noise which he had no doubt proceeded from the rattling of bricks. He followed the noise and found it proceeded from making an aperture through the wall under the cellar stairs into an adjoining house, which no doubt had been previously arranged and prepared to assist him in escaping. The officer found Daniel Fagg in a state of nudity except for his breeches, in the act of clearing away the bricks to escape into the adjoining house: his state of nakedness was, no doubt, to avoid being held, and he made a desperate resistance, but Bond at length succeeded in securing him by handcuffs, and conveyed him to Margate, where he underwent an examination before the acting magistrates and from the evidence produced, he is suspected of being the man who attacked Lieutenant Carr, rested his sword from him, gave him a desperate wound on his head, of about three inches in length, and afterwards threw the officer's sword in Pluck's Gutter. The lieutenant was knocked down and supposed to have been killed with the blow.

For better security Fagg was taken out to the *Severn*, anchored in the Downs, to await trial. By the time the Spring Assizes were held in Maidstone in March 1822 there were another five men in custody, making eighteen in all. These eighteen were indicted, together with four other smugglers known to the authorities but not yet taken, for having on

2 September last with other persons unknown, feloniously assembled together, armed with firearms and other offensive weapons, in the parish of St John the Baptist in the Isle of Thanet, in order to be aiding and assisting in the illegal landing and carrying away of uncustomed goods, and for having maliciously shot and wounded Washington Carr, Thomas Cook and John Brimen, being in the execution of their duty as officers in the Coast Blockade Service.

An interesting fact to emerge from the trial was that the whole party of about sixty men had been hired by a master smuggler called Stephen Lawrence, who had so far escaped arrest. The 'brains' behind the gang and supplier of the cash had presumably fled abroad soon after Taylor was taken into custody. The prosecution managed to prove that arms were carried by a number of men both before and after the affray, and this was of course a capital offence. The prisoner Taylor endeavoured to prove an alibi, and several witnesses were called to say that he was two miles off at the time of the affray. However, this was immediately quashed by the prosecution, who submitted to the court a written examination taken by a magistrate's clerk, in which the prisoner had given a different version of his movements on the night in question. The judge, Mr Baron Wood, summed up and after a few minutes' deliberation the jury found all the prisoners guilty. The death sentence was delivered but the judge afterwards reprieved all except Rolfe and Fagg, and two others, John Wilsden and John Meredith.

The execution of the four who were not reprieved took place in the morning of Thursday 4 April 1822 at Penenden Heath, near Maidstone. A huge crowd, estimated at about 40,000, had gathered to witness their end. A contemporary writer describes the scene on that spring morning:

> The unfortunate smugglers appeared perfectly resigned to their unhappy fate. The parting between these deluded men and their families was truly heartrending. After ascending the fatal drop, and joining fervently in prayer with the chaplain, they repeated several times to the spectators: 'God bless you all'. When the dreadful bolt was withdrawn they ceased to exist. There can be no doubt that these wretched victims were encouraged to the last moment by the hope of a rescue, either before or at the place of execution; and as is always the case among characters of this description, they were abandoned by their associates from the first hour of apprehension.

Strangely there was no jeering or cheering at this public spectacle.

An execution was still an excuse for a day off work but there was emerging in the nineteenth century more respect for life. The occasion was solemn and seems to have impressed on the folk of Kent that the hanged men had been found guilty of a crime that was no longer going to be tolerated by the authorities. 'Not a sound broke the awful stillness of the procession, nor was a word spoken, except by the clergyman, from the gaol to the gallows.' The message was getting home.

On 13 May the remainder of the prisoners convicted at the Maidstone Assizes were taken from the county gaol at Maidstone to Portsmouth for transportation to Van Dieman's Land; five for life, the rest for seven years. A Naval officer wrote soon after the trial, 'This dreadful example had the desired effect; for from that moment the heart of smuggling appeared to be Broken.' This may have been true for the north part of Kent but elsewhere smuggling continued for a few more years.

During this survey of open smuggling, it can be seen that whenever the authorities were at a loss for a lead that would bring the culprits of a particular outrage to justice, which was usually the case, a financial reward and a promise of a pardon were invariably offered to an accomplice. The researches of Teignmouth and Harper describe in fascinating detail how this reward was shared out after the trial of the North Kent Gang in 1822.

One of the first claimants was a man called Thomas Avis, who had once been a keeper at St Augustine's Gaol in Canterbury but had subsequently been dismissed. The authorities employed him earlier on during the round-up of the smugglers as his former occupation had made him acquainted with most of the disreputable characters around Canterbury. In fact he had apprehended one of the accomplices who later turned witness for the Crown. But on one occasion Avis had appeared at the magistrates' court in a state of intoxication and his further services were dispensed with. As he had already received an honorarium of £5 2s 4d, his claim for further remuneration was disallowed.

Another claimant was John Wixson, who was employed in the apprehension of several of the smugglers; he played a chief role in securing James Rolfe and John Buffington, but the solicitor appointed to adjudicate on these claims observed that 'it has been represented to me that in eight instances Wixson connived at the escape of several of the offenders whilst the officers were in pursuit'. Wixson was a gardener, who, when not hunting smugglers, earned three shillings a day. While assisting the authorities he was paid ten shillings a day. But as he had already received about £20, besides compensation for some windows alleged to have been broken, his claim was considered to have been met in full. The next claimant was a lady, Mrs Everitt of Canterbury, who gave information which resulted in the apprehension of three of the convicted persons. She cautiously demanded payment, which amounted to £17 15s 0d, before she imparted the information, and this sum was thought to be sufficient.

The solicitor adjudicated, 'The persons to whom the discovery and conviction of most of the offenders was due were the four accomplices viz. James Justice, Samuel Kirby, Thomas Meers and Thomas Powell. These men are entitled to share in the reward offered.' Robert Stride, an Excise officer of Canterbury, had already received £250 for his part in the smugglers' apprehension and his claim was thought to have been amply met. Two other claimants were a Peace Officer, William Fleers, who was reported to have died of a cold caught in consequence of his activity in apprehending the offenders and his widow and family were deemed 'deserving of a reward', and John Reynolds, who had been 'ruined in business through the displeasure of his neighbours at the assistance he rendered'.

The 'Scheme of Distribution' was not completed until 8 November 1822 or more than seven months after the conviction of the offenders. It was then decided that the £500 should be divided among twenty-eight persons, in sums varying from £100 to £5, the largest sum being awarded to the widow of constable William Fleers. James Justice, who made full disclosure of the names of the gang and did not carry arms on the occasion, received £50. Two other accomplices, whose evidence helped to secure convictions, received £40 each. Thomas Cook, a seaman of the Blockade who received a gunshot wound and recognised Taylor, was awarded £10. The only other participator deserving mention was a constable of Margate 'who was the means of getting several arrested by the conversations he overheard amongst those under arrest'.

The Crown solicitor acknowledged the important part played in the trial by Mr Boys, the Margate solicitor. A letter dated 20 February 1823 stated:

> The prosecution of Mr Snow's murderers failed for want of corroborating testimony, but in the present case the difficulty was overcome through the diligence of Mr Boys … who zealously co-operated with my agents and discovered corroborative evidence to sustain the testimony of four accomplices.

However, his professional zealousness made him very unpopular in his home town, where considerable sympathy was still shown towards the smuggling fraternity:

> Mr Boys was during the proceedings the object of almost general hatred in the town and neighbourhood of Margate that he was placarded on the walls as an informer and hunter after blood money and his house was frequently assailed and his windows broken and his person assaulted in the dark, and the fruit trees destroyed in his garden in the night.

Another large gang of smugglers operated in Kent at this time. They were known as the Aldington 'Blues' after the village between Hythe and Ashford. This group employed the same methods as the East Kent Gang on the stretch of coastline from Dover to Camber on Romney Marsh. They made many forced runs between 1820 and 1826 and were involved in several bloody encounters with the Blockade men. The worst incident occurred one February night on Romney Marsh in 1821. The Blues marched down to the pre-arranged landing place on the beach at Camber with an armed party of twenty-five men on each flank of an unarmed working party. This formidable army of smugglers was spotted by a Blockade sentinel who fired his pistol to sound the alarm. Three Blockade officers, MacKenzie, Digby and Newton, arrived just in time to see the smugglers complete the run and begin their retreat into the dark flatness of the Marsh. Undaunted the officers and several Blockade men followed and volleys of fire were exchanged with the smugglers, who were conducting a classic military retreat of turning, kneeling and firing together before retiring another few hundred yards. The smugglers were at a considerable advantage as they were being guided by 'lookers', farm labourers who had an intimate knowledge of the Marsh.

The running battle continued throughout the night, the last shots being exchanged just before dawn. By this time they were eight miles inland near Brookland. As daylight came to the Marsh, the sound of gunfire died away; the list of casualties was counted. Midshipman McKenzie had been mortally wounded and died soon after; another three officers and six seamen had been wounded. The bodies of four smugglers were found lying in the road and probably twelve more had been wounded. The Battle of Brookland was one of the bloodiest encounters between the Blockade men and the smugglers but more significant was that two supposed smugglers had been captured, both of whom had come up to the Blockade party in the dark, having mistaken them for their confederates. With two gang members in custody, the authorities had considerable hope of applying pressure on them until they disclosed their accomplices. But this was not to be.

At the Old Bailey trial on 17 April 1821, Richard Wraight, aged thirty-eight and Cephas Quested, aged thirty, were capitally indicted for assembling with others, armed with firearms and carrying goods liable to pay duty. They were not charged with the murder of McKenzie as both had been taken before the midshipman had received his fatal bullet at about five o'clock in the morning near Brookland. The case against Quested was pretty clear as he had been apprehended with a musket in his hand. However, Wraight submitted a long written defence in which he denied being involved in the run, accounting for his presence in the area by saying he had missed his way in the dark. The prosecution endeavoured to prove his guilt by drawing attention to the fact that powder and shot had been found on him after his arrest and that his face had been blackened to avoid detection. The defendant countered this by stating that he had been shooting rooks the day previous, and that by putting his hands into his pockets and then to his face, he had dirtied it. Several witnesses were called to corroborate this statement and testify to his good character. The jury returned a verdict of guilty against Quested but Wraight was more fortunate; the evidence against him was considered to be purely circumstantial and he was acquitted.

Quested was not hanged until 4 July 1821 as the authorities continued to hope to persuade him to reveal the names of his accomplices. Many of the 'Blues' must have spent an uncomfortable eleven weeks, but Quested, with the stubborn simplicity and loyalty of an uneducated rustic labourer, refused to inform on them. He was described as a 'great, strong blustering chap' and the prospect of adventure as one of the fighting parties appealed to his simple mind. He was a prodigious drinker of the spirits he helped to smuggle and one cold day he and a friend called Gardiner tapped one of the barrels and drank until they collapsed in a stupor. They lay out all through a frosty night, and next morning Gardiner, 'being a weakly sort of chap', was dead. Yet Quested appeared none the worse and, when told of the death of his drinking companion, remarked, 'Well, he died of what he loved.'

The Blues take the discredit for another bloody affray that happened in the summer of the same year, 1821. Lieutenant Peat, with a small party of three Blockade men, was on duty one night in June when, in crossing some fields by a Martello tower to the east of Folkestone, he noticed what he at first supposed to be a flock of sheep, from the irregular manner in which they were lying. However, on investigation they were found to be a party of smugglers, estimated at about 300-strong. The officer immediately called upon the nearest of them to surrender but, not surprisingly, the gang jumped up and ran away. The Blockade men pursued and when the smugglers refused to stop Peat ordered his men to fire, which they did. Thereupon the armed party of smugglers stopped, and about forty of them returned the fire. By their second volley all the Blockade party had fallen wounded. However, one of them had dragged himself into a crouching position prior to firing again, when a third murderous volley hit the group and he collapsed. The gun battle attracted reinforcements but by the time they arrived the smugglers had escaped. Quartermaster Richard Woolridge was found to be dead; his two fellow seamen were wounded. Lieutenant Peat had received no less than fourteen gunshot wounds according to the surgeon who examined him soon afterwards, but miraculously he survived. He was promoted and pensioned by the Admiralty, and astonished the inhabitants of Folkestone by appearing at the theatre in his uniform as a commander. At the subsequent inquest into Woolridge's death, because the smugglers had not fired first and had no uncustomed goods with them, after several hours of deliberation a verdict of wilful murder by some persons unknown was returned. Despite considerable investigation and the usual offer of reward and pardon, no one was brought to trial accused of his murder.

The hanging of four members of the North Kent Gang at Maidstone in April 1822, and the subsequent deportation of several others, appears to have had a sobering effect on the activities of their South Kent counterpart the 'Blues'. The years 1823 to 1825 were remarkably peaceful and no major confrontations were reported. Undoubtedly smuggling continued, but the forced runs had been temporarily abandoned. The Custom Commissioners heard that three smugglers in Dover Gaol were continuing their activities from prison and the Commissioners wrote confidentially to the Customs officer at the port requesting him to investigate whether Thomsett, Richards and Higgs were in the practice of giving bond to the gaoler and obtaining from him leave to go out at night and pursue their former smuggling transactions. They also believed that prohibited goods were frequently brought into Dover Gaol and bought and sold there. This return to less violent smuggling was short-lived and the forced runs and bloodshed appeared again in 1826 when Captain McCulloch of the Coast Blockade reported in short but dramatic fashion, 'The armed parties of smugglers are again appearing on the coast within the limits of the Blockade.' But the bell had been sounded to announce the final bloody round between the armed smugglers of Kent and the men of the Coast Blockade.

Runs occurred between March and June of 1826 but matters were brought to a head when Richard Morgan, a quartermaster from HMS *Ramillies*, was shot dead on 30 July when trying to prevent a cargo of contraband spirits from being unloaded near the bathing machines at Dover. He noticed a boat in the surf and ran forward to challenge it; the smugglers opened fire without warning and three shots struck him within three inches of each other in the left side near the heart. The whole consignment of spirits was carried away by the smugglers, and flushed with this victory they made another successful run six days later near Hythe. However, this time the smugglers had to leave one of their number behind. James Bushell had been wounded in the right knee-joint, and the Blockade men took him into custody. He was in no fit state to be interviewed as his wound necessitated the amputation of his leg but in time he could be persuaded to name his accomplices. In September Edward Horne, another member of the gang, was arrested near Walmer Castle. The 'Blues' were aware that two of their number were in the hands of the authorities; but they did not know that two other people were working actively against them. These two were William Marsh and James Spratford, both local men who had turned informers and were later rewarded £130 each for their assistance.

The leader of the Aldington Blues was a remarkable man named George Ransley. A stout, jolly hard fellow, he had started his working life as a waggoner for a farmer who lived near Brookland on Romney Marsh. He married a girl from Aldington and gave up work to devote his whole time to smuggling. He built a house called Bourne Tap and was a very capable organiser, employer and distributor. The men he employed to help in a run used to meet at his home and if they were short of money he would pay them in advance. This was a shrewd business gesture, for it created good feeling and also allowed the men to buy rum and gin which he sold to them illegally. Many of the smugglers he employed drank excessively but Ransley himself always kept a clear head. Stories about his daring exploits are legion. Once, when riding back from the coast with a consignment of contraband, he was spotted by a mounted party of Preventive men. Knowing there was a large ransom on his head, he deliberately rode towards them and boldly ensured they would recognise him before he veered off. The Preventive men gave chase to him, but both he and the contraband got clean away. On another occasion he was captured and placed in a Martello tower and, to deter his escape, all his clothes were removed. Undaunted, he went up to the roof of the tower and jumped over thirty feet to the ground and ran off, startling a ploughman with a not unreasonable request for something to wear.

Ransley's short career in the 1820s gave him a folk-hero status comparable with that of Dick Turpin. But like the famous highwayman, he was not immune from the law. When the authorities believed they had sufficient evidence they arranged for the nucleus of the gang to be apprehended, and one wild, stormy night in October 1826 eight of them, including Ransley, were arrested. They were completely surprised. Lieutenant Samuel Hellard of the Coast Blockade, guided by Spratford, the informer, and with a large party of men and two Bow Street Runners, arrested them all in their bedrooms, after cutting down the guard dogs before they had a chance to bark a warning. The prisoners were taken before Sir Richard Birnie at Bow Street and charged with the wilful murder of Richard Morgan and unlawfully assembling with arms, and with the intention of running smuggled goods; their trial was fixed for the Kent Winter Assizes at Maidstone in January 1827.

The trial caused a sensation throughout Kent as many anticipated a mass turning off. The judge, Mr Park, took the opportunity to condemn smuggling:

> If everyman, in whatever station he might be in this country, were to lay it down as a positive rule, to suffer nothing to come into his family that had been purchased of smugglers, the evil would soon be stopped. It was an old saying 'that the receiver is

worse than the thief', and he would say that persons buying smuggled goods were worse than the smugglers, and such should be his conviction to the hour of his death. Many people think that there is no harm in defrauding the Revenue but whoever breaks any law of the country is guilty of a great breach of moral law.

Apart from the eight arrested in October, eight more had been arrested subsequently and so there were sixteen Aldington men in the dock. A long and involved trial was expected with numerous witnesses ready to be called. However, counsel for the smugglers secured a deal for them: if the murder charge was dropped, then all the men would plead guilty to the other charges, on the condition that their punishment should be transportation for life, and not hanging. It was a very clever move; if the Crown agreed then the expense of a long trial would be saved. Not only that, a plea of guilty to unlawful assembly would have the required effect of permanently disbanding the gang. The Crown agreed to the deal.

The judge went through the formality of condemning fourteen of the men to death; the other two were acquitted as they had been accused only of Morgan's murder. Four days before the date of their execution the fourteen were reprieved and all were sent to Van Dieman's Land, for life. Despite this, the town of Maidstone was crowded on the day of the expected execution, 5 February 1827, with many people coming in from the surrounding countryside. The *Maidstone Gazette* reported, 'But being disappointed of their amusement, they went back about as wise as they came.' Ransley's organising abilities did not desert him when he reached the penal colony in the Antipodes. Once more he prospered, this time as a respectable farmer, and at his death in 1860 he was well loved and a trusted employer of convict servants.

The shift from the open running of contraband to the more ingenious methods of concealment signalled the end of an era; but, as shown, this end did not come suddenly nor peacefully. The decade 1820 to 1830 provided the bloody climax to the smuggling in this bold form. The affrays during this time were the final paroxysms of open smuggling, which had so often been tainted by violence in the past. Before things got better they had, for a time, got worse as the traditional trade gave way to the subtler business of deception. The Coast Blockade was finally paid off in 1831; it had been involved during its fifteen turbulent years in a great number of incidents but was mainly responsible for the break-up of the large armed gangs that continued until potential profit did not warrant the risks involved. Or maybe until the risks involved were greater than the potential profit.

There is no need for a summary or an epilogue to any history of smuggling. This book has dealt mainly with a period when contraband running was due as much to government greed as to the cupidity of free traders who relied heavily on the acquiescence of the general public. Yet there will always be such greed, cupidity and acquiescence, and what citizen today is fully aware of the origin of every object that makes up his or her own environment? How many willingly pay tribute to whom tribute is due, or render unto Caesar the things that are Caesar's?

Index